WATCHING SKIES

WATCHING SKIES

SKIES

STAR WARS, SPIELBERG AND US

MARK O'CONNELL

The
History
Press

First published 2018
The History Press
The Mill, Brimscombe Port
Stroud, Gloucestershire, GL5 2QG
www.thehistorypress.co.uk

British Library Cataloguing in Publication Data.
A catalogue record for this book is available from the British Library.

ISBN 978 0 7509 7019 8

Typesetting and origination by The History Press
Printed and bound by CPI Group (UK) Ltd

For Elliot – who lifts life like a BMX bike
flying against the moon.

CONTENTS

ABOUT THE AUTHOR

Mark O'Connell is an award-winning writer, author and Bond fan. As a comedy writer he has written for a wide range of actors, performers, and media. As a pop culture pundit, he has written and guested for *Variety*, Sky Movies, *The Times*, *The Guardian*, *OUT* magazine, Channel Four, Five, various news outlets and across the BBC. He was one of the official storytellers of London 2012, owns one tenth of a BAFTA, is also a travel writer and lives in England with his husband. He is the author of *Catching Bullets: Memoirs of a Bond Fan*.

markoconnell.co.uk
Twitter / @Mark0Connell
Instagram / MarkOConnellWriter

It is a dark time for the Hollywood System. A team of rebel filmmakers have managed to steal the secret plans to the SEVENTIES and have already begun a sequence of films with enough power to change cinema.

On the frozen planet of Britain, a young boy needs releasing from the vile clutches of boring toys, no siblings and a lack of home video.

In an attempt to rescue the boy and the childhoods of all like him, the rebel filmmakers are dispatching their movies into the farthest reaches of cinema with a special mission to kids the world over – watch the skies …

THE CALIFORNIA EXPRESS

The canary-yellow road lines of the Pacific Coast Highway stretch into the horizon like the opening crawl of a *Star Wars* movie. As the steady trail of cars, camper vans, motorbikes and cyclists threads along Highway 1 towards San Francisco, the cobalt blue skies of California in August match the Pacific's waves beneath. In a SUV rental the size of a space shuttle, my partner and I are not only pondering how the Pacific Coast Highway is hardly wide enough for a SUV rental the size of a space shuttle – we are reflecting too on the Los Angeles we have left behind, and the America we have already found.

We had seen the Grauman's Chinese Theatre, where black and white photographs of the 1977 queues for *Star Wars* became nearly as iconic as the film itself; we very nearly threw water over a dining Daryl Hannah's feet, just to see if she still had the *Splash* mermaid's tail and a sense of humour; I confused Al Pacino with my Limey accent and got the stony Corleone stare for my troubles; we wandered the very Paramount sound stages that housed *The Godfather*, *Chinatown*, *Rosemary's Baby* and *Star Trek III: The Search For Spock*; we had lunch at the Walt Disney Studios and a sneaky

Big Sur   15 mi 24 km
Monterey Peninsula   46 mi 74 km
San Francisco   162 mi 261 km

Driving the line to San Francisco and the home of *Star Wars*.

peek at its archives – despite nearly crashing said SUV rental into a security booth, much to the guards' amusement – and two-time Bond actress and *Octopussy* herself Maud Adams took us on a charming tour of Hollywood and Beverly Hills in exchange for some home improvement advice and a trip to various lumber yards. Our SUV was soon christened the *USS Maud* – in part tribute to its interstellar dimensions, but also because its satnav voice reminded us of the *Octopussy* actress and my 'co-star' on my previous book, *Catching Bullets: Memoirs of a Bond Fan*.

Trying to soundtrack our journey with the Californian sounds of Mama Cass, Joan Baez, The Byrds, Bread and the movie sounds of John Barry, Bernard Herrmann and John Williams, we travel along the very highways that were themselves the locations of new wave game-changers such as *Easy Rider, Chinatown, Play Misty For Me, Dirty Harry, Harold and Maude, American Graffiti* and *The Graduate*. It soon becomes ever-apparent that America is the one country whose cinematic reputation precedes it more than any other. Everything we think we know of America came from and continues to come from its movies. Station wagons, yellow school buses, cop cars, neon Coca-Cola signs, Cape Cod beach fences, protest marches on DC, newspaper stands, spinning wind pumps, the leaves of fall lapping white picket fences, lemonade stands, surfboards, top loading washing machines, baseball gloves, groceries in brown paper bags, piles of mash potato, mailboxes on

Taking the 101 to San Francisco, California.

poles, railroad crossings and all-night diners. These accoutrements of Americana were not just commonplace to us because we went there. They were commonplace because the movies came to us.

We are driving to San Francisco – the counterpulse city home of queer culture, Hitchcock, Pixar Animation, a thriving movie fan scene to maybe match no other, Industrial Light & Magic, abundant independent movie festivals, the brassy paddle steamer that is the vintage Castro Theatre movie palace, *Dirty Harry*, *The Conversation*, *A View to a Kill*, *Milk*, *The Towering Inferno*, *Vertigo*, Peaches Christ's wild and canny celebrations of cult and un-cult classics, all manner of underground and overground cinema, all manner of movie and media technology, and both the spiritual and production home of *Star Wars* and Lucasfilm Ltd. Having passed the shipping container cranes at the Port of Oakland – and how local legend loves to mythically suggest their gargantuan four-legged frames straddling the horizon were George Lucas's inspiration for the AT-ATs in *The Empire Strikes Back* – we are soon crossing the Bay Bridge into San Francisco. With that disaster movie stalwart that is the Golden Gate Bridge on our distant right, I glance to where the near-mythical Skywalker Ranch might be hiding in the Marin Headlands, and where in the city's Presidio Park the 23-acre headquarters of Lucasfilm Ltd and legendary visual effects house Industrial Light & Magic are now based.

Minutes later, we are taking a left into Folsom Street and driving past the very South of Market stretch where a late-1960s act of anti-Hollywood defiance saw a new generation of Northern Californian filmmakers begin to change the face of American and mainstream cinema forever. It was here, on the second floor of a warehouse at 827 Folsom Street, that moviemakers George Lucas, Francis Ford Coppola, John Korty, Walter Murch, Caleb Deschanel, Matthew Robbins, Willard Huyck, Howard Kazanjian, John Milius and others set up the first incarnation of American

827 Folsom, San Francisco – the site where George Lucas and his moviemaking pals began to change US cinema in a now long-gone warehouse.

Zoetrope. A response to the counterculture revolutions happening all around them, Zoetrope's agenda was to cultivate and support a moviemaking independence from Hollywood and its withering studio hierarchies. It was here amidst the recording studios, gay clubs, bathhouses, leather bars, stoner enclaves and experimental arts spaces of Folsom that Francis Ford Coppola worked on the post–production of *The Rain People* (1969) and pal George Lucas took his University of Southern California's graduation film project, *Electronic Labyrinth: THX 1138 4EB,* and developed it into 1971's *THX 1138* and the feature film whose genesis and DNA was vital to his future far, far away galaxies.

The Coppola Club II – the Sentinel Building at 916 Kearney Street and the home of American Zoetrope since 1971.

I am not sure when my love affair with America quite began. But I know what started it. The movies. And not just any movies. It was the second golden age of American cinema – the unplanned, often anti-establishment, and cinematically rich new wave of 1970s creativity whose first globally recognised and mainstream poster boy was Steven Spielberg's *Jaws* (1975). As the classical Hollywood system, its studios, stars and thinking slowly caved in on themselves amid a late-1960s of shifting demographics, budgets and tastes, the likes of *Bonnie and Clyde* (1967), *Rosemary's Baby* (1968), *Easy Rider* (1969), *Midnight Cowboy* (1969), *Woodstock* (1970), *Five Easy Pieces* (1970) and *The Last Picture Show* (1971) all laid vital foundation stones to an upcoming decade of movie hope and independence. Here was a new generation of movie-soaked filmmakers who did not just want a cinema that made us look inwards. They wanted us to look outwards. And skywards. It was now the time of *Star Wars, Superman: The Movie, Close Encounters of the Third Kind, E.T. the Extra-Terrestrial, Poltergeist, Gremlins, Raiders of the Lost Ark, Ghostbusters, Star Trek II: The Wrath of Khan, Alien, The Omen, Superman II, Jaws 2, The Empire Strikes Back* and *Return of the Jedi*. It was the era where the shark-skin suits and Pomade-slicked hair of old Hollywood were replaced by the fake sharks, jeans, long hair, checked shirts and branded baseball caps of a film-savvy younger guard. To movie-mad kids growing up on that frozen planet of Britain, the bearded triumvirate of Steven Spielberg, George Lucas and John Williams were household names before we could even spell our own household's name. Phrases and figures like ILM, Skywalker Ranch, Frank Oz, Margot Kidder, Richard Donner, JoBeth Williams, Amity Island, Chief Brody, Miss Teschmacher, Joe Dante, Lynn Stalmaster, Lawrence Kasdan, the Well of the Souls, Carlo Rambaldi, Tom Mankiewicz, the Daily Planet, Mike Fenton, the Salkinds, Rick Baker, CBS/Fox video, The Freelings, Ralph McQuarrie, Dennis Muren and Kathleen Kennedy were all part and parcel of our movie-watching parlance and playground chat. I could not tell you the line-up for England's 1982 World Cup hopes, but I could soon name at least three sound designers and production artists on films I hadn't seen yet.

Taking its cue from *Watch the Skies* – the original working title of what became 1977's *Close Encounters of the Third Kind* (which itself was a closing phrase from the 1951 sci-fi classic *The Thing From Another Planet*) – *Watching Skies: Star Wars, Spielberg and Us* is about American cinema of the 1970s and early 1980s. It is about how one era's cinematic output became a new rich age for a new Hollywood order whose key players were wilfully operating outside of itself. It is about how the mass spectatorship for these movies was soon offset by the very personal inroads into our childhoods, our cultural reference points, our most treasured movie house memories, our vacation routes and our toy boxes. It is about a cinematic sky that experienced a magnificent dawn with 1975's *Jaws* and a glorious sundown with 1984's *Ghostbusters* and *Gremlins*. It is a small window of cinema. But in barely a decade, that small window let in a hell of a lot of cinematic light. With the original *Star Wars* trilogy as both crowning glory and First Family, this book intends to reconsider a rich portfolio of key familiar titles, and the personal stamps they put on our movie souls as they continue to shape big and vital cinema to this day.

This is not about chronology. Just as we experience all cinema in different ways, in different times and in different orders, the stars in this movie firmament are dotted in different directions. This is not a volume about the extended universes of *Star Wars* or the elongated adventures of fan favourites with names like Jarab Puke or Putt Ferlangi. This is not going to happily tell you how the carved images of C-3PO and R2-D2 are visible on the Ark of the Covenant in *Raiders of the Lost Ark,* that *Return of the Jedi* was originally called *Revenge of the Jedi* or that Tom Selleck was originally cast as both Indiana Jones and the mum in *E.T.* This is not about fan theories of Kylo Ren being Admiral Ackbar's great-nephew. Vice Admiral Holdo being Poe Dameron's mother, or Mon Mothma actually being Emperor Palpatine's drag queen alias. This is not even going to spend too much page space sticking voodoo pins into a Jar Jar Binks doll. *Watching Skies* is about how these films work as movies. And experiences. It is not about the making of *Raiders of the Lost Ark* or trivia about a broken mechanical shark in *Jaws*. For many reasons, the movies of this era are still the benchmarks, the forerunners, and the templates. These movies were not just a fresh dawn of storytelling and storytelling wizardry. They

With the Hollywood sign looking on from Mount Lee, Paramount Studio's Stage 30 and 31 – the production home of one of 1970s cinema's key players, Francis Ford Coppola's *The Godfather*.

marked the beginning of a new thinking towards release patterns, the seasons of the movie year, how films were promoted, how films became franchises, the home cinema market, merchandising, how such films influenced the filmmakers that followed and how the movies now renovate, repair and reboot themselves. And with the now forty-year-old *A New Hope* and *Close Encounters of the Third Kind* officially middle-aged movies, Lucasfilm and Disney continue bringing that far, far away galaxy just that bit closer with a new *Star Wars* trilogy and standalone adventures; The Duffer Brothers' *Stranger Things* goes from strength to strength on television; Marvel Studios' *Guardians of the Galaxy* spins on an axis of Walkmans, *Knight Rider*, mixtapes and 1970s vinyl; a new genre of fan-led documentaries are looking at the affection and dedication these films engender on a lifetime (*Raiders!*, *Elstree 1976*, *Back in Time* and *For The Love of Spock*), the rise of Secret Cinema and the new immersive and wholly communal ways to honour our cinematic linchpins; and Steven Spielberg's *Ready Player One* is now uploaded onto movie screens, with its coyly pitched post, post, post-modern tale of a dystopian society where a social and gameplay currency centres on 1980s pop cultural references and nods to the cinema started by the likes of Lucas, Donner and Spielberg. It is as good a time as any to skip school, pick up those BMX bikes and watch the skies again.

As my previous book, *Catching Bullets*, is a very personal tale of watching James Bond movies, *Watching Skies* is a universal and affectionate tale about the personal remembrances stuck in all our R2 units' memory systems. It is about being one of the *Star Wars* generation. It is about how cinema was part of our formative years like never before. Before there was Bond for this writer, there was *Star Wars* and those titles that swiftly followed its movie jump to lightspeed. So maybe *Watching Skies* is a *Star Wars* prequel. What can go wrong?!

THE GREAT MUPPET OPENER

1980. It's time to play the music. It's time to light the lights. That was probably my earliest memory. Of anything. Well, that and the soaked socks and leather sandals I got when my 4-year-old foot slipped into a tiny garden pond and I thought I was going to drown in a 1970s information film warning of the vagaries of unattended ponds. Before I was a Bond fan or a *Star Wars* fan or an Indiana Jones fan or a Superman fan, I was a Muppets fan. My favourite toy was a very well-worn Kermit the Frog bendy toy made of rubber with properly unsafe 1970s wire limbs, and my 6th birthday cake had Henson's characters carefully iced all over it. *The Muppets* and the Peanuts gang were my world. Every Friday night at 7 p.m. I would hesitate in the bath with one ear on the lounge TV until Gonzo's trumpet blast heralded that *The Muppet Show*'s opening theme had finished. The overture and its bounding blue monsters, orange-haired ghouls in tuxedos and the lank-haired Miss Piggy quietly terrified this 5-year-old. But once Kermit came out to invite me into Jim Henson's fuzzy Beatnik universe, I was there, dripping wet and ready to meticulously eat the one black cherry yoghurt from the Keymarkets' multi-pack I would always dutifully save for a Friday night. Black cherry yoghurts were always the best.

The Muppets and the Peanuts gang were my first touchstones to that place called America. The Snoopy TV shows and comic strips underpinned a 1960s sense of West Coast Americana – of white picket fences, milk and cookies, baseball mounds and a sunny afterschool Californian suburbia. But it also served up a valuable cynicism, lessons in how the world does not play fair, a sense of comedy, a presentation of broken families and the faceless vagaries and fears of adulthood. Meanwhile, on the other side of the American map, Jim Henson and *The Muppet Show* were mining a whole East Coast heritage of burlesque, cabaret and vaudeville. That mix of West Coast Americana and a folky, East Coast Beat Generation was prescient stuff for this 1980s kid.

I was born five years earlier, at the very end of September 1975. *Rebel Without a Cause* was being shown by BBC1 – to no doubt commemorate James Dean, who had died on a stretch of road

Breakfast at Kermit's and a late 1970s childhood of Spielberg kid hair, great cousins and wood panelling.

off the Pacific Coast Highway twenty years to the day – and the famous 'Thrilla in Manilla' boxing match was about to kick off between Ali and Frazier. Sydney Pollack's *Three Days of the Condor* was number 1 at the American box office, and was the first film all summer to knock *Jaws* off the top spot it had stayed at since its US release on 20 June 1975. In California, George Lucas was drafting and designing *Adventures of the Starkiller* – a little-known film which eventually evolved into a very well-known film called *Star Wars*. Steven Spielberg was prepping a UFO movie called *Watch the Skies*. Bond director Guy Hamilton was developing a movie of *Superman*. And Richard Donner was just a few miles down the rural Surrey roads, about to start filming *The Omen*.

I was an only child. And I still am. I lived with my mum and dad and our three dogs in a sleepy house-lined lane just outside a Surrey village called Cranleigh. Mum was a primary school teacher and my dad worked in the airline cargo business. Unbeknownst to me at the time, the movies were already a lot nearer my life than I would realise. In fact, very near. It was a few years yet before I got to fully appreciate how my grandfather, Jimmy O'Connell, had already spent the majority of his working life in and around the movies by the time I was 5 years old and starting school. Jimmy worked for James Bond producer Albert R. Broccoli and the 007 creative house, EON Productions. He was the Broccoli family's chauffeur, house-sitter, car-sitter, child guardian and more. His intermittent jaunts to Los Angeles and the former Broccoli family home in Beverly Hills, and his more regular trips back and forth from South Audley Street in London's Mayfair to Buckinghamshire's Pinewood Studios, put him in the eye of a moviemaking world he was always notoriously quiet about. The Broccolis were never anything but supportive and looked after Jimmy way beyond his retirement. On my first trip to Los Angeles many years later, and before I took in the movie culture and history of the town, my partner and I went with the lead actress from the first Bond film I ever saw – 1983's *Octopussy* – to pay brief tribute to the Broccolis, my grandfather, the house he sometimes looked after and the movie maelstrom that is Hollywood. Cinema has the power to do that. It gets very personal, very quickly.

The first film I saw at the cinema was a Disney re-release of *Snow White and the Seven Dwarfs*. It was December 1980 at the Guildford Odeon. I was 5 years old. I remember the sadness of the titular heroine alone in her glass coffin with a bereft Dopey waiting nearby, and being transfixed by the animated light reflections bouncing off the cigarette-stained ivory of the art deco interiors of the 1935-built cinema. But by that time, America itself had already come to my home in a rather curious and random fashion. In 1977, President Jimmy Carter's hand-picked American ambassador to Britain, his entourage and Stars-and-Stripes-bearing car twice visited our humble Surrey bungalow. So far, so very Robert Thorn and *The Omen*. The brilliantly named Kingman Brewster Jr. had not long finished his modernising tenure as president of Yale University, which of course irritated a few vocal and less progressive folks such as President Richard Nixon and the then Secretary of State, Henry Kissinger. The Brewsters were now looking for a new family pet and my mum had already built up a sound reputation for breeding Golden Retrievers. Unfortunately, the Anglo-Irish politics of late-1970s Britain and the mainland activities of the IRA meant the O'Connell surname was somewhat of a dicey one where American dignitaries and friends of President Carter with the highest diplomatic position outside of America were concerned. With all the blacked-out security of a lurking government car in *E.T. the Extra-Terrestrial*, Brewster Jr. had to remain inside his as the security staff came indoors instead, had a cup of tea, met the litter and then picked a puppy which Kingman and his wife took home to his palatial address in Regent's Park a few weeks later. There is every likelihood that at least one American president met one of our dogs. And ten dollars says it wasn't Richard Nixon.

Our parents' post-war, baby boomer generation learnt about America through rock and roll, chewing gum and hamburgers. Theirs was a generation where they went to the movies and found America through music, the radio, denim and vinyl. Mine was when the movies and America came to us – a time when home video and film merchandise took on a bedspread, figurine and collector's sticker album life of its own. It all changed when a great white shark terrorised the waters of Cape Cod, the comfort zones of Universal Pictures' financiers and movie house owners who thought they knew how summer audiences worked. Instead of the musicals, westerns, Biblical epics and social dramas of our parents' generation's moviegoing, now America was presenting its movie self via more adventure, fantasy and science fiction. The age-old sense of spectacle is unaltered. The widescreen might and wonder of cinema does not change in the 1970s. The background cameo tributes to *Pinocchio* (1941) and *The Ten Commandments* (1956) in *Close Encounters of the Third Kind* are tribute and testimony to that. Yet, maybe science fiction and the fantasy movie came of age in the decade of Watergate, various energy panics, the three-day week and Dolby Stereo. It certainly moved from the communistic allegories and nuclear age fears of our parents' teen years and its B-movie heyday.

The first inkling I had of the science fiction genre was not from the cinema at all. It was from our local big town's shopping centre, The Friary. Guildford's gleaming new hive of retail and adjoined parking had just opened in 1980. Like all brick-interior British shopping centres housing the futuristic likes of C&A, Clockhouse, Athena, Tammy Girl and Tandy, ours was also held up as the zenith of suburban shopping. However, in the December of 1981 it was briefly known as 'Zondor'. Such was the futuristic vision of the newly opened shopping centre and its revolutionary system of escalators, that BBC space opera *Blake's* 7 came to town to shoot a sequence for its penultimate episode, 'Warlord'. *Blake's* 7 was one of British television's reactions to *Star Wars*. It was a sort of human *Pigs in Space* – which to date had been the only other future world I had experienced before. And even that unnerved me. I had a long-standing problem with Henson's pig puppets and their human-like eyes. It took me a long time to not break out in a cold sweat whenever felt-covered swine did Rodgers and Hammerstein chorus numbers in unison.

The Friary shopping centre's pivotal role in the 1981 episode of *Blake's* 7 depicted bad Federation soldiers picking off spaced-out civilians on their way up and down the escalators. Having shopped there again recently, it was quite an apt forecast. Wearing curiously familiar Tatooine moisture farmer robes, said victims were no doubt heading to the sales at Clockhouse and Tammy Girl when they were so cruelly lasered to death. Despite being too young to properly take in Guildford's brief moment of sci-fi immortality, I do recall a subsequent 'make' on British kids' TV stalwart, *Blue Peter*. By way of the standard disclaimer 'get a grown up to help you', host Janet Ellis instructed viewers in how to make a *Blake's* 7 teleporter wrist bangle thing out of a plastic soda bottle. I tried to make one. But it just looked like a plastic soda bottle bangle from a show that had actually ended a few years before but the repeats were doing the rounds again.

Like a lot of science fiction and its need to reflect current times through its various futures, Guildford's cameo in *Blake's* 7 was fairly metaphorical for life in Britain at the time. The 'Winter of Discontent' of 1979 and its government-blaming trade union strikes were still a recent, sore memory. As young British kids entering the 1980s with only three television channels, one landline telephone under the stairs, three flavours of crisps, one Thatcher in Parliament and nine and a half months of grey weather a year, we were constantly being trained to be fearful of British electricity pylons, Bonfire Night sparklers and crossing a suburban road anywhere near a parked Bedford van. Oh, and stagnant pools of water housing hidden shopping trolleys just waiting to grab the feet of passing young kids. For a time, we only ever had publicly-funded kids'TV shows demonstrating just how to make film and television merchandise from the household rubbish our refuse trucks were on strike from collecting. All I had was a height chart from *The Magic Roundabout* and a *Muppets* annual, in which I had folded over any pages featuring any felt pigs with creepy eyes.

Because of all that drudgery, warning and pallid living, we would get extremely excited about new space-age developments within our reach, like escalators and pedestrian walkways that would go over traffic lanes. No wonder *Blake's 7* thought Guildford was the future – albeit a dystopian Home Counties one whose shops only sold beige slacks and which all closed on a Sunday and at lunchtime on a Wednesday. Thinking about it, science fiction really had it in for our neck of the planet. Not only was Guildford twinned with some tyrannical alien state called Zondor, but *The Hitchhiker's Guide to the Galaxy* (1978) and Douglas Adams made sure lead character Ford Prefect initially claimed he was from Guildford for maximum dullard effect, *Doctor Who and the Silurians* (1970) did location battle on our local heathland whilst the Doctor blocked the traffic in nearby Godalming with his faithful souped-up yellow car Bessie, and one of the key fathers of science fiction, H. G. Wells himself, was more than happy for *The War of the Worlds* (1897) and its alien invasions to trash nearby Woking and the surrounding towns and villages.

TOYS. TOYS!

CLOSE ENCOUNTERS OF THE THIRD KIND

1977. A fearless small boy's imagination and toys run riot when midnight alien visitors lay siege to his Alabama home – engulfing the skies around his house in dazzling orange illuminations and his single mother in total fear.

○———————○

The cinematic skies of 1982 were rich with sci-fi landmarks and immortal game-changers. *Star Trek II: The Wrath of Khan, Blade Runner, First Blood, The Thing, Poltergeist, The Dark Crystal, Tootsie, Rocky III, Das Boot, Conan the Barbarian, The Sword and the Sorcerer, The Evil Dead, Max Mad 2, Tron* and of course *E.T. the Extra-Terrestrial* all took their first bow in 1982. It was a year marked by the Falklands War, the Greenham Common nuclear protests, *Dynasty*, Princess Diana's unique fashion sense and the space shuttle's first manned mission. But if any year of my childhood should have a big canary-yellow Irwin Allen disaster movie font over its foyer, then it is '1982!' Just like the disaster movie genre itself, my parents' marriage didn't quite survive the turn into the new decade. And just like any young kid watching *The Towering Inferno* or *The Poseidon Adventure* on TV one Sunday afternoon, I don't really remember the perilous build-up or the dangerous cracks appearing – just the final-act fireworks and capsized emotions. We had gone from being the Brody family of *Jaws* to the Kramers of *Kramer Vs Kramer* – whose original Avery Corman novel my mum had a well-worn copy of, complete with the then obligatory '8 pages of film scenes' which may have accounted for my Meryl Streep obsession and scrapbook in later years.

The summer of 1982 had hardly got off to a good start. Not only did the Pope not actually visit our school and bless our new television room and its plush diocese-financed carpet as the very wild rumours had promised, I was then snubbed by Admiral James T. Kirk and the entire crew of the *Enterprise*. A neighbour pal was having a *Star Trek II: The Wrath of Khan* cinema birthday trip I clearly wasn't invited to, as the other boys from the road and their packed lunches carpooled into various cars without me. In hindsight, maybe I should have waved them off wearing a Starfleet insignia pin rather than an 'I heart Pope John Paul II' badge we had to buy at school, no doubt to prove our allegiance to the good ship Jesus. I certainly recall that the 1981 assassination attempt on the Pope's life guaranteed us Catholic foot soldiers attended the neighbouring church for days and weeks to pray for his soul, safety and new popemobile. I have still not forgiven the nuns for leading no such vigils a year later, when Captain Spock also put his life on the line behind some protective glass for a much greater good. The birthday party snub was the first of a few at that time, one of the possible side effects of the Surrey mum circuit thinking the kid from the broken – or breaking – home was damaged goods. Or something like that.

It is worth remembering that in 1982, it was only those cinematic skies and their screens where we could watch our films. Us junior school kids of Thatcher's Britain may well have been positioned in a glorious Kessel Run of Reaganite-era movies and American culture – but this was not an era in which we could actually see those films. Not at will, anyway. Home videos and the machines to play them on were still a form of wizardry, that had yet to fully infiltrate all the homes of Britain with those three TV channels, prudishly timed closedowns and daily warnings about turning off your television sets before going to bed. There were no *Star Wars* boxsets, Sky Movies HD on demand or anniversary Blu-ray editions of *Jaws*. There were no teaser trailers, video blogs or live streamed interview panels at Comic Con. It was an era when the quality of a film was judged by watching it and its story skies, not the online hit rate or reaction of a first photo or still from a teaser's teaser. We would only know of a new movie via a half-page black and white ad in *Look-In* magazine or some crude greyscale image of a lightsaber in the newspaper flanked by, 'Now showing at the Odeon Marble Arch and leading cinemas throughout the country.' But no one would actually tell you just where those 'leading cinemas' were.

One of the greatest movie summers of all time, and the nearest I got to it was some repeat matinee screenings of *The Cat from Outer Space* (1978) at the 1936 monoplex that was our trusted local cinema, the Cranleigh Regal. To be fair, a great many of those summer American releases didn't reach British shores until the autumn – or 'the fall', as the movie campaigns like to call it. But in 1982, if you didn't have a cousin with a mate whose neighbour had a video player, then you were pretty much like Han Solo in *A New Hope* – digging your heels in and resisting the very notion that such home entertainment sorcery existed. Us Spielberg-generation sky kids were still part of the Old Republic – bound to television schedulers, TV holiday premieres, theatrical re-releases and birthday cinema party invites. Going to the movies was still a rare treat – even rarer if, like me, you had detaching parents and no siblings around to up the odds of Panda-orange-fuelled family trips down the cinema. The cracks were certainly showing in my mum and dad's lives together. *Kramer Vs Kramer* was not far off the reality – minus, perhaps, the Central Park trike rides, badly made French toast, five Oscars and Vivaldi.

When the summer holidays came, Mum and I left our Surrey bungalow and flew up to Clydebank to stay with family in her childhood home near the River Clyde and the John Brown shipbuilding history my grandfather and his siblings had once been such a proud part of. My aunt and uncle had moved into my grandmother's house since the early death of my grandfather, James. Not only had they created an upstairs lounge – which blew my 1982 mind with its upstairs stereo, upstairs sofas, upstairs coffee percolator and upstairs television – when it came to new home technology, my uncle Tommy was somewhat of a pioneering Glaswegian Jedi Knight, minus the man bun. My older cousins, Maureen and Mark – I was known as 'Wee Mark' – had cassette players in their rooms, knew all about Dr Pepper *and* owned a Grandstand 6000 Colour video game centre. Not only did it understandably boast '10 Games' including the groundbreaking likes of *Gridball*, *Soccer*, *Basketball* and *Tennis* – which was a *Pong* rip-off in all but name – it also had the added analogue glory of two attached joysticks *and* a console slider score tracker.

Attaching wires and things to the back of a TV and having a picture that was not BBC1, BBC2 or ITV – which you were controlling – was tantamount to joining the dark side. Admittedly, for quite a while I thought Ceefax was some CIA computer system only our TV had access to. Not that I wasn't at the cutting edge of gaming technology myself in 1982. My other uncle, Gerald, had recently sent me a newly-released *Donkey Kong Jr.* Game & Watch all the way from Australia. Not only was this pocket-sized console offering a Game A *and* Game B option, it also had an inbuilt alarm clock *and* stand. I may have secretly wanted the *Snoopy Tennis* Game & Watch with its rather fetching puce veneer and ability to see Snoopy ace like Billie Jean King, but to this day *Donkey Kong Jr.* remains the only Nintendo product I have ever owned – even if it was ultimately easier to use a Grandmaster 6000 to hack into the Pentagon and play *WarGames* than to learn how to swing for that sodding jungle key at the end.

My aunt and uncle's previous house was once owned by one of the inventors of television itself, John Logie Baird. It seemed apt that the evolution of television and technology had now made them the first in our family to own a video recorder and the Polaroid VHS cassettes to go with it. Possibly the first Logie-Baird-style demonstration of a video player I'd ever witnessed was during that August 1982 visit, when my uncle put on a video of my cousin Mark appearing on a recent episode of BBC kids' show *Why Don't You?*. Imagine a kids' TV summer show set in the basement of an asbestos-ridden warehouse with the dullest regionally-selected kids known to humanity sat on hay bales, picking through a weekly mailbag rich with suggestions as to how you can really shake up your pineapple and cheese party snacks by replacing the pineapple with more cheese, viewers' letters detailing such anecdotal gold as the time Janet from Hartlepool once pulled the beard of a vicar as a baby, and my cousin Mark nervously guiding us through Glasgow's turn-of-the-century trams. Yes, that was *Why Don't You?* – and the first time I jumped to home-video hyperspace was watching cousin Mark nervously extoll the virtues of reversible tram seats on behalf of the Scottish Trams Union Society. Looking very much like a teenager from *Jaws 2*, minus the sailing injuries and Cape Cod tan, Mark did a grand job in making *Why Don't You?* almost watchable as the nation waited for *Battle of the Planets* to kick in afterwards. I was quietly agog at how the very fabric of time itself could be altered by fast-forwarding a programme to any point in history – well, the history of time between *Hong Kong Phooey* and *Battle of the Planets* one August morning in 1982. I was equally transfixed by the lights and buttons on the video recorder and how the 'tape' would vanish inside the machine only to re-emerge like a big piece of Pez candy. Our PYE push-button TV set back home was a rather sedate, mahogany box of mono sound, three channels and a repository for all those kitschy pottery vases our parents seemed compelled to buy on holiday in the 1970s.

My uncle Tommy was certainly the family flag bearer for all things video, stereo, sound and vision. He would have magazines lying about with centre spreads on the Dolby advancements in movie sound and which movies were available for 'home rental' that month. I didn't even know what 'home rental' was. But it was at this time during this summer visit that I first encountered *Close Encounters of the Third Kind* in a magazine, and became quietly transfixed by the stills of the 'mothership' and that iconic tsunami of blue light, orange beams and silhouettes. I had started to watch television that didn't always star the Muppets or *Sesame Street*. Already landmark titles like *Close Encounters* and *Star Wars* were circling our worlds and our TV culture. I was also an only child. Too often – and gloriously so – my siblings or sleepover pals would be TV shows. They were certainly my breakfast, teatime and a lot of school holidays. My mum's regular insistence on watching *Little House on the Prairie* evolved into *Dallas* and then I got hooked into *The Dukes of Hazzard*, *CHiPS*, *Diff'rent Strokes* and repeats of *Wonder Woman* and *The Incredible Hulk*. Letters like NBC, CBS and ABC became as familiar as Thames TV, LWT and ATV. We could memorise the television schedules and when *CHiPS* was broadcast on a Saturday afternoon quicker than we did our times tables.

Well, I could. But I was having a Larry Wilcox fixation at the time that would immediately switch into a Bo Duke one on the other channel an hour later.

Very soon, we were the generation who knelt at the altar of Aaron Spelling, Glen A. Larson, Stephen J. Cannell and all the American TV production houses whose end credit logos we could recite in our sleep. We were also not averse to taking our movie and TV play out of the lounge and into the back gardens, side alleys and suburban streets of Thatcher's Britain. It would almost always involve bikes and the hierarchy of who owned a racer versus those on a Chopper. Before the 1982 school holidays had started – and energised by American teatime TV shows like *The Red Hand Gang* and *CHiPS* – a bunch of us neighbourhood kids had recently, and somewhat controversially, been exploring an abandoned industrial estate and its scope for wheelies, jumps and screeching halts. It was a school night and we all very quickly made the mistake of ignoring our parental teatime curfews. That magic witching hour of dusk, the ochre sundowns, our flared Lee denim on the pedals and our indie locks, was a heady mix when the suburban Californian adventures of TV shows like *The Red Hand Gang* had emancipated us to venture a bit further and a bit later. When we finally could not eke out another minute, we returned home only to find a line of

Never underestimate the wonder of a bike, summer evenings, movie-inspired adventures and having Spielberg kid hair.

our concerned parents stood like FBI agents mounting a roadblock. And there was no director's cut replacing their fury with walkie-talkies, as befitted the twentieth anniversary modifications of 1982's *E.T. the Extra-Terrestrial*. At least three of the fuming mums looked ready to throw down a stinger strip, and one dad was one glare away from using tear gas on our Rebel formation.

All in all, I had not had much luck when it came to bike play. A year before, in the July of 1981, my 5-year-old self was cautioned by a policeman on the night of Prince Charles and Lady Diana's wedding for failing to use lights, reflectors and a red, white and blue plastic bowler hat in a built-up area. And an acne-ridden, glue-sniffing kid once threw a high-speed apple at me from his racer and nearly knocked the white plastic basket off my first bike. He was probably quite justified in said attack on my bike basket and he probably wasn't actually a glue-sniffer. But anyone in early-1980s Britain who was a local enemy with bad acne must of course be a Copydex-snorting fiend. *Grange Hill* and those terrifying 1980s anti-fun information ads saw to that.

But here in Glasgow another bike incident was to inadvertently set me on a path to the Force. An early summer evening visit with my mum and cousins to pals of theirs resulted in an accident that finally set in motion a series of events which made me a *Star Wars* kid. Just as the visual effects touches were no doubt being done on *Return of the Jedi* and its speeder bike chase back in California, I did a backie on the seat of a 16-year-old boy's racer and within a few metres tore my right ankle open in the pedals. He was mortified and shaking as he carried me valiantly into the nearest hospital in an adult-fearing panic. His name was Paul Logan, a talented musician and the older teen brother straight out of a 1970s Spielberg movie with his dark mop of hair, skinny T-shirt and Dunlop sneakers. He was also one of my first misplaced crushes. Or maybe it was just the mindful older brother figure I had always wanted, but seemed to only have for just one evening. He stayed with me as the doctors sewed up my ankle, and later carried me in his arms, in what felt like the dead of night, to my grandmother's house in Old Kilpatrick. Two summers later, when I was back in Glasgow and *Supergirl* was 1984's summer cinematic obsession, I overheard my cousin Maureen mention how Paul Logan had drowned in a diving accident. It was news that dropped like a quiet geranium petal that only I noticed.

Such an injury was obviously a badge of honour to a nearly-7-year-old. My mum was less keen, possibly kicking herself and a bit more agitated that it happened on her watch at a marital time which had little house space for more drama. Going outside was, of course, now limited. Maybe it was now time to avail myself of Tommy's magical upstairs VHS emporium. One particular title still fascinating me was *Close Encounters of the Third Kind*, its talk of motherships, UFOs and all those lights. And Tommy had it, taped from ITV when Spielberg's original version was first shown in the evening of 28 December 1981. I don't recall if he started the film at the beginning, and I was more enthralled by the lights of the VCR rather than those filling out Ralph McQuarrie's on-screen mothership. But as far as losing my video tape cherry goes – having my first VHS encounter of a movie kind with *Close Encounters of the Third Kind* was no bad thing.

'I am a lineman for the county,' sings Glen Campbell in his 1968 hit, 'Wichita Lineman', 'and I drive the main road searchin' in the sun for another overload.' Searching in the sun and watching skies is the very essence of Steven Spielberg's 1977 opus, *Close Encounters of the Third Kind*. And none more so than for its central character, county lineman Roy Neary, played with blue-eyed, blue-collar brilliance by Richard Dreyfuss. If 1982's *E. T. the Extra-Terrestrial* is about a childhood stood facing adulthood, *Close Encounters* is about an adulthood contemplating childhood, as everyman Roy is soon both infatuated, consumed and enchanted by the orange-flavoured 'ice cream' lights bounding about the skies of Indiana. *Close Encounters* is about artists. It is about sculptors, painters, translators, musicians, communicators, photographers and science visionaries. It is a film that celebrates language in all its earthly, interstellar and visual forms. It is about holding a vision – whether it is Neary's or Spielberg's – and seeing it through to its natural and not always clear-cut conclusion.

Close Encounters is also vital to the sequence of *Watching Skies* movies. The very phrase 'Watch the skies' is of course an overheard piece of advice in the film, the name lent to the film's publicity promo campaign and one of its initial working titles. Very much like its spiritual cousin *E. T.*, *Close Encounters* initially unfurls like a suburban horror movie. A young boy's house is plagued at night by an otherworldly force, sending his toy trucks into a creepy frenzy and the contents of a fridge spilling onto the floor to remind all UK audiences we still do not have refrigerators or milk cartons that big. A panicking mother later pushes through a dark, cricket-heavy forest looking for that son. A single 'star' follows a truck across the Indiana highways. A pristine squadron of Second World War torpedo bombers is found in the Mexican desert with unspoiled cockpit photos of the sweethearts back home. An old-timer whistles 'She'll be Coming Round the Mountain' whilst ignoring the young boy stood perilously on the canary-yellow lines of a mountainous road. Other locals huddle with a kindred yet ever so sinister unity to evangelise the skies for reasons that so far evade both us and them. And as the whole of Indiana is left in a haunted state of high alert, very soon our hero Roy Neary is in the grips of an obsessive breakdown and marriage break-up.

To be the one who splits the family in a Spielberg film and to get away with it as chief protagonist is no mean feat. The families in a Spielberg movie are often already broken – with those responsible often cast off into the story wings. However, with his Falstaffian lunges of mud at his Devils Tower sculpture in the lounge mixed with that dogged independence of *American Graffiti*'s Curt and the unhinged spontaneity of *Jaws*' Hooper, Dreyfuss has only to arc those baby blue eyes up at the skies and we buy it. Add a touch of beatnik, on-the-road scruffiness and a Rockwellian humility, and the lineman for the county becomes an intuitive sculptor-cum-interstellar ambassador with a face 'like a 50/50 Bar'. Key to the film's titular close encounter, Roy is of course a belligerent bull in the authorities' china shop. But as the recent political memories of Watergate and Nixon dictate, no government official is to be trusted, despite the UN flags getting events off on a benevolent footing. The officialdom of the film is the scientists working above the law and the extra-terrestrials clearly trust Roy. It is his determination and final-act attendance which possibly validates the whole mission continuing on the aliens' terms. He is both ambassador and chief witness, and it is one of Dreyfuss and Spielberg's fundamental performances.

Jaws, *Close Encounters* and *E.T. the Extra-Terrestrial* are Spielberg's career-defining 'everyman trilogy' – a key sequence of movies vital to their cultural zeitgeist, key to Steven Spielberg and key to American cinema of the 1970s. Like Tom Hanks and Mark Rylance after him, the suggestion is that Richard Dreyfuss is of course an extension of director Spielberg himself. But in *Close Encounters* – which is the first and only time Spielberg gets sole screenwriting credit on a film he has directed – the director is also there in Bob Balaban's cartographer-cum-translator Laughlin ('are we the first?!'), the wide-eyed innocence and lack of judgment of Cary Guffey's pre-schooler Barry Guiler ('you can come and play now') and undeniably Francois Truffaut's Claude Lacombe ('Major Walsh, it is an event sociologique'). That casting decision, to place a trailblazing film director of French new wave cinema at the mainstream end of an American new wave in a role that celebrates both Truffaut's personal gravitas and his passion for cinema, is a delicious beat of *Close Encounters*. As Lacombe masterminds and supervises the Devils Tower landing project, he does so like an overexcited film director on set – commanding his sound levels, keeping the cameras rolling, positioning his lights and quietly allowing on-set visitors to stay and watch the skies unfold. For Truffaut, Neary may as well be Spielberg.

Close Encounters of the Third Kind is dripping in a late-1970s Americana, and it was a heady mix to a British kid with milk bottles not cartons and fridges not refrigerators. We had torches. America had flashlights – with the longest beams dramatically cut through with that Spielberg cold breath and mist. We had Panda Pops. America had Dr Pepper. We had our dinner already on the plate. America had bowls of food in the centre of the table to help yourself. We had three TV channels. America had multiple TV channels, *Looney Tunes* for breakfast, a whole button of local news, *The Ten Commandments* playing on tap and remote controls. Add to that the mailboxes with their plastic semaphore flags, railroad crossings, bridge-playing grandmothers with their cat-eye spectacles, lone trucks ploughing across midnight freeways, khaki-clad generals on portable phone units, fly doors, the clapping cymbals of a Musical Jolly Chimp, mounds of mash potato and those canary-yellow road lines never that far away from the drama, and you have a fierce and lucid Spielberg sense of post-baby-boom America. It's a textured blue-collar world – handing American cinema a working-class baton that continues in the likes of *The Deer Hunter* (1978), *Blue Collar* (1978), *Norma Jean* (1979), *Alien* (1979), *Silkwood* (1983), *Mask* (1985) and arguably *The Terminator* (1984).

Unlike *Jaws*' Chief Brody (Roy Scheider), who is on a police promotion with a decent Cape Cod home, amicable colleagues and a car 'in the yard', Roy Neary's world is one of intolerant bosses, coupons, being at the mercy of middle management and getting fired. Yet this is still a 1970s Spielberg movie. *Close Encounters* still operates in the same domestic world as that of the Brody family in *Jaws*, with its Snoopy poster in the kids' bedroom, Marvin the Martian on TV, a *Star Trek USS Enterprise* model hanging in the lounge, Ronnie Neary cutting out and hiding a local paper's UFO news flanked by a report on the unexpected box office success of *Star Wars* (complete with parochial news typos and misspelt actors' names) and the military hides its UFO-welcoming infrastructure in plain sight behind branded Baskin-Robbins, Coca-Cola and Piggly Wiggly trucks.

Spielberg's films are often predicated on passions – whether it is those that look beyond the stars, into the woods, under the waves, along the benches of the Senate or newsrooms of DC, into the darkest recesses of European history or those that are simply about getting home. Notions of home are tantamount to many a Spielberg movie and many a *Watching Skies*-era movie. *E.T.*, *Superman*, *Star Trek II: The Wrath of Khan*, *Poltergeist*, *Gremlins* and *Star Wars* are all pivoted on the home or a guiding sense of it. And when Barry Guiler impulsively opens that front door as his home is besieged by a terrifying display of domestic mayhem, juddering ovens, wild vacuum cleaners and an unsolicited Johnny Mathis on the record player reminding all mothers in *Watching Skies* movies to flee the house when they hear the tones of said knitted crooner (Frances Lee McCain clearly took no such note in 1984's *Gremlins*), Vilmos Zsigmond's orange horizon cutting across the trees is as instantly ingrained into the psyche of 1970s cinema and its sense of home as John Wayne opening that door to an altogether different American frontier in John Ford's *The Searchers* (1956). Yet, the visual orchestrations of *Close Encounters* are not all fairy lights bombast and lens glare splendour. If one assumes it was *Jaws* and 1975 that properly ignited Steven Spielberg's moviemaking credentials and the box office fortunes of a whole decade's movie output, one is already overlooking how large-scale and finely orchestrated *The Sugarland Express* and *Duel* are too. Large-scale visuals in *Close Encounters* are not just the mother lode of the mothership, but the exodus chaos of panicking hoards pushing onto freight trains with their gas masks and all those future echoes of *Schindler's List*, cars convoying out of sight along those canary-yellow lined roads, UN trucks bouncing over the dunes of the Gobi Desert and hundreds of villagers scampering to tell their story in Northern India. Spielberg is adroit at putting a national event on a local, personal scale. And vice versa. *Sugarland* is a prescient and true tale of a criminal action being lent a state-wide and snowballing celebrity. *Close Encounters* is telling a soon-to-be-global story from its initial, almost small-town beginnings. If anything, of Spielberg's first three theatrical features – *The Sugarland Express*, *Jaws* and *Close Encounters* – the one about the shark is the smaller, more intimate picture.

Whilst it is a mix of time, life and the story subjects Spielberg settles upon in his movie timeline, as the 1980s continues and he no doubt settles down to raise Neary and Brody kids of his own, it is arguable that the women in his films shift away from that contemporary passion and zeal. After Whoopi Goldberg's turn as Celi in *The Color Purple* (1985) and Holly Hunter's Dorinda opposite Dreyfuss in *Always* (1989), Spielberg's movies possibly surrender that 1977 suburban and domestic edge. *Jurassic Park* (1993) and *The Lost World: Jurassic Park* (1997) are steered by modern science and corporate cynicism, but also pinned to a timeless Indiana Jones safari world where mothers and girlfriends are absent (unless one counts the mothering instincts of the T. rex in *The Lost World*).

After *Jaws* and its high seas machismo, here Spielberg's own script pins protagonist Roy between two resilient women – both of whom end the film as single mums. Jillian Guiler (Melinda Dillon) and Ronnie Neary (Teri Garr) are immediately part of a rich line of key women in Spielberg movies, which by 1977 has already notched up *Something Evil*'s Marjorie (Sandy Dennis), *The Sugarland Express*'s Lou Jean (Goldie Hawn) and *Jaws*' Ellen (Lorraine Gary). And they would soon be followed by *Raiders of the Lost Ark*'s Marion (Karen Allen), *E.T.*'s Mary (Dee Wallace) and *Poltergeist*'s Diane (JoBeth Williams), Tangina (Zelda Rubenstein) and Dr Lesh (Beatrice Straight). And despite being released forty years after *Close Encounters*, it is curious how one of Spielberg's key female roles is now *The Post*'s Katharine Graham (Meryl Streep) in a story which not only examines the Pentagon Papers and less fictional government cover-ups of 1971 but also the gender politics of 1970s America from a prescient 2018 standpoint.

'Don't you think I'm taking this really well?' remarks housewife and kids'-tantrum-wrangler Ronnie Neary as she strives to be enthused by husband Roy's early morning fixations with watching skies. Whilst Ronnie ultimately refuses to share her husband's journey down the UFO rabbit hole in favour of protecting her family, artist Jillian almost understands the extra-terrestrial long game at play as her son Barry is taken by the skies for a greater good. The manner in which a traumatised Jillian is hounded by men and reporters at a press conference scene – restored by Spielberg in the 1998 Director's Cut – is wholly uncomfortable as she is thrown to the press wolves and the ever-so-jealous Ronnie chooses to sit quietly by and not defend a mother trapped in government headlights. One of the screenplay's skills is that Roy's burgeoning friendship with Jillian is barely a romance. They share more in common than not with the thumb-trippin' pair in Spielberg's student short, *Amblin'* (1968), as the likeminded souls Roy and Jillian are flung together because the skies watched them too. Like *Poltergeist*'s Diane and *E.T.*'s Mary, there is a sense with the artist Jillian of a distant ex paying the bills and a late-1960s, possibly rebellious student life at Boston University – as seen on son Barry's T-shirt. Whilst the broken home motif is often a pertinent one to Spielberg, that is not what *Close Encounters* is about. For a film that starts in a foreign language, has no discernible villain and sees all its kid characters taken away, the film is also *not* about the creation of a romance. It is too preoccupied with those *2001: A Space Odyssey* cosmic conundrums encasing our place in the universal scheme of things. And cinema.

Melinda Dillon's role was nominated for the Academy Award for Best Supporting Actress in a year that saw co-star Dreyfuss become the youngest actor at the time to nab the Best Actor Oscar for Neil Simon's *The Goodbye Girl* (1977). He was barely 30 years old and even younger when he shot *Jaws* and *Close Encounters*. Without doubt Melinda Dillon, Teri Garr, Lorraine Gary and Goldie Hawn can all stand tall in a crucial decade of American movies where the bearded, long-haired and plaid-shirted director geeks from film school were now dictating the course of mainstream cinema – and often via female protagonists. Jane Fonda in *Klute* (Alan J. Pakula, 1971), Karen Black in *Five Easy Pieces* (Bob Rafelson, 1971), Ellen Burstyn in *The Exorcist* (William Friedkin, 1973) and *Alice Doesn't Live Here Anymore* (Martin Scorsese, 1974), Gena Rowlands in husband John Cassavetes' *A Woman Under The Influence* (1974) and *Gloria* (1980), Louise Fletcher in *One Flew Over The Cuckoo's Nest* (Milos Forman, 1975), Talia Shire in *Rocky* (John G. Avildsen, 1976), Sissy Spacek in *Carrie* (Brian De Palma, 1976), Faye Dunaway in *Network* (Sidney Lumet, 1976), Diane Keaton in *Annie Hall* (Woody Allen, 1977) and Meryl Streep in *The Deer Hunter* (Michael Cimino, 1978) and *Kramer Vs Kramer* (Robert Benton, 1979) – these are all vital notches in the timeline of 1970s cinema, and all with a contemporary zeal heavily predicated on women.

When watching these movie skies and asked to believe that these shark infested galaxies far, far away can fly, we are also repeatedly watching the labours of women – the crucial ladies both behind and alongside the cameras of this American new wave. Often tutors, classmates and creative allies from the film schools and movie circles frequented by the likes of Spielberg, George Lucas, Francis Ford Coppola, Peter Bogdanovich, Lawrence Kasdan, Walter Murch and Martin Scorsese, these movies of the *Star Wars* generation – like the Bond series – never operated in a male vacuum. Universal Pictures' Vice-President Verna Fields edited *The Sugarland Express* and *Jaws*. She had previously cut *American Graffiti* (1973) with Marcia Lucas before she went on to co-edit her husband George's sand and stars opus, *Star Wars: A New Hope*. Carol Littleton edited *E. T. the Extra-Terrestrial* and collaborated on screenwriter Lawrence Kasdan's later directorial work such as *Body Heat* (1981), *The Big Chill* (1983) and *Silverado* (1985). Likewise, Tina Hirsch edited *Gremlins* (1984) and Scorsese's legendary editor of choice – Thelma Shoonmaker – cut *Raging Bull, The King of Comedy* and many a Marty picture since. Screenwriter Gloria Katz co-wrote *American Graffiti* (1973) and later *Indiana Jones and the Temple of Doom* (1984) with her husband Willard Huyck; Melissa Mathison, the future spouse of Harrison Ford, wrote and produced *E. T. the Extra-Terrestrial*; and Aggie Guerard Rodgers costume-designed *American Graffiti*, *The Conversation* (1974), *Return of the Jedi* (1983) and *The Color Purple* (1985). After becoming the first female producer to win the Best Picture Academy Award for *The Sting* (1973), Julia Phillips followed that up with *Taxi Driver* (1976) before producing *Close Encounters of the Third Kind* with her husband Michael. And perhaps one of the most familiar and loyal names of the eras of both Lucas and Spielberg is producer Kathleen Kennedy – staunch flame-holder of the new *Star Wars* and sidebar movies.

Spielberg is a self-confessed Bond fan. One reading of *Raiders of the Lost Ark* (1981) is that it is his partial response to not being able to direct a Bond movie. And another reading could cite how *Octopussy* (1983) was Bond's reaction to Indiana Jones. When 007 producer Albert R. Broccoli and United Artists respond to the box office sovereignty of *Close Encounters of the Third Kind* and its 1977 bedfellow *Star Wars* with subsequent Bond bullet *Moonraker* (1979), it is not just the ingredients of space, spaceships and the stars that Broccoli and EON Productions want for their man James. It is the effects themselves — that very statement of production, ambition and scale. *Close Encounters'* world of officialdom nervously monitoring TV screens, aircraft radars and gargantuan secret airfield bases replete with tannoys, men in boiler suits, modern technology looming from rock faces, gantries and control pods is nothing if not culled from the production ethics of a Bond movie as designed by Ken Adam. At one point, *Moonraker* even uses John Williams' five-note *Close Encounters* motif for an entrance pad tone.

The likes of *Close Encounters of the Third Kind*, *Star Wars* and *Superman: The Movie* nurtured our cinematic palates for effects-driven movies. But they did not just give us a taste and appetite for these effects-strewn movies with their signature walls of light burning through venetian blinds, keyholes and fireplaces. They gave us an opinion on them too, and a very quickly forged lounge sofa authority on what worked and what didn't. Just as a visual effects pioneer name like Ray Harryhausen had been familiar to our parents' generation, we were soon accustomed to the visual effects family surrounding the work of Lucas, Spielberg and Richard Donner. Names such as Dennis Muren, John Dykstra, Joe Johnston, Phil Tippet, Richard Edlund, Stan Winston, Rick Baker, Ben Burtt, Ken Ralston and Douglas Trumbull fast became the familiar roll call of a team of California-based movie sorcerers whose names were just as familiar to some of us as those of our school teachers.

In just one six-month period, *Star Wars* and *Close Encounters of the Third Kind* set a bar that is arguably still the DNA of movie effects and testament to their successful application.

Of course, other SFX movies emerged in 1977. Though few of us schoolkids had any lunch boxes or bubble-bath bottles from *Demon Seed, Damnation Alley, Prey, Starship Invasions, Capricorn One* or the very British antics of the Children's Film Foundation's *The Glitterball*. I was quite obsessed with that last one in the 1980s. For quite a while I couldn't walk down a supermarket aisle without expecting a tsunami of alien ball bearings wreaking a stop-motion havoc. But if they were not *very* pre-*Star Wars* sci-fi B-movies, they

Close Encounters of the Third Kind and its mothership still hang over Hollywood's Dolby Theatre with knowing, stereo pride.

were often dollar-inducing hopes of wringing out the returns on previous 1970s hits without fully gauging what made those originals work. Step forward 1977's underwater pretenders to the throne – *Orca* and *The Deep* (written by *Jaws*' Peter Benchley and starring Robert Shaw), *Airport '77*, the box-of-frogs crazy that is *Exorcist II: The Heretic* and all their attempts to catch the lightning of those early 1970s originals back into the jar, with diminishing results.

As my uncle Tommy's home tech magazines attested in that summer of 1982, *Close Encounters of the Third Kind* is certainly a film which felt aligned to the advancing cinema technology of the 1970s. Its movie peers *Superman* and *Star Wars* made great play not just of the FX powerhouses they were in their day. The movie theatres of America and eventually Britain – well, those 'leading cinemas throughout the country' – made great play of the new developments in theatrical sound too. The sound design of *Close Encounters* is particularly noteworthy – with the inane chat of idle television sets commenting on dialogue-free scenes, the power station hums of overhead UFOs, the improvised chatter, the unnerving use of a *Sesame Street* educational album when interplanetary visitors first drop in on the Guiler household, the physics of delayed soundwaves from the mothership, the busy tannoys of the landing site and those most *Watching Skies* of Spielberg tropes – the simultaneous conversations, frenzied radio panics and the crickets of nightfall. It is an aural template Spielberg still uses forty years later in *The Post* (2017) with its Pakula-savvy newsrooms, buzzing typing pools and multi-delivered dialogue vying for attention. The very term 'Dolby Stereo' became a high street parlance and marketing tool with *Close Encounters* as one of its leading lights. A new Dolby-endorsing billboard featuring the film's mothership still perches atop the Dolby Theatre in Hollywood – the current home of the Academy Awards ceremony.

Like *Jaws* before it, with the dismembered head of Ben Gardner, and later *Jurassic Park* and the rippling waters of the first T. rex attack, *Close Encounters* plays with and partly banks on how it knows it will be discussed on the walk home from the movie theatre. It knowingly starts with mysterious headlights in a sandstorm soon revealed to be just that. But when those less earthly headlights later rise above Dreyfuss and his parked truck *that* is the moment that lingers as the playfulness and wonder of *Close Encounters* is summed up in one rousing beat. Being tailgated by a truck bigger than you, wading into the water on a beach, waving approaching headlights to veer around you and a starry night resting behind the dark silhouette of a mountain – three or so films in and this crucial first act of Spielberg's career has already left indelible marks on the psyche of cinema and its audiences. That *Close Encounters of the Third Kind* has retained its command, power and glory like one of those Flight 19 torpedo bombers returned intact at the start of the movie is sheer testament to Spielberg and his creative team's wisdom, labours and artistry. Instead of American arrogance and military might leading humankind's welcoming party to extra-terrestrial life, *Close Encounters* leaves the audience with a template of benevolence and a wish upon a star that any real-life first contact would be exactly what Spielberg depicts here in 1977. There is no cynicism in Roy Neary, *Close Encounters of the Third Kind* or its officialdom and scientists. The film may exist in a world before camera phones and videos become the chatter of YouTube comments and Facebook shares. Yet four decades later its many lights are not diminished. The kids and their familiar mops of hair, boot-cut denim and skinny tees aside, Spielberg's ode to the star men in all of us arguably feels more contemporary than J.J. Abrams' *Super 8* (2011) and its gallant, Spielberg-produced homage to that 1970s world of American moviemaking. And all the *D.A.R.Y.L.* meets *Close Encounters* drives of a film like *Midnight Special* (2016) just serve to remind us of the original's humanity and poise.

This was a film whose very movie culture was turned on its head during post-production when *Star Wars* emerged onto American movie screens in May 1977 and fired its blaster at all previous patterns of spectatorship, exhibition and movie consumption (even the ones *Jaws* had rewritten just two summers before). The very fact that *Close Encounters of the Third Kind* doesn't pale in comparison to *Star Wars* – despite achieving similar visual effects milestones, cultural footprints and trouncing *A New Hope* to the Academy Award for Best Cinematography – is one of its glories. Although, we may have to lay some blame at the rubber alien feet of *Close Encounters* and its (then) rare 1980 Special Edition for possibly giving George Lucas the notion of special editions, extended editions and directors' cuts. Hopefully a third encounter of a re-edited kind is enough now for Steven and his 1977 piece of movie perfection. Political without resting on any real anti-Watergate or anti-Washington laurels, domestic without being cosy, and uplifting without being cloying – *Close Encounters of the Third Kind* is still one of the masterworks of American cinema.

OBI-WAN FLEW OVER
THE CUCKOO'S NEST

A week later. With my mum's larger-than-life Uncle Willy carrying my heavily bandaged ankle and I through Glasgow Airport before I then received the airside VIP wheelchair perks normally reserved for Elizabeth Taylor – a tartan knee blanket and a colouring book – the time came to bid goodbye to the mothership of Glasgow for now.

With the understandable strains and pains of a marriage break-up clearly getting to both my parents, I spent the end of the summer with my pal Gareth and his family. His mum was a childhood mate of Mum's and Gareth had already been a good wingman at my birthday parties. The hushed conversations and phone calls were still some whispering Greek chorus to the three-act separation that endeavoured to play out without me noticing. That tactic somewhat failed, and homesickness and restless nights at Gareth's ensued. But there was salvation. And it was a plastic redemption sent all the way from Cincinnati, Ohio to possibly put a purpose to my broken home and torn ankle. In truth, it was only licensed in Cincinnati, Ohio. It was actually produced in an English industrial town called Coalville, North West Leicestershire. Since the early

1920s, the company, which had begun producing celluloid-based household products, dolls and toys, had been based out of the former mining town of Coalville. It went by the name of Palitoy. Talking Daleks, Tiny Tears, Action Force, *Star Trek* figures, Care Bears and Action Man – they were all Palitoy products in the UK. I already had the flock haired and eagle-eyed Action Man with the infamous gripping hand motif, blue plastic Speedos, a deep-sea diving suit – complete with weighted boots for bath-time play - and an assault helicopter with accompanying navy-blue jumpsuit. Next to my *Superman: The Movie* flask, it was probably the butchest statement of my formative years. And quite a few that followed in their wake.

However, Palitoy was about to be even more synonymous with our early-1980s childhood – as recognisable a name as Spielberg, Princess Diana, Mattel, J. R. Ewing, Margaret Thatcher or Ronald Reagan. For it was Palitoy who were the British face of *Star Wars* toys. They had been granted the licence from America's famed Kenner Products and Lucasfilm Ltd to produce and distribute a plastic fantastic universe of 3¾-inch figures, playset worlds, poseable creatures, battleships with batteries not included and tiny plastic blasters ready to be lost up the Hoover or in the backyard in three days flat. Palitoy's 1978 Death Star playset would not only prove to be one of the eventually rarer and niftier of Palitoy's *Star Wars* range – Kenner produced a different Death Star playset for the American market – but my friend Gareth had one. It was the first physical piece of merchandise or reference to *Star* Wars I had ever encountered. In a front-lounge den we made from a bedsheet, a plastic clothes horse and some dining table chairs, Gareth laid out the elusive Death Star on the carpet. Like all cardboard games of the time, it of course needed unfolding, clipping and opening out to bring it to life. It was a two-level base – three if you count the X-Wing-ready gun turret platform on the top – held together with plastic pegs and complete with painted dividing panels depicting the control boards, pipes, gantries, blast doors and the working life of the Death Star and its Stormtroopers and Star Destroyer Commanders. It had those undeniable Galactic lozenge-shaped mesh partitions and that most deadly of all Empirical design statements – hexagonal corridor entrances. Gareth filled some of the partitioned rooms with a Stormtrooper or two and a Ben Kenobi figure took his place near a traction beam. And who the hell was this other guy, *Obi-Wan*?!

This wasn't all just a galaxy far, far away to me. I had never experienced these worlds before. When it came to the characters, movies, planets and toys which had been gripping the older end of my generation, I was still a naïve farm boy from the Cranleigh System, kicking through the dust of my only child homestead making modest dens and wondering why I had to go to bed in the summer when it was still light outside. My world had been backstage at *The Muppet Show*, my *Dukes of Hazzard* Barnbusters playset and Bo Duke fixation and how the pages of my *Peanuts* comic books matched my Snoopy bedspread. But here – here was someone who knew of the Rebellion against the Empire. He knew of Stormtroopers, Jedi, Jawas, TIE fighters, R2 units and Death Stars. It was all happening on his lounge floor and upstairs – where a vacant, staring black mask you could open up and store plastic figurines inside perched on a shelf with its sinister and immobile triangular mouth and bolted jowls. That was the 1980 Darth Vader Collector's Case. And the white-font names of those figurine compartments were fascinating – easily discernible with their strange, but clearly good or bad identities such as 'Death Star Droid', 'Princess Leia', 'Luke Skywalker: X-Wing Pilot', 'IG-88 Bounty Hunter' and 'Chewbacca'. Slowly, surely and without much resistance, I found myself being seduced by the Dark Side, the Light Side, Hand Solo and this Death Star. A few us got Han

Solo's name wrong for quite a while – the 1982 downside of having no *Star Wars* figures, books, movie or end credits to replay over and over.

Suddenly my Lego police station never had a backstory. My waterproof Action Man didn't have a movie the world knew about. My blue bike had just been a blue bike, not a part-time Landspeeder. And *Sesame Street* had just been brought to us by the letter 'C' and the number '3', rather than C-3PO. How apt that a toy company charged with firing our movie imaginations from the skies of the big screen to our bedroom, lounges, kitchen tables and stairwells started out life making products from celluloid – the infamously flammable plastic that was once the very physical constituent of cinema itself. Because of this debilitating ankle and the lounge floor tour of the Death Star, I had just entered a fraternity – one with 'Palitoy' on its box and 'Lucasfilm' on the soles of its plastic feet. I am reminded of that early family scene in *Close Encounters* when Roy Neary wants to win over his restless kids with the promise of a Disney movie at the local movie theatre or Goofy Golf – 'Tomorrow night you can play Goofy Golf, which is a lot of standing in line and shoving and pushing and probably getting a zero, or you can see *Pinocchio* which is a lot of furry animals and magic, and you'll have a wonderful time. Okay? So let's vote.' 'Goofy Golf!' reply his kids with rapid fire. Sorry Roy, but *Pinocchio* was our parents' childhood. 'A lot of standing in line' for a new *Star Wars* movie or piece of merchandise was exactly what us sky kids were going to be all about. But in the fall of 1982, and without any re-release or home video access, my chances of seeing *A New Hope* were very much without hope. One particular film was everywhere. It had ingrained itself into a globe of moviegoers' memories and passions and I could not watch it. I cannot even make a quip here about leaving a distress message in the memory banks of an astromech robot, as I didn't even know that pivotal beat of 1970s culture had happened. But in October 1982, that began to change and through the most unexpected of ways.

We are now told that depression is what happens when someone has 'just been strong for too long'. It is a cloying fridge magnet of a sentiment, but like all decent fridge magnet one-liners, it packs a truth. Life and the unexpected loss of a parent dealt my mother a bad set of cards in the early 1980s. The night before I was meant to start school for the first time, my grandfather suffered a fatal heart attack in sudden circumstances. Despite being given a brand-new *Superman: The Movie* flask and lunch box, it was not easy standing in the September dew coating our front lawn about eight hours later for that suddenly less important 'first day at school' photo. It was probably best my mum did not try to be strong for a while. When the cracks started to become splinters and my bike injury didn't help, my mum ended up in a hospital – the sort of hospital they had less-kind labels for in 1982. Mum was actually very low down on the scale of needing treatment. Today, she no doubt would have been offered decent counselling. Very much like my ankle, Mum just had a broken spirit. As I was discovering the world of *Star Wars* and leaving my family home, not entirely unlike at least two generations of Skywalker boys – albeit with less podracing and interventions by ex-Jedi Knights of the British stage – my mum was recovering. I don't recall the no-doubt veiled and concerned whisperings of whether it was suitable for my 7-year-old self to go and visit my mum in hospital. But I wanted to. And needed to.

The hospital in question was a former shining beacon of the British mental health system – one that was so big it once had its own fire brigade, chapel, gasworks and ballroom. Less a shining beacon to the British health care system of the twentieth century, more a labyrinthine hospital designed by Stanley Kubrick in the early 1970s – a sort of Clockwork Melange. It never ceases to perplex me why people felt the smallest glitches in people's minds required the biggest show of architectural might to heal them. Yet, looking back, it was also a vital community for the long-haul and permanent residents. And possibly a better one than the 'community' Margaret Thatcher's government decided should provide free 'care', whilst her Cabinet was pounding a wrecking ball through the spine of many a community.

But there it was – this twice-weekly behemoth of towers and windows stretching forth like a council-run Jabba the Hutt's Palace. It quickly became an odd playground for this 7-year-old – one that very soon never seemed that bizarre. As kids, we all got left with Mum's pal down the road or a crazy neighbour lady we couldn't quite work out. My weekends and two evenings a week were no different. My babysitters and new friends were recovering alcoholics, manic depressives, schizophrenics and broken artists with dark and telling stitches from ear to ear. It was like happy hour at the Mos Eisley Cantina. Just with less space-age lounge music. And then there were those who didn't have any visitors. They were often the life and soul of the place, the rebel rousers turning up the radio to stem the awkwardness and rule-bound windows of visiting time. I would be quite over-dressed with my Muppets T-shirt, flared jeans and Luke Skywalker locks as all around me was a sea of cigarette-ash-stained dressing gowns and striped pyjamas. Beat author Ken Kesey's *One Flew Over the Cuckoo's Nest* and Milos Forman's subsequent Academy Award-winning movie of 1975 were not just the template of people's perceptions of such institutions. It was the reality of those living it. And those visiting. The wards would have curious names all culled, it seemed, from

1950s drag queens like 'Barbara' and 'Florence'. Who would call a ward for the mentally bruised 'Barbara'?! Okay – I think I might. It sounds wild!

Thanks to the ping-pong table on the second floor, my table tennis backhand gradually improved to nearly Chinese Olympic levels – assuming the seriously alcoholic men tutoring me were having 'a good day'. Without the panic that would curb such encounters nowadays, I would be given squashed chocolate bars from older patients just desperate to reach out with some kindness to somebody young. And some kind soul made me a beautiful blue wooden stool in woodwork classes that I have to this day.

Like the patients, I soon learnt the routine of the tea trolley, sharing their anticipation of a biscuit and hot chocolate in those thick NHS enamel cups and saucers. It was a weekly routine that would coincide with Sunday night television and a cup-clutching exodus into the slightly yellowing TV lounge and its out-of-reach screens nailed hard into the corners of the high ceilings. As much as it would be most surreal to witness the patients collectively heckling the fortunes of Sue Ellen Ewing as she ended up in 'the nut house' in a *Dallas* cliffhanger freeze-frame, it was the loyal Sunday TV exodus into the TV lounge to watch British World War Two incarceration drama *Tenko* that sticks in the mind. You could have heard a pin drop – assuming pins were not confiscated by the staff – whenever actress Stephanie Beacham and her sinewy neck were trying to make a three-course meal out of a thimble of rice and a dead rat. Maybe it was *Tenko's* all-women story or the Japanese concentration camp saga that struck home for the patients? I do not recall any cruel Death Star commandants on Barbara Ward, but I do remember hearing stories of escaping inmates making a beeline for the local shops in ward gowns and slippers, and visiting priests soon learning to check the boots of their cars when leaving. It was clear Han Solo's old smuggling tricks were familiar to some of the patients. But not me. Yet.

However, on the night of Sunday 24 October 1982, there were no such great escapes planned. With *Tenko* and *Dallas* controversially jettisoned, the channel-changing stick reached high for the third button down. And at 7.15 p.m. sharp on ITV, Obi-Wan Kenobi flew over, under and into the cuckoo's nest as *Star Wars* received its British television premiere. In a total reversal of how British audiences had to wait months and months for *A New Hope* to reach the cinema screens of January 1978, here the first *Star Wars* movie was being premiered on prime-time network television one and a half years before its inaugural network broadcast in the States. It had been available on some pay-per-view services since the winter of 1983, but British TV still got to shoot first. It wasn't until the evening of Sunday 26 February 1984 that *Star Wars* first screened to network audiences on CBS.

The very first time I ever clocked the real Darth Vader was not on a lunch box, a figurine card, a duvet set or even in a Death Star playset. It was in a smoke-filled TV lounge of a psychiatric ward in a Victorian-built hospital. Suffice to say, the viewing was soon interrupted by the cantina bar dramatics of some of the more restless patients, the end of visiting hours and a school-night need to get home early. As I walked away on that October evening along a corridor that heralded such fun signposts as 'ECT Department', 'Occupational Therapy' and 'Mortuary', John Williams' Stormtrooper theme echoed into the cold night. It was the first time I left not just thinking of Mum and the next visit. I was thinking of that film with the shiny black villain and those robots.

My mum thankfully soon recovered and came home before Christmas to a renewed life, and an eventual new marriage. She spent time feeling guilty for exposing me to that world. Yet when you are 6 years old, *anything* is a world. A makeshift Death Star base under a dining table. The ability of polystyrene packaging to be a Rebel headquarters. Even the strange corridors of a psychiatric unit echoing to some Sand People's attack cries before a commercial break. Those worlds are ours to do with in our own minds as we want. Finding a strange good in what can be deemed by others as bad is surely one of the powers of childhood. Just look at the young kids who loved *The Phantom Menace*.

HE CAME TO
ME TOO

E.T. THE EXTRA-TERRESTRIAL

1982. A 10-year-old boy hastens through his Californian neighbourhood after a lost creature flees his backyard in a panic. With growing wonder, the boy pauses by a set of kids' swings and watches the night sky above with a cautious smile at the adventure ahead.

○————————○

The late 1970s and early 1980s was a time when our American films were often delayed on their journey to Britain. Despite its now sainted 25 May 1977 opening date in the States, *Star Wars* actually took eight months to reach mainstream UK cinemas – seven if you lived in London. That's right – eight months. Eight of 'em! Thankfully, in May 1980, *The Empire Strikes Back* made British fans wait a more acceptable four days. *E.T. the Extra-Terrestrial* was released in America on 11 June 1982 – a full six months before Elliott, E.T. and that BMX bike flew over the moon and the Atlantic for the UK's 10 December opening.

With the *Star Wars* publicity machine two films into its original cycle, it was clear Universal Studios wanted a bit of that merch action for their brown rubber alien. Images of said spaceman being flanked by wild bracken and Spielberg in his *E. T. the Extra-Terrestrial* baseball cap were almost as commonplace in the early 1980s as Diana's puff-sleeve blouses, the miner's strike on the TV news, *He-Man*, *BBC Breakfast Time*'s news reports on the Cabbage Patch Kid craze, the Mary Rose excavation and posters for Bob Marley's *Legend* album on every derelict high street wall. The 'Flying' main theme from *E. T.* was released in Britain as a single in December 1982 and spent ten respectable weeks in the charts (in the curious company of Toto's 'Africa', performed by John Williams' son, Joseph). In January 1983, 'Flying' peaked at number 17 where it was ably flanked on either side by The Stranglers and Wham. Despite a 1977 guilty-pleasure of a space disco version by Meco reaching numbers 1 and 7 in the US and UK charts respectively, not even Williams' landmark 'Star Wars Main Theme' made the chart grade in the way *E. T.* did. The film later garnered John Williams his fourth Academy Award – he had previously won for *Fiddler on the Roof, Jaws* and *Star Wars*, and would later have a fifth win for 1993's *Schindler's List*. And to this day it is still California State Law that cues from the *E. T.* score must accompany every post-commercial-break crane shot of the Oscars telecast.

In 1982, *E. T. the Extra-Terrestrial* was a fully-fledged cultural event propelled by shining reviews, expectancy, merchandise and that theme. *E. T.* lunch boxes, torches, extendable-necked figurines, View-Master slides, Pizza Hut tumblers, pyjamas, Topps candy, Pez dispensers, Christmas baubles, William Kotzwinkle's bestselling novelisation, colouring books, Kuwahara BMX bikes, Panini sticker albums, vinyl soundtracks, chewing gum, posters and photo books were having their own fairly lucrative adventure on Earth. The covers of *People, Rolling Stone* and nearly every other 1982 magazine featured a coy E.T. lurking in various fake ferns; and Michael Jackson and Quincy Jones produced a short-lived vinyl narration of the film which was pulled almost as soon as it was released for fear it would damage sales of an imminent, little-known album called *Thriller*. The next time Spielberg had an event movie approaching the global hold of *E.T.* was *Jurassic Park* (1993) – a film whose deliberate and playful on-screen branding, lunch boxes, T-shirts, plush toys and baseball caps were as much a nod to the marketing phenomenon of *Star Wars* and *E.T.* as Richard Attenborough's drive-in dinos. This 7-year-old desperately wanted a plush leather E.T. doll, but had to settle instead for a dodgy knock-off from some market and the mandatory, more pocket money friendly Panini sticker album.

Because it wasn't just an extra-terrestrial that had separation issues in 1982. I was taken very separately to see *E.T.* twice in one week – by my mum and then my dad. The first parental trip was a partial treat from Mum for my recent sterling work in St Cuthbert Mayne's nativity play, *Noah's Ark*. To be fair, as 7-year-old Catholic frogs in unforgiving green nylon leotards go, not even *E.T.*'s Elliott himself could have saved this school frog from a critical mauling. It was not a patch on my previous year's innkeeper triumph, or the following year's *Xanadu*-inspired archangel with a nun-goading, gold-trimmed miniskirt ensemble. Yep, 1982's frog was the least of my crimes against nativity. And as a cinematic reward for said performance, one rainy December afternoon in 1982, Mum and I ignored the Christmas shoppers and their Argos-bound quests for Tefal sandwich makers, Tomytronic 3D game handsets, Major Morgans and maybe a new rose-patterned plastic clock for the kitchen and headed to Guildford's Star Cinema.

After the 1935 art deco behemoth that was the town's Odeon, the Star Cinema's Studio 1 was Guildford's support-act movie house – and where I later saw *Indiana Jones and the Temple of Doom* in 1984 and some arduous, badly dubbed *Jesus* movie that the local bishop had clearly found some cheap prints of down the market. As the ticket line for Studio 1 trailed out of sight towards the cracked plastic 1970s Santas making up Guildford's Christmas lights, *E.T.* became the first film I remember queuing for. And in the subsequent movie years of the 1980s, I rarely queued ever again – but only because I became most insistent at always being the first in line in case the seats ran out. There was no pre-booking in 1982. The only interaction with the cinema beforehand came down to listening to an unenthusiastic answerphone message from the projectionist's wife, detailing the two showings a day of 'hit new movie *Krull* – rated PG', where best to park and how 'the left half of the aisle is now unfortunately non-smoking'. You couldn't even buy tickets in advance in person. Could you imagine the abject terror of not being able to pre-book any seats for the first night of *The Force Awakens, The Last Jedi, Solo* or *Rogue One*?! That is partly why the blockbuster genre and its literal block-busting queues awoke with such force during these sky-watching years – you had to be at the cinema hours before or you ran the risk of total disappointment. Or watching *Sophie's Choice* as your Christmas movie treat. There were not even any seat allocation checks in 1982 – just a Saturday girl traipsing along the damp queue with a clicker counter, a stack of emergency plastic chairs and a home perm.

Together with its contemporary siblings *Jaws* and *Close Encounters of the Third Kind, E.T. the Extra-Terrestrial* completes that career-defining 'everyman trilogy' for Steven Spielberg. Flanked by the Second World War hijinks of *1941* (1979), *Raiders of the Lost Ark* (1981) and *Indiana Jones and the Temple of Doom* (1984), *E.T.* represents a marked return to a contemporary grit and domestic

Steven Spielberg finally got his Hollywood Walk of Fame star twenty years after *E.T. The Extra Terrestrial.*

resolve Spielberg has – arguably – rarely achieved since. Henry Thomas's Elliott is easily cut from the same everyman cloth as *Close Encounters'* Roy Neary (Richard Dreyfuss) and *Jaws'* Martin Brody (Roy Scheider). Despite their chronology, *E. T.* feels almost like a prequel to *Close Encounters* – where Elliott later grows up to be Richard Dreyfuss in any number of Spielberg movies. Aside from 2008's *Indiana Jones and the Kingdom of the Crystal Skull* – the only instance of Spielberg doing UFOs in a historic setting – it seems the director prefers a modern-day context for his alien encounters. He only properly returns to the genre as director two decades later for *War of the Worlds* (2005) for its altogether less benevolent aliens and their stark warnings about ignoring your flu jab in the fall.

From the opening frame of a night sky and all its story promise to a generation whose movie adventures often launched on a vista of stars (*Star Trek, Star Wars, Superman*), *E.T. the Extra-Terrestrial* reportedly developed from an early urge on the part of Steven Spielberg to make a film about childhood, and one hampered by separating parents. Tapping into his adolescent obsessions of UFOs and the divorce that displaced his own youth, the young Steven nurtured the idea in various directions over the years. As our titular botanist gets easily distracted and strays from the pack – there is always one who ignores what time the coach party leaves the car park – *E.T.* starts with an almost Penderecki sense of musical foreboding. With clusters of ominous, discordant tones reminiscent of how composer John Williams also opens *Close Encounters* and *Jaws, E.T.* launches on a dark note of musical fear as Spielberg very nearly pitches this as a horror film for kids. The initial spectacle of visiting aliens is met with heavy church organs, the roaming E.T. is soon dwarfed by a Gothic cathedral of trees, and the arriving government agents are dealt an ominous leitmotif not unlike the Empirical cues from *Star Wars*. And it is not just in space that no one can hear you scream. The speechless Elliott's first moonlit encounter with E.T. is a creepy cacophony of scattering limbs, dropped flashlights and an outer-worldly musical pulse straight out of *Alien*. But as that alien follows the bait of Reese's Pieces like breadcrumbs in a Brothers Grimm fairy tale to the boy in the red riding hoodie, it is John Williams' own musical breadcrumbs which supplant the audience's trepidation with softening strings, harps and a gentle trust. As Henry Thomas's Elliott demonstrates his *Star Wars* toys, *Jaws* merchandise and Pez dispensers for his new interstellar pal, Williams affords the scene one of his greatest tracks, 'E.T. and Me'. Just as Williams captures that sense of Americana and home for the Smallville scenes in *Superman: The Movie* (1978), in *E.T.* he underscores the fleeting sanctity of a childhood home as kind harps accompany the extra-terrestrial listening in to Mary (Dee Wallace) reading *Peter Pan* to her daughter Gertie.

Any examination of childhood – be it *E.T.*, *Empire of the Sun*, *Hook, Kes, The BFG* or Richard Linklater's *Boyhood* – cannot help but look at adulthood and parenthood too. Elliott's brother Michael (Robert MacNaughton) is a juvenile father figure to his younger siblings, forever trying to jostle Elliott and Gertie (Drew Barrymore) into remembering their mother's frayed emotions and resources. Government investigator Keys (Peter Coyote) very quickly takes Elliott, his family and their heartbreaks under his wing. And one of the tender turning points of the film is when you realise it is E.T. who is now being the surrogate parent to Elliott. From an adult concern over the boys teasing their sister Gertie and her rag doll in the closet, to a later moonlit moment when E.T. simply extends a kind, chin-up finger to his young charge with a reassuring smile, Melissa Mathison's script revels in not just how the kids adopt this extra-terrestrial into their after-school world, but how it is he who ultimately guides them.

With the same suburban California of new builds, parched grass verges, arid backyards and child-busy driveways of its 1982 cousin *Poltergeist* – which Spielberg also wrote and co-produced – *E.T.* also populates itself with the same 1960s student baby boomers-cum-disillusioned nine-to-five parents. *E.T.*'s Mary (Dee Wallace) and *Poltergeist*'s Steven and Diane Freeling (Craig T. Nelson and JoBeth Williams) are unsure suburbanites not always certain of when or how they grew up. With her husband's belongings resigned to the garage, Mary's marriage has crumbled with the off-story affair he is continuing in Mexico. And the Freelings try to keep their flower-power minds open as husband Steven gets to incongruous grips with a joint and a bedtime book about Ronald Reagan. It is a sense of disillusioned domesticity not wholly apparent in the warmer dinner-table milieus and exchanges of *Jaws* and *Close Encounters*. Whereas the open-minded Diane Freeling is trying to embrace the early paranormal activity creeping up on her home, single parent Mary has long lost all sense of wonder and cannot even notice the 'man from the moon' in her kitchen.

Mary and the Freelings were also the same generation as my parents. My mum had experienced that 1950s childhood framed by American music, politics and movie influences. She had been that 1960s university student hearing the news of JFK's assassination and remembering how the campus paused in midnight tribute when a lone nun played 'The Star-Spangled Banner' on the university chapel's grand organ. She too was a mum to a little mop-haired kid entering a 1980s of *Star Wars*, *Sesame Street*, *Superman* lunch boxes, Rubik's Cubes and a Golden Retriever or two by his side. She was also in the hard midst of a divorce.

Maybe it was because Steven Spielberg himself experienced a broken home, or because I was too and you later make these observations, but a founding and ever recurring trope of the director's work is absent fathers. From Mann (Dennis Weaver) trying to make amends on the payphone to his wife in *Duel* (1971) and absent family man Donovan (Tom Hanks) in *Bridge Of Spies* (2015), via the incarcerated Clovis (William Atherton) in *The Sugarland Express* (1974), the surrogate father figures of Harrison Ford in *Indiana Jones and the Temple of Doom* (1984), John Malkovich in *Empire of the Sun* (1987), Sam Robards in *A.I. Artificial Intelligence* (2001), Tom Hanks again in *Catch Me If You Can* (2002), Mark Rylance in *The BFG* (2016) and arguably *Ready Player One* (2018), to the ever-busy protagonist dads of *Jaws* (1975), *Close Encounters*

(1977), *Indiana Jones and the Last Crusade* (1989), *Hook* (1991), *Jurassic Park: The Lost World* (1997), *Munich* (2005), *Indiana Jones and the Kingdom of the Crystal Skull* (2008), *Lincoln* (2012) and *The Post* (2017) – the patriarchal motif Spielberg began in the 1970s is still a constant. It is one that has clearly grown too, as the director himself has. Comparing the parentally reckless and incarcerated Clovis in *The Sugarland Express* to the calm and law-abiding parental granite of Donovan in *Bridge of Spies* forty years later, the father figures of Spielberg's *oeuvre* have no doubt evolved with their director and his own experiences of being a parent to seven kids. It is a trope that is tantamount to *Superman: The Movie* (1978) – where both Clark Kent's star and Earth fathers are soon sorely absent, *Star Trek II: The Wrath of Khan* which puts Admiral Kirk somewhat through the wringer of bad-dad shame, and the *Star Wars* saga – whose key personal dramas are of course hinged on fathers, sons, mothers and daughters.

My father was never absent. He was separate. And as *E.T. the Extra-Terrestrial* proves, separate is still hard. What the likes of *E.T.* and Spielberg underscore is the new normality of this fragmented family unit. Gone are the classical Hollywood family units of *It's a Wonderful Life* (1946), *Meet Me in St Louis* (1944) and *Old Yeller* (1957). By the time of *E.T.*, the Republican family nirvana has already been cinematically pricked by the likes of *The Godfather* (1972), *The Texas Chain Saw Massacre* (1974), *The Omen* (1976), *Kramer Vs Kramer* (1979), *Ordinary People* (1980), *The Shining* (1980) and the Skywalkers of *Star Wars* (1977). In the 1970s, American cinema sees new wave filmmakers challenge movie family templates with *their* family templates.

Whilst single parents are nothing new to the timeline of cinema (1921's *The Kid*, 1940's *Pinocchio* and 1962's *To Kill a Mockingbird* are all predicated quite brilliantly on single fathers), it was ironically the 1980s and the time of Ronald Reagan's dangerously nostalgic pushes for 'traditional' family values that saw cinema – that very medium that gave the President his fame – opt for something a bit more in keeping with the audience's own experiences. *WarGames* (1983), *Footloose* (1983), *The Karate Kid* (1984), *The NeverEnding Story* (1984), *Cocoon* (1985), *Explorers* (1985), *Pretty in Pink* (1986), *Teen Wolf* (1986) and of course *E.T.* all pin their lead kids to lone parent homesteads without fanfare. Divorce was Spielberg's world. Divorce was my world. And it was the world of a great many kids of my generation who just picked up their Millennium Falcons and *Superman* View-Master reels and got on with it. Just as divorce became its own Oscar-baiting genre, and dysfunctional families were either the fall from family grace of A-listers (*Mrs Doubtfire*, *Stepmom*) or the kooky mainstay of indie cinema (*The Royal Tenenbaums*, *The Squid and the Whale*, *The Kids are Alright*), *E.T.* presents the honesty of it.

Until the 1950s and the rise of the 'teenager' as a new demographic ripe for the box office picking, the previous Hollywood child-star likes of Shirley Temple, Elizabeth Taylor, Judy Garland, Jackie Cooper and Roddy McDowall were often cute and endearing, because they were kids acting like small adults in a nostalgic world. As Hollywood and its coffers sat up to rethink sidetracking children's stories to the kids' table of cinema, the timeline of kids' stories in European filmmaking was faring somewhat differently. Despite the later live-action and more contemporary American likes of *Freaky Friday* (1976), any number of 1970s Disney movies charting Jodie Foster's denim-heavy adolescence, *Escape to Witch Mountain* (1975), *The Bad News Bears* (1976) and 1979's *The Black Stallion* (penned by *E.T.*'s Melissa Mathison), *E.T. the Extra-Terrestrial* ultimately has more in common with Ken Loach's *Kes* (1969) than not. Likewise, the European influences of Francois Truffaut's *Le 400 Coups*, Victor Erice's *The Spirit of the Beehive* (1974) and Bryan Forbes *Whistle Down the Wind* (1961) are all over *E.T.* In 1959's *Le 400 Coups*,

Truffaut – who Spielberg, of course, had already hand-picked to play benevolent UFO expert Lacombe in *Close Encounters* – also shoots at a child's height. He too glories in the note-passing culture of kids, their classroom desks and that afterschool world versus the authority of an adult's desk and detention, the mixed freedoms and dramas to be had from a stolen typewriter and the parents' lives continuing almost on sidebars.

Just as Truffaut here peppers his kids' worlds with an adolescent jumble of pinball machines, smuggled pin-up mags, bubblegum and chaotic movie houses, Spielberg ups his realism with identifiable touchstones of the *Star Wars* generation. From a Halloween-night procession of Yoda cameos and home-made Mos Eisley-inspired freaks to *Dungeons & Dragons* board games, *Sesame Street*, Reese's Pieces candy, Lego sets, an Incredible Hulk sleeping bag, Atari games, Palitoy's Imperial Probe playset and Kenner's Cloud City twin-pod car from *The Empire Strikes Back*, Coors beer cans, space shuttle toys, Plasticine, View-Master projectors, Milton Bradley's Big Trak truck, Speak & Spell games, a *Jaws* grabber-wand and an Elvis Costello poster – if this wasn't the vital oddments of Elliott and his sibling's world, it could well be the Autumn/Winter 1982 Argos catalogue. *Superman: The Movie* director Richard Donner calls it 'verisimilitude' – the quality of feeling real, of a sense of believability. It is also a guiding trope in the cluttered worlds of many a title of this *Watching Skies* era – from *Alien, Jaws, Close Encounters* and *Blade Runner* to *The Deer Hunter, Kramer Vs Kramer, Ordinary People, The Dead Zone* and *Silkwood*. The universality of *E.T. the Extra-Terrestrial* emerges from one of early Spielberg's most striking tropes – the domestic milieu of childhood. When Elliott yells at his pals to 'get the bikes!' in a last-act attempt to save E.T. from the authorities, the audacity of the resulting chase is all about the boys' gameplay and adventure references. Every kitchen-table game of *Dungeons & Dragons* and every bout of Atari down the local arcade has come to this moment. The unkempt kids' bedrooms of *E.T.*, *Poltergeist* (1982), *Gremlins* (1984) and *The Goonies* (1985) were all our bedrooms. We too had an X-Wing hanging from the ceiling, an Incredible Hulk sleeping bag, abandoned Simon Says games and Death Star playsets we really shouldn't have taken out of the box. The decisions production designer James Bissell and set decorator Jackie Carr make to pepper *E.T.* with the minutiae of early-1980s domesticity the world over are just as key to the creative triumphs and authority of *E.T.* as John Williams' master score, Carlo Rambaldi's E.T. design, Ralph McQuarrie's mothership and Melissa Mathison's screenplay. Thirty-three years later, in 2015's *The Force Awakens*, director J.J. Abrams and writer Lawrence Kasdan (*The Empire Strikes Back, Raiders of the Lost Ark*) do not just rely on John Williams' score to suggest their new protagonist Rey is a kind, everyman soul. She has a messy bedroom and kitchen – complete with home-made X-Wing pilot dolls, a scavenged Rebel helmet for those cosplay moments and a repurposed AT-AT of her own. In a film and production that deftly got the fan communities on side in about twelve parsecs, Daisy Ridley's Rey is coyly pitched as a *Star Wars* fan too – one who is about to rescue a cute and skittish off-planet outsider she has just discovered in her backyard.

Just like the everyman likes of *Jaws* and *Close Encounters of the Third Kind*, *E.T.* was shot during the beginnings of a Republican presidency. And the character of Elliott was himself born during the ill-fated Richard Nixon tenure. There is a tiny sense of the hero versus 'the Man' – of meddling bureaucracy attempting to stifle the human spirit because it knows what is best for us. In Spielberg's *The Sugarland Express* (1974), it is Ben Johnson's police captain Tanner trying to commandeer some sanity into the chat and actions of the impulsive, gun-toting Texan townsfolk and county officers. In *Close Encounters of the Third Kind*, it is keen academics and ennobled officials wowed by the zeal of the human spirit in the face of outer-worldly contact. By the time of *E.T.*, Washington and 'the Man' have become less benign and more officious. They are now circling invaders crossing the line between science and security as they push into a family home with faceless menaces and hermetically-sealed safeguards. Later on, as those escaping BMX bikes are pushed along those canary-yellow road lines by John Williams' swirling flutes and excited strings in a moment of sheer 1980s movie majesty, this grand suburban opera sticks a joyous finger up at 'the Man'. But it is a defiance of childhood, not politics. Spielberg doesn't do politics. And rarely political judgment. Instead, he examines the politics of the human spirit. Even the bigger presidencies and affairs of state of *Amistad* (1998), *Munich* (2005), *Lincoln* (2012), *Bridge of Spies* (2015) and *The Post* (2017) are are about the statutes of tolerance and truth, not who is in charge. Despite President Reagan's 1982 signing of a new anti-piracy law, five years to the very day that *Star Wars* hit US cinemas, that particular Presidential gesture failed to halt *E.T. the Extra-Terrestrial* fast becoming one of the most pirated films of all time. The bootlegging of *E.T.* was purportedly a major factor in the film not being officially available on the home rental market until October 1988. In a time when our movies hit Blu-ray, digital download and DVD in what feels like six weeks after theatrical release, that six-year gap before home release would now be unheard of.

With the end credits rolling on a somewhat difficult autumn – and year – I was desperately hoping the Santa Claus of 1982 had clearly been influenced by *E.T. the Extra-Terrestrial* and would furnish me with a brand-new BMX bike. As we drove north back to Glasgow that Christmas Eve I kept a blanketed, backseat vigil for Santa and that precious bike – ever fearful that the family upheaval and last-minute decision to spend Christmas in Scotland would hinder the man in red from knowing where

I was that very night. For hours, I nervously scoured the stars through the back window of our Ford Cortina, the ever-elapsing motorway lights flickering like amber sprocket holes on a film reel. Unlike *E. T.*'s Elliott, I did not have good luck when it came to bike play.

Hoping that luck had indeed changed, and with Glasgow's illuminated Erskine Bridge looking like a mothership straddling the nearby River Clyde, my bare feet cautiously navigated the sharp stair rods of my mum's childhood home to a Christmas morning jackpot of that BMX. Okay, it wasn't strictly a BMX. It was technically a Raleigh Grifter XL – a design sibling of the more iconic and very 1970s British staple the Chopper, and a slightly faux BMX the Raleigh company no doubt introduced when *E. T.* helped whip up a global BMX frenzy. Mine was fiery red with chunky black rubber handlebars and a pinched rubber seat that would not take any prisoners. Or backies. I would later attempt to adapt my Grifter into a Speeder Bike – complete with cardboard front steering fins, blaster cannons and thrust flaps. Suffice to say, the Empire didn't commission Raleigh to design an open-air, repulsor-lift Grifter for very good reason.

As much as *E. T. the Extra-Terrestrial* is that commanding essay on childhood, when John Williams' score reaches its final operatic cue and Elliott watches those night skies with an older, less innocent mind, one realises that *E. T.* is not only one of the best motion pictures about childhood. It is one of the most incisive movies about the end of it. As Henry Thomas watches the mothership zip triumphantly across the night sky with a rainbow flourish, and the orchestral curtain goes down on John Williams' magnificent grand suburban opera, it is adolescence that is Elliott's next adventure. It was certainly going to be mine one day, with Henry Thomas and that character becoming the first time my 7-year-old self woke from a dream thinking about a boy and not knowing why. I dreamt

Thomas had come to our school as a new kid and needed someone to show him around – because naturally all Californian kids who star in the biggest film of all time seek out a nun-based Catholic education in the freezing corridors of the South of England.

I later marry a man called Elliot. With one 't'.

And just as there were perhaps fewer warm dinner-table milieus evident in Spielberg's personal sonnet to broken homes, *E. T.* marked a point in my childhood where I no longer remembered my mum and dad being together. As divorce besieged our lives like those officious Feds in NASA space suits, I don't recall *any* of our dinner-table moments. Unlike Spielberg's on-screen kids, I had no recollections of mimicking my dad at the table, playing with piles of mash potato to the dismay of my mum or futile arguments about staying out late on our bikes. Yet, I do remember the sobering punctuation point in my childhood that *E. T. the Extra-Terrestrial* embodied for evermore. When Elliott pleads to his initially cynical family about the 'goblin' in the backyard and how 'Dad would believe me', his mother Mary kindly snaps, 'Maybe you ought to call your father and tell him about it.' 'I can't,' confesses Elliott, 'he's in Mexico with Sally.' At that same moment when Elliott's mother loses her composure, my own mother – also called Sally – looked down at me and my lapful of Munchies with private tears in her eyes. Nothing more was said or even needed to be. In that single moment, two of the central drives of Spielberg's classic ode to childhood came crashing home to me – empathy and separation. The blonde, mop-haired kid who looked like Luke Skywalker suddenly understood the raised voices, the hushed whisperings of over-kind teachers and the tears down various phones to doctors and family. You grow up quick as an only child in the eye of Hurricane Divorce. Without fully appreciating just yet how your parents are sort of kids themselves navigating an adult world and all its vagaries and disappointments – like Mary in *E. T.* – you become desperately sensitive to your parents' emotions. So much so that when my dad wanted to take me to see *E.T.* again at Brighton's ABC Savoy the following Saturday, I pretended I hadn't yet seen it. I didn't have the heart or parental bias to tell him otherwise. It was the first of many kind fictions you learn to navigate divorce with – like telling a white lie about your trick-or-treat plans, or faking a temperature to spend a day off school with a stranded alien.

Is there anyone out there

Some people think that its true about UFO's People make films with monsters but they are not real.

An aliens

'Is there anybody out there' because this 7-year-old sky kid is armed with crayons.

A BRIGHT CENTRE
TO THE UNIVERSE

STAR WARS: A NEW HOPE

1977. With twin moons dominating the horizon of a distant desert planet, a restless farm boy watches the skies of sundown with a contemplation of his childhood, his home, and his future.

1983. 'Some people think that it's true about UFOs. People make films with monsters but they are not real.' That was the corker of insight I wrote on one page of a space project we had to complete for primary school. I got a 'Very Good' for my efforts. Quite right. But the truth was it was a rushed, last-minute job, completed that morning as I watched the recently launched *BBC Breakfast Time*. No doubt spurred on by *Star Wars* and *Close Encounters*, space exploration and the American TV coverage of it was highly prevalent in the early 1980s. In the wake of *Jaws*, *Star Wars* and *E.T.*, the 1980s already felt a particularly American decade for us British kids. When not covering space shuttle launches, our television screens were dominated by *Dynasty, Dallas, Cagney & Lacey, Diff'rent Strokes* and *The Fall Guy,* our school satchels and Saturday teatimes were all about *The A-Team* and *Knight Rider,* our television news was forever circling President Reagan and the Cold War, our music was often hinged on Michael Jackson, Madonna, Prince and *Rocky III*'s 'Eye of the Tiger', our denim and Day-Glo fashions were straight out of a John Hughes movie and it was of course American cinema that took starring roles in our Christmas Day TV schedules, birthday cinema trips and weekend VHS rentals. Space was already another very American product to us sky kids. We were aware of the

My space shuttle design – the USS Childhood, 1983.

moon landings of 1969 and beyond. However, we didn't grasp that they had ceased in 1972. Blame *Superman II* (1980) for that. Space, the exploration and the television presentation of it, was always through the Stateside filter of bulky white spacesuits emblazoned with eagles and swooshing stars, the American flag on the moon and the side of rocket boosters, golfing astronauts, moon buggies, Florida launches and radio comms links with California.

And just like *Star Wars*, the very Californian space shuttle programme finally went into orbit in 1977, after years of dedicated planning and design wrangling. NASA and the first Shuttle had already tapped into American sci-fi lore by calling the first prototype *Enterprise*, and Bond producer Albert R. Broccoli helped too by putting the Shuttle into space in 1979's *Moonraker*. And like its Paramount Studios *Star Trek* namesake, this *Enterprise* never actually flew in space, but instead completed valuable flight research missions within the confines of Earth. That was followed by *Columbia's* first manned flight into space in April 1981 and a second similar mission in November 1983. In April 1983, the *Challenger* Shuttle launched for the first time. It was during our lunch break at junior school. The teachers and nuns wheeled in the school's all-important television and the launch played out over the eating of Spam fritters and some disgusting lemon sponge concoction. It was usually only popes and space shuttles that our Catholically-funded television set was allowed to screen. That and the Wimbledon Men's Final, as it always clashed with the school's annual summer fete and Björn Borg's short shorts and thighs were like catnip to Surrey mothers on their second glass of summer fete wine.

Talking of school fetes, legs and flesh – one does not fully understand mortification until one has got the bus home on your own, aged 6-and-a-bit, dressed as a dice and knowing full well you only have some football underpants on underneath. That was how I left one of St Cuthbert Mayne's fancy dress summer pageants, vowing to never again have such chagrin repeated. A cardboard box with limb holes and dots was the standard, most easy parental contingency plan when fancy dress events loomed with no warning and no one at home had the engineering skills to fashion a space shuttle out of a cardboard box nicked from the back of Bejams. I wouldn't have minded had there not been at least five other dice marching around the school field like a terrible Catholic Vegas supper show. Once a year the nuns, teachers and the parish priest would hook up a 1950s sound system to play Irish marching band music as us kids paraded for the mums and the lone stay-at-home dad watching from the plastic hall chairs we had to carry out beforehand. There were prizes – usually a *My First New Testament Colouring Book* – and it was often a fiercely contested event. There was always one pushy mum who would go to town. Or another that would court the nuns' favour by dressing their son up as a waving Pope, complete with mock bulletproof glass. However, I was not repeating the walk of shame home in broad daylight dressed from head to backside in a black and white dice costume ever again. I had better plans for 1983. And they involved the fully-fledged return of a Jedi.

Picking 'Tatooine farm boy' as my theme for this year's pageant, I set about a proper cosplay statement a full two and a half decades before anyone had even heard of the phrase 'cosplay'. Alas, I was no Aunt Beru when it came to domestic chores. My sartorial plans for that year's must-have Luke Skywalker ensemble somewhat fell apart at the drawing table. I cut up an old white sheet and wrapped it around my skinny frame like a pashmina. There were no boots or trousers so I went barefoot, but I did have a home-made lightsaber. A strip of new fluorescent lights for our kitchen had recently come packed with a long, thin tube of polystyrene packaging. I wrapped duct tape around one end to make a handle and attached orange

Flanked by two Imperial Robin Hoods, this fancy-dress-pageant Jedi had it all. Almost.

sticky paper around the saber. It was not bad for my first attempt. Making your own lightsaber is a rite of passage for many a young Jedi – although the youngsters of Lucas's galaxies probably didn't have to contend with an elegant weapon from a more civilised age that bent in the middle when it accidentally got left near a radiator. I secretly hoped that sharing a first name with the actor who plays Luke Skywalker would somehow mask my attempts to mirror his *Episode IV* Tatooine regalia.

Unfortunately, they fell somewhat short for a Stormtrooper and a Catholic kid about to face the fancy dress jury. On the afternoon itself I got myself ready, and no doubt threw a 'help me Virgin Mary – you're my only hope' stare at the resident Virgin Mary statue flanking the dining hall, fully aware that I was once again wearing a revealing costume in only my underpants. Wrapping the pashmina-style sheet around my torso I was less a Jedi Knight in waiting, more a pasty-skinned Mahatma Gandhi holding a bright orange lightsaber. My slight disappointment was not helped by a teacher pairing me up with an amazing Darth Vader costume some clever fancy dress pageant mother had slipped under the radar. Admittedly, the boy in question was considerably shorter than my tall self, which made our shared height altogether more awkward, but his costume and Vader helmet were truly a work of art. As the parade started to a gurgling 1950s cassette tape of the 'Floral Dance' and the pair of us nervously walked out, soon to be followed by two Robin Hoods, I leant down to the diminutive Sith Lord with an 'I think we're going to win this' whisper of confidence. It was a sentiment I leant in and promised during every lap we did that day. We didn't win. Instead we got thrashed by some girl dressed as a Dutch milkmaid. Not even close. Before the day was out I had thrown that homemade lightsaber over my shoulder in anger a full 34 years before the real Luke Skywalker did the same in *The Last Jedi*. Maybe the nuns and priest were just not yet ready for *Star Wars* cosplay on their very doorstep, despite *The Last Jedi*'s Lanai caretakers being the nearest to the disgruntled wimple-wearing nuns our childhood was most familiar with. The same nuns and priest that wore black Empirical robes all day and made the altar boys dress in white robes for every Mass. Some of the gathered mums certainly looked at me with confused pity. Divorcing parents and a bad Jedi cosplay outfit are never a good mix. It was probably the last dip I had in the cosplay waters – barring trying to dress up as Roger Moore for a birthday party in September 1985.

One friend who joined me on that particular movie-themed birthday was new pal Inigo. He had joined our junior school in 1983 when his parents took over a local Cranleigh wine bar. Every Monday afternoon Inigo and I would narrowly avoid altar boy practice to sprint back to his parents' to catch *He-Man and the Masters of the Universe*. Inigo's mum would make amazing ham sandwiches and the wine bar cola button was merely a flight of stairs away. As childhood friends go, Inigo was quietly revolutionary to mine. Not only did he have full access to free cola, live merely three minutes' walk from our local swimming pool *and* own an Atari 2600 – he also introduced me to 1981 sci-fi cartoon epic *Ulysses 31* and its epic theme tune way before British TV and kids had even heard of it. Added to that, it seemed Inigo had a private line to toy makers Mattel and the *He-Man* world of Eternia. He had the fold-out Castle Greyskull, a 'power punching' He-Man, Skeletor, Battle Cat, Man-at-Arms, Trap Jaw, Savage Cat complete with purple felt fur effect, Orko, Beast Man and Zoar the bird with flapping wings mechanism. Naturally I was utterly envious and reciprocated by haggling my mum into buying me a He-Man and Skeletor of my own – when the truth was that I was not totally into the chest-harness-wearing gym bunny with the iffy pageboy do that was He-Man. I wanted a Sorceress figurine with her amazing feathered sleeves, or an Evil Lyn complete with her bitchy, evil skull cap costume. Though I was never a fan of *She-Ra: Princess of Power* – the *Masters of the Universe*'s later side project for girls and queeny boys. She was always too needy – like the high school princess who was just a bit *too* popular. Although, as distractions go, her trusty tache-wearing and highly closeted archer pal Bow was a buff revelation.

More crucially, however, Inigo's parents also had a video machine. And it was not just any video machine. It was a Betamax player – as Inigo's dad swore the days of VHS were numbered. My family still did not have a video player. A mix of funds and inclination had so far kept me out of that home cinema revolution. But not only did Inigo's parents have a video player, cola and ham sandwiches seemingly on tap. They had a copy of *Star Wars*. Like a proper, real 1982 copy of *Star Wars* – complete with commercial breaks, title cards, mono sound, those analogue broadcast tan lines, an announcer promising another repeat of *Catweazle* next week, that little top right revolving square indicator thing that said the ads were coming, and all the glorious widescreen skies of George Lucas's vision cropped to a 4:3 square of themselves. And do you know what? It was perfect.

The cinema that made *Star Wars* and queueing around the block a twentieth-century icon – the Mann's Chinese Theatre (now the Grauman's) on Hollywood Boulevard.

A long time ago, before prequels and sidebar movies were needed – or even heard of – a film called *Star Wars* changed cinema, childhoods, adulthoods and popular culture. *Star Wars* opened in America on 25 May 1977. It wasn't even called *A New Hope* yet – that came a year or two later, when George Lucas was finally able to make his playful homage to the multi-episode world of *Flash Gordon* he had planned. Two days later, *Smokey and the Bandit* became the bravest film ever in the history of cinema when it opened just forty-eight hours into the first of *Star Wars'* many victory laps of the American box office that year.

As American kids made movie fan folklore by queueing in the Hollywood sun for the Mann's Chinese Theatre, the Coronet Theatre in San Francisco and many a movie house across the land, Britain's impatient sky kids meanwhile had to settle for the newly released soft-core flesh flick, *The Blazer Girls*. Failing that, the likeminded *Come Play With Me* and *Stand Up, Virgin Soldiers* were still doing the fleapit rounds, with only *The Prince and the Pauper*, *Are You Being Served?* and *The Many Adventures of Winnie the Pooh* on the imminent cinematic horizon. It was enough to make scared and pleading blue holograms of us all. That was a gap of 217 – no doubt very long – days. And that was only for the 27 December 1977 London release. The nationwide roll-out didn't happen until 29 January 1978 – rounding off the wait to a neat, but no less painful, 250 days. That's a lot of parsecs, patience and desperately entering every Marlboro cigarette packet competition for a Concorde trip to New York. *The Empire Strikes Back* was already deep into pre-production in California when British audiences braved the 1978 Hoth winter to finally watch the skies of George Lucas's eagerly-awaited space opera. The ever-so-very-weird and now very excommunicated *Star Wars*

Holiday Special (1978) was almost more imminent than the British kids' opportunity to finally experience *Star Wars*. Of course, that delay worked wonders at generating anticipation, merchandise fever and anchoring all those 'I can remember queueing round the block after school' memories, real or otherwise. Without a war, moon landing or a World Cup Final to personally remember, queueing round the block for *Star Wars* is a whole generation's only mutual touchstone.

Star Wars is a saga built on the metallic shoulders of androids. C-3PO and R2-D2 are not only our eyes and conduits into the story – they are the guardian angels of George Lucas's world, bearing quiet witness to the vagaries of war and the ramshackle resilience of good souls. From that now-quintessential opening shot of a preying Star Destroyer consuming the frame and the minds of 1970s sky kids for evermore, one of the early script tricks of *A New Hope* is not how its overture sequence underlines the potency of the Empire, but how it very soon breaks away to the plight of the androids. The mind-searing image of that Rebel blockade runner being pursued across the Galactic skies before being consumed by the Destroyer of course tells us everything we need to know about the spectacle and widescreen intent of *Star Wars,* the 1970s sci-fi film. However, the act that then follows involving the protocol droid C-3PO and the astromech unit R2-D2 tells us all we need to know about *Star Wars* as a story world and saga. With the two androids jettisoning blindly to a desert planet and soon being picked up by the cost-cutting robot dealership that is the Jawas and their Sandcrawler transport, Lucas and his script very quickly step back from the temptation to only fill his skies with lasers and spacecraft. Instead, we have a metallic Merry and Pippin in *Sith Lord of the Rings.*

With future echoes of the anti-Mecha 'Flesh Fair' in Spielberg's *A.I. Artificial Intelligence* (2001), as soon as we are aboard the Jawas' mobile and shadowy repository of mechanical automatons, ex-Empire stock robots and various semblances of a mechanised evolution, George Lucas begins presenting an off-story timescale and history to his universe. The opening act of C-3PO and R2-D2 eventually being placed in the ownership of farm boy Luke Skywalker at a robot thrift sale allows everything that has come since in *Star Wars*. That sense of verisimilitude and interstellar domesticity, of battle-worn androids, scavenging Jawas, a meagre family business, the scrap metal detritus of robots waiting to be repurposed, the meddling diktats of Stormtroopers, dive bars housing motley racketeer aliens, delinquent sand people and the social hierarchies, survival tactics and gossip of sparsely populated communities. *That* is *Star Wars*. That is why it is a canvas that has extended into three movie trilogies (so far), spin-off films, television movies, animation features, cartoon serials, a myriad of computer games and a Death-Star-sized hoard of extended universe novels and comic books of varying quality and relevance. This is why *The Force Awakens* played like a secret *Star Wars* film that was made in 1985, but only just released thirty years later. Director J.J. Abrams and writer Lawrence Kasdan knew their *Star Wars* principles were founded in *A New Hope*. When it comes to *Star Wars*, the world of *A New Hope*, the drama of *The Empire Strikes Back* and adventure of *Return of the Jedi* are what *Star Wars* films forget to their detriment.

This world of *A New Hope* wears its history. Everything we need to know about the economy and freedom-zapping exploits of the Empire is there in the tin-pan Jawas and their knock-off androids, the dinner chat politics and chores of the Lars household and the Third Reich style ghetto raids of the Empire. There is almost a Victorian sense of social detail and hierarchies gently hinted at in *A New Hope*. It is a Dickensian western – a universe with its own struggles, poverty, petty trades, economies and law enforcement. This is not a nylon white science fiction world. This is not making some statement about 1977 via spacesuits and intricately shot models. John Barry's production design ensures the walls of the Millennium Falcon are grimy and battered. 'Maybe it's another drill,' remarks an idle Death Star Stormtrooper with one eye clearly on the end-of-shift clock. It is an interstellar blue-collar world not dissimilar to the same year's *Close Encounters*. There is a dirt and experience to the Falcon, intricate minutiae that suggest a wealth of off-story experience and adventures as yet untold. It is a rich, late-1970s evolution of American science fiction that continues with the truckers-in-space ethic to Michael Seymour's production design of *Alien* (1979), Joe Alves' work on *Escape From New York* (1981), John J. Lloyd's art direction of *The Thing* (1982) and the waterlogged neon of Lawrence G. Paull's work on *Blade Runner* (1982). In one production design swoop from Lucasfilm and its Californian creatives, suddenly the over-bright likes of *Logan's Run* (1976), *Starcrash* (1978), *Laserblast* (1978), *Battlestar Galactica* (1978), *The Black Hole* (1979), *Galactica 1980* (1980) and *Battle Beyond the Stars* (1980) are woefully outmoded. With curious attempts to get 'star' somewhere in the poster of these budget-starved movies, and as fun as they end up being – in hindsight, they are still often antiquated, reheated episodes of the original *Star Trek* TV ethic. Us British sky kids would still lap them up and TV channels got good *Star Wars* baiting ratings for years off the back of their broadcasts. I have a majorly fond memory of one typically colourless Sunday afternoon being well and truly lit up by *Battle Beyond the Stars* on ITV. In lieu of *Star Wars*, I was very much into the television exploits of *Battlestar Galactica*. I desperately wanted to hang out with Apollo and Starbuck, and just walk down corridors wearing a jaunty space cape. But again, *Galactica* was as much about the sunny, late-1970s American backdrops mixing *Star Wars* and *Star Trek* and its attempts to make itself known through merchandise as it was any success at beating *Star Wars* at its own game. There was even a curious Italian-produced American film called *Sheriff and the Satellite Kid* (1979) starring *Close Encounters'* Cary Guffey as an alien kid – a sort of *Third Kind* meets *Smokey and the Bandit*. But often these overly gaudy movies do not know if they want to be *Star Wars* or *Star Trek* and end up falling somewhere in-between. Granted, it is not a bad place to be posited. They have their place and imitation is the sincerest form of flattery – even in late 1970s space where no one can hear the screenwriters scream. Yet, there was a very noticeable difference not just in how these non-Lucas tales of space princes and mask-wearing overlords fared with audiences, but in how the production ethic and understanding of cinema that George Lucas was quietly nurturing was clearly alien to his imitators.

In 1977 – and before its own movie series was up and running – *Star Trek* was pure television. *Star Wars* was pure cinema. The Starship Enterprise may soon have its own box office presence in the form of *Star Trek: The Motion Picture* (1979) – a somewhat strange title for such a motion-free movie, without the momentum yet of its far superior sequels. But the creative flourishes of this first *Star Wars* movie are all about the motion of pictures. For all his detractors and critics who lay prequel-shame at George Lucas's feet for being all about the technology and the gigabytes, *A New Hope* demonstrates a shrewd understanding of cinema – its scope for spectacle, movement and emotion via the most basic tenets of passing on stories about good versus evil. Until *Star Wars*, it was not normal for the Academy Awards to nominate a science fiction movie for Best Picture – even if it had made a lot of money for Hollywood and American investments. Until *Star Wars* it was not a God-given right to have a sci-fi sequel. If *2001: A Space Odyssey* is about a new dawn of science fiction cinema, then

Star Wars is its glorious matinee afternoon and the moment it gets to its feet.

But just as it refuses to be a campy, vampy romp or even a dystopian warning like *Westworld* (1973) or *Rollerball* (1974), *A New Hope* was a science fiction line in the Tatooine sand. Its motifs, action and design are not tied to the real procedures of space exploration which dominated the news screens of the previous twenty years. Barely eight years after the first men walked on the moon, that sense of exploration is not needed in a cosmos where men, women and Wookiees have been walking on many moons for centuries. From the get-go, there are no elongated docking sequences in *A New Hope*. It doesn't make great slo-mo play of hatches and decompression safety doors being opened. This is not sci-fi as predicated on the imagined future of NASA. 'Days' and 'hours' are mentioned, but the real science of those *Star Wars* galaxies are kept at a lightsaber's length. Explosions and blasters in space are lent the full Ben Burtt sound treatment rather than the silence of real science. There is no playing with gravity until 2005's *Revenge of the Sith*, which – a bit like the eye-rolling mention of the blessed midi-chlorians in *The Phantom Menace* (1999) – doesn't need those reminders of a logical reality the original trilogy did quite well without. Cue General Leia's floating in the void of space moment from *The Last Jedi* which strangely feels like a deleted scene from *Superman IV : The Quest for Peace*.

There are no planets to be explored in the *Star Wars* universe. This is not about the furthering of humanity. The explorations, habitations and mining have all been done. The creatures of Mos Eisley are first presented as unsavoury drifters and beer-swilling pirates rather than being slowly revealed as non-Earthlike wonders. There are no awe-making, *2001*-inspired Dawn of Man sequences in *A New Hope*. A Land Speeder cutting across the rocky desert is enough. Nor are the aliens open to interpretation. It is more pressing for Lucas to make the Jawas, Sand People and the first extra-terrestrials he presents us with familiar delinquents and robbers. That is more recognisable to 1970s kids and audiences than grand pronouncements about the evolution of the universe. Echoing the vegetation of *Return of the Jedi's* Forest Moon of Endor, here the Yavin jungles and green flora denote the good in *Star Wars* whilst the Empire is dealt the greys of gravestones and school uniforms. Compared to the wall-to-wall industry of the Empire, the Rebel base on the fourth moon of Yavin only holds the vaguest impressions of technology with its transparent screens, lack of a physical hierarchy and kind-faced bearded men watching attentively like the Devils Tower scientists from *Close Encounters*. That other 1970s Spielberg trope is ever present too – the busy, feverish radio chat between Yavin and the X-Wings.

The Death Star, meanwhile, is the magic, haunted castle staffed by marauding pirates keeping a princess in the dungeons that the farm boy and his dodgy smuggler pal must try to rescue. Lucas always cited Akira Kurosawa, and particularly 1958's *The Hidden Fortress*, as an influence on *Star Wars*, some of its characterisation and action beats. Likewise, the DNA of J.R.R. Tolkein is there too – with resourceful, well-intentioned underlings delivering freedom from industrialised tyranny. But Lucas also uses the age-old tropes of the golden era of the 1930s and 1940s classical Hollywood cinema as a shorthand for his vision. Luke and Leia 'Errol Flynn' their way to freedom across a bridgeless Death Star chasm, the various versions of *The Thief of Bagdad* are all over the Landspeeders and the wide-eyed dashing derring-do of Mark Hamill, and the bickering fizz of Bogart and Bacall is there in Leia and Han's verbal jousting. And whilst *A New Hope* is a marked progression from the stop-motion work of effects pioneer Ray Harryhausen (*The Clash of the Titans, Jason and the Argonauts*), his swagger of dusty skirmishes, false perspectives and ancient lore is key to the addictive bluster of

Star Wars. The casting of Peter Cushing as Grand Moff Tarkin is no accident either. Partly to humanize the senior villainy of the piece, the Hammer Films veteran Cushing brings that Conan Doyle style baronial authority to key scenes involving the expression-free Vader. Cushing is an expert in selling a line and a scene that maybe had not earnt it on the written page. And he is the only one to bark at Vader and not get choke-dropped to the shiny Elstree floors of the Death Star for his troubles. The curious digital retrieval of Cushing for 2016's *Rogue One: A Star Wars Story* is up for debate. Whilst maybe not as jarring as Japanese sex doll Princess Leia at the final flourish of the same film or that floating Leia in *The Last Jedi*, the 'performance' is still an animated version of a character and actor long dead – even it was wholly welcome and cool to be surprised by a new *Star Wars* film.

Another curio is perhaps the greatest sole creative contribution to the momentum and cinematic glory of the *Star Wars* movies. With the chevron moustaches of the 1977 Yavin Rebels matching those of many a San Franciscan young buck strutting his denim stuff down the Castro to a disco soundtrack, along comes composer John Williams to lend a golden age Hollywood score to a year whose music was decidedly not looking to the stars and Gustav Holst for its beats. The chart and movie music of 1977 were all about spinning glitterballs, not exploding Alderaans. Marvin Hamlisch's work on *The Spy Who Loved Me*, Lalo Schifrin's score for *Rollercoaster*, *ABBA: The Movie*, John Barry working with Donna Summer on *The Deep* and of course The Bee Gees' *Saturday Night Fever* soundtrack – they were all a very different movie sound to what went on to win the 1977 Oscar for Best Original Score. In any other galaxy, the score for *A New Hope* would have been loaded with instantly dated electronica, layered with nineteenth-century classical pieces or peppered with era-specific funk like Jerry Goldsmith's funk soul score for *Escape from*

Planet of the Apes (1971). The disco leanings of the blacklisted *Star Wars Holiday Special* of 1978 quickly demonstrated just how it was not in the saga's duty to go too contemporary. But – and no doubt spurred on by his genre-defining work on disaster movies *The Poseidon Adventure* (1972), *The Towering Inferno* (1974) and *Earthquake* (1974), and the three scores and one Academy Award Williams had already reaped for Spielberg's *The Sugarland Express*, *Jaws* and *Close Encounters of the Third Kind* – here Lucas opts for a fiercely orchestral sound at utter odds with the contemporary wizardry and technological advancements at play. But it works. And magnificently so. From the small screen likes of *Lost In Space* (1965), *The Time Tunnel* (1966) and *The Land of the Giants* (1968), the then-known Johnny Williams was already the proven master of the TV theme and its brief, precise window to get emotion, character and a swagger across in small minute bursts. His jazz cues and turtle-necked lounge sense of easy listening later marks the Martini-marinated scores for *Penelope* (1966), *How to Steal a Million* (1966), *A Guide for the Married Man* (1967) and *Daddy's Gone-A-Hunting* (1969). However, it was possibly his western-skewed work on *None but the Brave* (1965), *The Reivers* (1969), *The Cowboys* (1972), the feminine sounds of TV movie *Jane Eyre* (1970) and his Oscar-winning turn orchestrating *Fiddler on the Roof* (1971) where Williams really opens out his scores to the widescreen, orchestral palette that marks his work for evermore.

The score for *A New Hope* is not just a landmark piece of movie composition. It comes from a richer, broader canvas of characters, emotions and themes than Lucas or Williams had achieved before. The trinity of those earlier multi-character, multi-story disaster movies – *Poseidon*, *Earthquake* and *The Towering Inferno* – certainly gave Williams a fertile schooling in balancing numerous character cues, romance, villainy and adventure. Yet, it is in *Jaws* and *A New Hope* that he really leaves those Americana harmonicas and that cocktail-hour jazz to the side for a work that is a symphonic feat of classical movie brilliance. Whereas *Jaws* has its spirited out-to-sea scherzos emphasising its seafaring antics and of course the deep, portentous heartbeats of those two underwater notes, the score for *A New Hope* lends an even richer soul to multiple storylines, multiple tones and multiple characters. The solo French horns, flutes and eventual violins of 'Princess Leia's Theme', the multitudes of brass of the Empire, the playful woodwind and oboes of the foraging Jawas, the spiraling optimism and strings of the 'Rebel Fanfare' and the soaring violins of a hero watching the skies of a binary sunset – it is all a key component of the regality and grandeur of *A New Hope*. It is a European sense of majesty, imbued with the classical influences of Richard Wagner, Edward Elgar and Gustav Holst as Williams' optimistic strings combat against the deep brass of Vader and the Empire. 'Princess Leia's Theme' takes the form of an English summer as scored by Erich Korngold, X-Wings cascade towards their target under the baton and musical influence of Sir William Walton and Benjamin Britten, and Holst's *The Planets* is of course all over the skies of *A New Hope* with its adventurous musical odyssey of the stars coming from the darker musical recesses of 1918 and the Great War.

As bedroom turntables spun to Pink Floyd, Fleetwood Mac, ABBA, the Sex Pistols and David Bowie, along comes a project of music that becomes *the* classical adagio of our childhoods. It wasn't 'Dancing Queen' or even 'God Save the Queen' that a great many British kids of the late 1970s were humming as they did battle down the Death Star trenches of their back walls. It was the 'Rebel Fanfare' or a hand on the hip as the sun went down with a hum of the Luke Skywalker keynote. Bill Murray and friends would ape the *Star Wars* main theme on *Saturday Night Live*. Suddenly every classical album on sale at Woolworths had a starscape on it and every nineteenth-century composer had their name up in a chunky sci-fi font. Meco's disco take on the 'Main Theme' hit number 1 in the American Billboard Hot 100 in October 1977. And for the first time ever, kids, their parents and cinema audiences had a film composer who was a household and high street name. It was a work that earnt John Williams an Academy Award, a Golden Globe, a BAFTA and three Grammys. It was also one that ensured a great many subpar movies of the 1970s that Williams happened to score were watched on rainy Sunday afternoon television with more enthusiasm than was warranted.

This wasn't just a good score for a good movie. Williams' work on *A New Hope* became part of the lexicon of popular twentieth-century music. Its romantic sweeps, symphonic momentum and wistful sense of home got under the skin of a whole generation of kids and young adults. I didn't join the recorder lunchtime club at school because I wanted to play 'Frere Jacques' horribly out of tune. I joined the recorder lunchtime club because I wanted to play the 'Princess Leia Theme' horribly out of tune. Alongside maybe John Barry's arrangement of the *James Bond* theme, Bernard Herrmann's work on *Psycho* and Williams' previous *Jaws* motif, the *Star Wars* score is not only forever destined to feature on bad Leipzig Philharmonic movie hits collections for the rest of time, it significantly revived and prolonged classical film composition – as a filmmaking choice and a record store must-have. As the likes of Giorgio Moroder, Vangelis, Tangerine Dream and director John Carpenter were flexing their new electronic movie sounds and synthesizers, John Williams and *Star Wars* take cinema back to the notion of leitmotifs, full orchestras and cutting-edge adventure cinema dressed in 1940s symphonic sounds. And all this was the same year Williams produced his score for *Close Encounters of the Third Kind* – which one could argue is even more of a technical tour de force than *A New Hope*. Science fiction cinema was no stranger to decent scores. Bernard Herrmann's theremin-heavy work for *The Day the Earth Stood Still* (1951) is a divine, quivering delight. Jerry Goldsmith's percussion-laden score for *Planet of the Apes* (1968) was Oscar nominated. And *2001: A Space Odyssey* soars partly due to Kubrick papering the film with European classical music standards to equate the science and evolution of man with the musicality of man.

Over forty years later, John Williams' work on *A New Hope* has not aged. A simple piano rendering of 'The Princess Leia Theme' hanging in space for emotional resonance forty years later in *The Last Jedi* is testament to that. The same cannot be said for the score for *Dark Star* (1974), *Logan's Run* (1976), *The Humanoid* (1979) or *Flash Gordon* (1980). In creating a score for a far, far away galaxy that is out of our time, the *Star Wars* cues are naturally ageless. As is Hollywood's insistence ever since for science fiction scores from top composers. Very soon after *Star Wars* John Barry is scoring Disney's *The Black Hole* (1979), Jerry Goldsmith is bringing some of that *Planet of the Apes* musical discord to his skin-curdling work on *Alien* (1979), Elmer Bernstein scores *Firefox* (1982) and Ennio Morricone is tasked with *The Thing* (1982). It is no longer curious that a big Hollywood name like Elmer Bernstein would later score *Ghostbusters* (1984). Or that the on-screen fortunes and successes of the original *Star Trek* movies were arguably elevated by composer James Horner's dazzling work on *The Wrath of Khan* (1982) and *The Search for Spock* (1983) – defining 1980s scores whose DNA can easily be traced back to the romantic glories of John Williams and *A New Hope*.

All science fiction is about its source era. The likes of *It Came from Outer Space* (1955), *Plan 9 from Outer Space* (1959) and their atomic age B-movie cousins are of course about a very 1950s fear of nuclear conflict, a fear of communism and a fear of the other. An easy reading of *A New Hope* is that it is a reaction to Second World

War, which Lucas was born into in May 1944. His childhood – very much like Steven Spielberg's – was no doubt dominated by war heroes, war stories and war movies. But that was his parents' war. And there is more to *Star Wars* than Second World War. The McCarthy witch hunts, the Civil Rights movements, President Nixon and Watergate's stolen plans, the age of the automobile and jet-engine, the vicious purging of villages in Vietnam, and of course the Space Race – these not so far, far away influences of American mid-twentieth-century history are all evident in *A New Hope*. With the opening beats of young heroine Jyn Erso framed in the watery reeds of Lah'mu, its sidebar prequel *Rogue One: A Star Wars Story* (2016) starts out almost as a Space Race meets Vietnam movie allegory as director Gareth Edwards echoes *Casualties of War* (1989), *Platoon* (1986) and even a bit of *The Bridge on the River Kwai* (1957) – with caped weapons developer Orson Krennic (Ben Mendelsohn) barking at his prisoners of war to complete their Death Star construction project.

When watching the skies of *Episode IV* today it is almost impossible to see past the phenomenon and movie iconography of what Lucas created. Unlike the subsequent *The Empire Strikes Back* and *Return of the Jedi*, *A New Hope* is especially bound to its own glories. Not only is it the iconic beacon of its own franchise, but it is also irretrievably bound to the history of American cinema and popular culture of the twentieth century. The starry warfare aside, it is still a particularly indie film with a soulful, almost folky spine. For a film that is often discussed as being the one which points a Death Star super-laser at American independent cinema of the 1970s, it is curiously still very much aligned to the self-regulating habits and tropes of that decade. This remains a film with an improvised texture forged in the creative heartlands and impromptu warehouses, lock-ups and parking lots of Van Nuys, San Rafael and San Francisco, and realised in a British film studio situated in an outer-rim suburb of North London. Not only is George Lucas endeavouring throughout to build and maintain his film production model that is very much outside of Hollywood both physically and mentally, that new wave sense of the individual against 'the Man', with an often domestic backdrop, is key to *Star Wars* too. As much as *Episode IV* swipe-cuts to the special-effects vistas of Star Destroyers, Death Stars and the Empire, it more slavishly cuts back to C-3PO and R2-D2 getting to know the kind-minded Luke Skywalker and calm hermit Ben Kenobi in both their homesteads. Even the scenes between Darth Vader and Peter Cushing's Grand Moff Tarkin take their time, and are the longest exchanges we see of our Sith Lord in the whole saga. Just like Krypton in the following year's *Superman* (1978), that sense of home and the destruction of it is particularly focal to *Episode IV*. The mettle of Princess Leia (Carrie Fisher) is tested when her home planet of Alderaan is destroyed by Peter Cushing, and Luke's sinking panic about the androids leading the Stormtroopers back 'home' comes too late as he soon discovers the burnt-out bodies of his aunt and uncle in a grim tableau that was deeply shocking for us kids at the time.

Star Wars shares that 1970s American movie penchant for nostalgia in youth-skewed stories, as seen in *Grease* (1978), *The Warriors* (1979), *The Last Picture House* (1971) and *I Wanna Hold Your Hand* (1978). It is a trait of *American Graffiti* too – as the older generations talk of wars and the younger crew cruise around town in their first cars, becoming ever restless to spend time with their friends. George Lucas got labelled with the science fiction tag early on his movie career. But as *Star Wars* and a lot of his work proves – he understands how younger audiences tick. The evil in *A New Hope* is all centred around older male autocrats. That is possibly another factor why the later prequels hit more troubled times with audiences. The sky kids of the 1970s and 1980s grew up

Inspired by *American Graffifi*'s hub of youth and motor cars, Mel's Drive-In now operates on Van Ness Avenue, San Francisco.

with a young and heroic mop-haired Mark Hamill and a sardonic scoundrel in the form of Harrison Ford – not a petulant villain of a mulleted teenager in Anakin Skywalker (Hayden Christensen). Even the younger treachery of *The Force Awakens*' Kylo Ren (Adam Driver) still sits in a very different template to the original trilogy, as both he and Domnhall Gleeson's Admiral Hux become young villains fighting veteran heroes alongside Rey and Finn in a flip of *Episode IV*'s youthful dynamic. There is a buoyancy to Hamill in *A New Hope*. Carrying none of the story weight of *The Empire Strikes Back*, *Return of the Jedi* or even *The Last Jedi*, he stares in mop-topped wonder at events like the older brother in a 1970s Spielberg movie. It is an optimism from a different era and one that not even the kind-pitched Rey can pull off in the darker pitched *The Force Awakens*. A West Coast boy, from California, Hamill doesn't always get the credit for selling a character to a movie and political world that was still reeling from Nixon, Vietnam, an oil crisis and falling cinema admissions. But it is Hamill's blind faith in the role that makes it work. Cut very much from a 1970s cloth of mop-haired wonder without being too specifically '1977', and under the auspices of Oakland-born Mark Hamill, Luke Skywalker is one of the least cynical movie characters of all time.

American Graffiti (1973) showed George Lucas could handle youth-skewed stories made up of disparate characters in different parts of the one town – or planet. Just like *Graffiti*, *Star Wars* is also a film about velocity, movement, souped-up old wrecks no one has any faith in, checking your wing mirrors for approaching trouble, diners, the hushed conversations at the local hop and speed trials. The younger Carol (Mackenzie Philips) bickering with a secret fondness at the slightly older John (Paul Le Mat) on the bench-seat of his prized, yesteryear Ford Coupé is a dress rehearsal for Leia and Han aboard the Falcon. *American Graffiti* even has its own Harrison Ford as the rather *Star Wars* sounding Bob Falfa peacocks about town from the cockpit of his 1955 Chevy – 'Hey, you're supposed to be the fast thing in the Valley, man' – before coming unstuck in the last reel as he is unable to win a dawn road race in less than twelve parsecs. If the original *Star Wars* trilogy is a three-act rite of passage for Luke Skywalker, then *A New Hope* is his final weekend before college.

PLASTIC FANTASTIC

1977. A gold protocol android takes a much-needed oil bath as his twitchy new owner plays with a plastic model of a spaceship and berates his life.

o———o

May 1983. In the week that *Return of the Jedi* returned *Star Wars* to the movie screens of America, my mum, stepdad, two Golden Retrievers and I moved house. As I went to school that Thursday morning I left the road of 1960s houses in a 1970s English suburbia with 1980s dressing, the various kids dotted throughout the street and some sadder memories, but many more great ones of making camps, building igloos, riding bikes after sunset and watching *The Muppet Show*. It was a home of my childhood, but not *the* home of my childhood. As the sky kids of America were queueing up around their movie houses in their skinny denim, sneaker pumps and raglan tees, I left school that afternoon in my charcoal-grey shorts and returned to a new, bigger home. We were in the same village, but a more rural, quieter and greener end of it. We now had stairs, a massive garden, a mini Endor woodland, surrounding fields, too many apple trees and fluctuating TV reception should it be windy. I was a bit of a lone Tatooine farm boy for all the years we remained there, but that never mattered. I also had a long, meandering private drive – perfect for bike stunts, Speeder Bike pursuits, sledging, screeching brake halts and imaginary tracking shots with plastic X-Wings.

With maybe a fear that I was being rehoused after a harsher previous year, my mum and stepdad tried to ease me into my new quarters. As I walked around the empty, echoing 1930s house, I went up to my new bedroom ever fascinated and scared by our very *Poltergeist*-inspired open stairs. A lone new *Star Wars* figure was sat on the windowsill forming a solo welcome party, and as a special treat we had that rare 1980s indulgence of a takeaway. Just down from the Regal Cinema and its tantalising front of house posters for the imminent *Return of the Jedi* – it was a single-screen theatre, but always had window space for eight plush, quad-sized film posters of all genres, ratings and cinema – was a small takeaway café called Hot Ice. That night was the first time I had pizza, and the first time I had takeaway pizza. Already America was clipping at my childhood heels, albeit in a yellowing polystyrene pizza box.

In the very first *Star Wars* movie *A New Hope* and in one of his very first scenes, Luke Skywalker sits in his basement den briefly toying with a model toy ship. It curiously resembles one of toy company Kenner's upcoming *Star Wars* Imperial Shuttles and reminds that the toy project of *Star Wars* was – like those Jabba skiffs – flying parallel to the films from the outset. *A New Hope* is so aligned to the toy re-enactments of kids across the globe that the merchandise and films are immediately two sides of the same box office dollar

– an instant and often profound marriage of product and produce. It is a trait that *Rogue One* echoes too as the young Jyn drops a Stormtrooper doll when fleeing the despotic Krennic in the film's overture.

Like a lot of sky kids of my age and generation, our maiden voyage into the movie world of *Star Wars* was not in the May of 1977 as we all like to remember and wish it had been. As fandom timelines go, I am sure some die-hard *Star Wars* fans queueing for Comic Con in San Diego would today seize my arm in anger like a disgruntled cantina bar stalwart on hearing how I first watched *A New Hope* barely a few weeks before *Return of the Jedi*, and a whole year and a half before the fates finally, finally let me experience *The Empire Strikes Back*. If the truth be told, I am not entirely happy with that admission myself. But it was the non-Netflix, non-Blu-ray analogue galaxy we lived in – mixed with different types of affordability and availability when it came to video players and disposable income.

Despite my (then) golden flowing locks and recent starring role as young Skywalker on that Catholic fancy dress catwalk – where I was so cruelly beaten by a Dutch milkmaid – I didn't really want to be Luke. If anything, I would flounce about the school playground with my flattened palms and locked elbows attempting to be the butch vessel of masculinity that was the golden droid, C-3PO. Yes, out of all the soldiers, fighters or pilots of the Outer Rim I could have been, I chose the camp butler with the pigeon-step walk and the ability to talk Bocce. What I really wanted to be was one of the Palitoy kids – those mop-haired, white-teethed cherubs charged with flanking the packaging and TV commercials of the *Star Wars* ships and playsets like Gulliver overseeing some intergalactic Lilliputians.

With that voiceover man straight out of a royal wedding commentary, and not wholly familiar with names like 'Princess

Leah' and 'Chief Chirp-her', they made good play of various backdrops found in any British home. Well, assuming your home had a penchant for chintzy lampshades, blacked out windows and allowing the kids to fly X-Wings around nan's best crystal tumblers. I think a lack of pine furniture and parquet flooring seriously limited my chances of being a Palitoy boy. It was a well-known fact that parquet flooring was like Kryptonite to Vader and his 3¾-inch soldiers. But we had linoleum. And 1970s linoleum the previous owners hadn't changed yet, and neither had we. Our Golden Retrievers did not help either, as they were forever found nursing a chewed Biker Scout between their paws like slightly well-groomed Rancor Monsters. I had a face for toy packaging, I'm sure I did. I could have been the poster boy of Kenner's *Star Wars* promotional campaigns in Europe, cherry-picked by George Lucas himself to come over to San Francisco and get properly fitted for some Palitoy boy dungarees. At this very moment, I could be sat tidying a pile of glossy 'then and now' headshots on a signing table at a *Star Wars* Celebration or Comic Con. Harrison Ford would come over and say, 'So you're the kid that changed the face of *Star Wars* toys?' and Mark Hamill would get all emotional and start hand-fanning away those nostalgic tears over a selfie. Maybe.

Hindsight has proved the Palitoy adverts were also sometimes different to the American Kenner ones. Now, they really were angelic kids, with their LA dentists, white picket fences, spacious front-porches and sun-drenched backyards. My dental track record was not quite the American advertising dream. Us Brit kids had cheap plastic garden furniture festooned with ashtrays and crushed cans of Hofmeister beer. The British Palitoy ads would opt for blacked out bedrooms and tables and no sun. Or they would overdub British accents onto the American footage. But we were wise to that. We were always bombarded with ladies' ads for hair removal packs featuring stunning Stateside commercial actresses all incongruously dubbed in Britain by some Linda from Kent. The American kids not only all sounded like Linus Van Pelt from the *Peanuts* cartoons, they got proper dialogue, clearly a script, and they also had the company of girls. That was unheard of in Britain. We may have had a lady Prime Minister, but only boys starred in *Star Wars* commercials and girls had their place in the *My Little Pony* adverts. The American kids had coiffured indie-boy surfer hair. We had pageboy bowl cuts. The American kids not only got to live in California in their big sunny houses and look like *The Red Hand Gang*, but they probably got to keep their toys. The British ads no doubt made all minors sign for theirs. And I bet the American kids got proper catering trucks whilst the Brits had to bring their own cheese sandwiches and Wotsits.

With a beige, faux leather overcoat, compounded insect-like eyes, a cuboid-shaped rifle and a plastic chest harness-cum-bum bag, the first ever *Star Wars* figure I owned was a galactic bounty hunter by the name of 4-LOM. And it was he that formed a lone welcome party that first moment I stepped into my new bedroom in our new house. In hindsight, I really wanted to be able to say it was an X-Wing Fighter Pilot Luke Skywalker or Bespin Outfit Han Solo. Or even the AT-AT Commander (I loved their square Imperial hats). But, no. It was 4-LOM – a particularly peripheral character from *The Empire Strikes Back* and one that I later found out was a toy company amalgamation of two bounty hunters, so was not even technically a character anyway. He was the only figure the Cranleigh Toy Shop stocked when I broke off from my mum's path to the supermarket one Friday morning, and I had held out long enough from that plastic toy revolution. I desperately wanted anything Luke Skywalker. But unless you bought into the figures and their cleverly packaged cardboard world, you were almost literally lost in space – especially if you were on the outer rim of a nearly rural outpost that saw the 1983 introduction of takeaway pizzas as groundbreaking. The teasing photos of other ships, creatures and vehicles always adorned all the Palitoy packaging. As soon as you bought one figurine, you had a glossy cardback that would have numbered lists and photo line-ups of other available figures from the (then) two *Star Wars* films. And once you had one cardback in your possession, it wasn't long before you needed another Rebel fix. It was 'Made in Hong Kong' plastic crack for kids aged '4 and over,' and now you knew where your dealer lived – Guildford high street. My mum and stepdad's Saturday afternoon ritual was almost always 'the shops'. As soon as Rob got in from work at midday on a Saturday and I had finished watching *The Fall Guy*, we would drive into town and yours truly – wholly distracted by the *Star Wars* toys quest at play – would have to climb out of the car and help save a parking space as the multistorey car parks became Rebel bunkers under attack from impatient Austin Allegros and mullet-wearing Saab drivers.

Kenner, Lucasfilm and Palitoy pulled a blinder with the 'collect them all' mantras. With enough pocket money all worked out in advance, next on my list was the rather dashing 3¾-inch Luke Skywalker in his tight-fitting beige Bespin fatigues. Not only did that figure have a mop of blonde hair to rival my own, the cardback movie image of Mark Hamill in full blaster-pointing glory was oddly intriguing to this sky kid. 'That's a really good look for him,' I pondered, before venturing with hope into the Guildford Tesco and the veritable Shangri-Leia that was Level One and its substantial *Star Wars* toy range. It seemed to have more Palitoy floor-space than its Debenhams rival and the whole level reeked of that sweet plastic resin bouquet that accompanied all *Star Wars* products. It was the smell of 1980s toys, of Skywalkers and Scout Walkers, yellowing Hoth Wampas, pocket money, Christmas and Saturdays. To this day, I have been known to declare just how much a new plastic household accessory 'smells just like *Star Wars*'. To which my other half – who never had the figures or toys – throws me a look of domestic incredulity as I breathe in a new potato peeler or ice tray. I found most of the stores would never stock the whole range of figures – which tallied ninety-two by 1983 and the release of *Return of the Jedi* – but lots and lots of duplicates. Tesco endeavoured to be tidy and hung their available figures in lines with a large box underneath that would catch the fallen Klaatus, Gamorrean Guards and Tusken Raiders. It very quickly became a glorious *Star Wars* figure soup – a plastic Sarlaac Pit of upturned androids and mustachioed Rebel officers awaiting rehousing. Very soon we became experts at delving deep and pouring scorn on the torn, figureless cardbacks that bad kids had plundered mercilessly whilst clearly ignoring the bulbous, terrifying department store CCTV cameras that always resembled hovering Death Star interrogation probes. Like Canto Bight croupiers, we could flick through the cardbacks at great speed. No dull Hoth Stormtrooper we already owned three of could be left unturned, in case there was a rarer Yoda, Emperor Palpatine or General Madine hidden underneath. And then there he was – Luke Skywalker. In his Bespin fatigues. And complete with a dashing photo of Mark Hamill being all pointy and dashing with his blaster pistol. Result. Well, nearly. I still had to have another quick scan to see if there were any more Luke Skywalkers in his Bespin fatigues with a less creased cardback. I never knew what was worse – having no choice of figures each week and only another Hoth Stormtrooper to take home, or too much choice and that till-queue fear you have picked the wrong one that Saturday.

My tenure as a *Star Wars* sky kid really jumped to lightspeed during the run-up to the June 1983 release of *Return of the Jedi*. 4-LOM and Bespin Luke were soon joined by Han Solo in his Hoth parka, Princess Leia in her Cloud City kaftan, Princess Leia in her Boushh bounty hunter leathers, R2-D2, the C-3PO whose limbs could all fall apart (not easy for display purposes at the end of play), Darth Vader and his red condom-shaped lightsaber, the Emperor's Royal Guard in a rather dashing red felt robe, Jabba the Hutt's tentacle-necked front of house manager Bib Fortuna (who also had a rather dashing felt couture robe of his own), an AT-AT Commander and a Tusken Raider to keep the others on their plastic toes.

Those founding fathers of twelve figures soon swelled to a toy collection of a Speeder Bike, two Scout Walkers, two Hoth Wampas, two X-Wings and a birthday AT-AT. The duplicates were often a direct result of the gift buying habits of two separated parents, a kind stepdad and my lack of principles when it came to receiving the same *Star Wars* toy twice. Around the summer of *Return of the Jedi*, the British toy company Palitoy soon released smaller, more allowance-friendly spin-off vehicles. For three pounds of my pocket money I soon lapped up these 'Mini Rigs' with a monthly relish. Suddenly my bedroom had a growing armada of a Vehicle Maintenance Energizer (a repository for all the guns, tools and blasters we had already lost in the back garden), a CAP-2 Captivator (complete with suction pad feet that would never unstick if you pressed too hard on your bedroom window), an Imperial Shuttle Pod and an INT-4 Interceptor. I desperately wanted a Snowspeeder and a TIE fighter. And the Ewok Village playset. And the Jabba the Hutt playset. And Sy Snootles and the Rebo Band. And a Tauntaun complete with its 'open belly rescue feature'. Oh, and a Millennium Falcon. And a Yoda and an Obi-Wan Kenobi. But definitely a Millennium Falcon. See. It is impossible to discuss *Star Wars* toys without listing what you had – all with a quiet sadness that you didn't have more of them, and any of them now.

It was hard work being a *Star Wars* kid. It was even harder being an only child who 'surely had enough *Star Wars* ships already'. Siblings would multiply the household fleet and arsenal of figures and ships. Only-child sky kids had to fight for the resistance singlehandedly. I was like Saw Gerrera in *Rogue One* singlehandedly defending the Rebel Alliance from afar, just with less bitter baggage and breathing apparatus. An early life with *Star Wars* involved a great deal of parental negotiations, budgetary summit meetings over the breakfast table and improvised birthday treaties. But despite not seeing the middle and most important act of the original trilogy – it was just 'the trilogy' to us, if that – it was my world. Or my galaxy. These figures were precious plastic idols, badges of childhood honour and a direct link to a global cinematic phenomenon. A few cloth-uniformed exceptions aside, these were hardy and durable 3¾-inch play pals that could stand rain, snow, being stepped on, drawn on, pulled in tug-of-loyalties, drowned in the bath, dropped down the toilet, driven over, Sellotaped to the spokes of our bikes, and being accidentally thrown into the washing machine. They even mostly survived the sharp canine teeth of Golden Retrievers. There was a shorthand to being a *Star Wars* kid and the toys and figures were its language. A weekend sleepover would always be preceded by 'can I take my AT-AT?' and playground nepotism based on knowing who owned what ship or rare figure was rife. There was always the darker-minded kid who had all the Empire's villains, Commanders and Stormtroopers. He would be invited to a play-off with anyone who had a Luke or three, and if you had a Han Solo with a Chewbacca you had instant leverage.

I was somewhere in the middle – enjoying the richer designed figures that were key to the films rather than sub-characters with zero screen time. And by the time of *Jedi*'s third outing, the figures had become a little more film accurate. The 1978 Han Solo no longer looked like a spindly toddler, gone were Ben Kenobi's bootcut slacks, Lando finally got a proper cape for his Rebel pilot look rather than his 1980 Elvis-collared housecoat, and the Stormtroopers kept their white veneer rather than looking like a smoker's finger over time. Incidentally, why did the Hoth Wampa's torso eventually also go a bit yellow whilst the legs stayed pristine white, lending a sort of 1970s pantsuit look to the otherwise fearsome Yeti-like creature?!

Like *E. T. the Extra-Terrestrial*, *Close Encounters of the Third Kind*, *Jaws*, *Superman* and the very trilogy from which they came, the *Star Wars* figures and toys became archetypal to a generation's childhood. Yes, they were all merchandise-minded by-products. They were a business strategy, and a very good one at that. But like all good products they needed a design strategy too, and the designers at Lucasfilm, ILM and Kenner Products did not just create movie magic for the big screen. They sanctioned the physical grammar of our bedroom floors and those all-too-brief magical spaces under our Christmas trees. After time, these toys become loaded with a different and powerful aesthetic – one of nostalgia. Those of us that had the foresight or forgotten loft space to still own our *Star Wars* toys now realise their potent ability to time-travel our minds back to a 3¾-inch childhood of bases and dens and ships and flying. A vintage *Star Wars* figure is now as evocative and haunting as the smell of a real pine Christmas tree or that Turtle Wax air freshener in your dad's car.

Some kids were, of course, into the complete *Star Wars* world and its merchandise. I was always drawn to the parka hoods, snow goggles and boots of the ice planet Hoth, and the modish, dandy swagger and terracotta pinks, navy blues and capes of the Cloud City tailoring – all from a movie I hadn't even seen yet. My Princess Leia figure in her puce Bespin evening wear was always a favourite, and the founding queen of my figurine collection. In hindsight, of course it was high camp – as was Lando Calrissian's nylon, high-collared and sleeveless rain mac number that doubled for the cape he wore in *The Empire Strikes Back*. Maybe it was *Episode V*'s Nordic, European backdrops that appealed to this Surrey boy from the frozen moon of Britain. It was a greater touchstone than the parched and distant deserts of Tunisia and Arizona. For half a year Britain was usually as grey, damp and murky as Dagobah. And we all traipsed through the winter snow to school in a navy blue parka like Han Solo, whilst our kneeling AT-AT sat in the back garden covered in ice. I would have worn Leia's Bespin puce kaftan too, if the nuns were not still reeling from some of my nativity ensembles. Although, whilst the *Star Wars* figure world was a particularly progressive and inclusive one, it wasn't too wise to boast of wanting or even having that many Princess Leia figurines. I eventually had three Leias – though her Endor combat poncho from *Jedi* did end up as a divine must-have for one of my Biker Scouts, who just wanted to lead a hipster life at the gay end of the redwood forest with his long-term partner and Speeder Bike repair shop.

And then there were the kids who took their *Star Wars* figures on holiday abroad. Because there is nothing key players in the Rebel Alliance, the Jedi Council and the Galactic Empire love more than a package holiday to a Greek island. But in the May 1983 half-term I did indeed take my twelve plastic 3¾-inch friends on a week's break to Crete and the town of Hersonissos. Bespin Luke even accompanied me through security at Gatwick Airport, whilst his eleven travelling companions no doubt splintered off into the good and the dark side of my suitcase having stocked up on duty-free Cinzano, two-for-ones Blue Stratos and a multipack of Camel cigarettes. And before we'd even left British soil I had spent a wedge of my holiday spending money in the Gatwick WHSmith's on the grand and rather brilliant *Return of the Jedi* photo storybook. Written by 1980s film tie-in legend Joan D. Vinge, it was a glossy recounting of the story I hadn't yet seen. Who cares about spoilers when you have a portable gallery of new images from a factory-fresh *Star Wars* film in your hand?! As we flew over Europe, I pored over each and every page of that 'storybook based on the movie' like Bib Fortuna checking out a recently arrived R2 unit. When we arrived at our typical late-1970s Mediterranean hotel in Hersonissos, I was still obsessed. As my parents checked in at reception, I sat at a Space Invaders table arcade game complete with beech veneer and the scope to leave three letters of your name on a scoreboard should you win. I was so ensconced in the book I ignored the other passing kids and their incredulous faces at how someone would be sat in prime position on the arcade game table and not bother to play it. I did later venture to have a go one morning, but my shooting skills were hardly X-Wing Academy ready. But I did get to type in three letters of my name for future virtual-forensic teams to pore over in centuries to come. All that effort, and all you got to do was shorten your name to an unrecognisable three characters for later strangers to totally ignore. Soon, Bespin Luke was accompanying my parents and I on a coach trip to the ancient palace of Knossos, totally overlooking the historical irony that one of *Star Wars'* key influences is Greek mythology, Theseus and the Minotaur in the labyrinth – which Greek legend suggests all unfurled in the very crumbling corridors and catacombs Bespin Luke and I mentally transformed into Jabba's Palace with somewhat sacrilegious haste.

Instead of just taking photos of my family and the Greek sights on holiday, I spent our valuable camera exposures also taking photos of photos of the Scout Walkers and Boba Fett in my *Return of the Jedi* book. And Bespin Luke and I were having quite the summer fling. We shared a bedroom, we hung out on the beach and I got Bespin Luke over his fear of stuffed vine leaves. He even accompanied me to one of those hotel basement nightclubs that have no customers, just kids and their *Star Wars* figures quietly fascinated by the fluorescent lights making everything white glow like green Kryptonite. But it was also time to let 4-LOM, Bib Fortuna, Darth Vader, the androids and Leia in her Cloud City kaftan out for a bit of Grecian sun in our third-floor Crete apartment room. With some high-end production design of tinfoil, some upturned glass tumblers and a white bedsheet, I set about my Crete photoshoot on our apartment balcony without wondering once why we would have brought tinfoil with us on holiday. Naturally, Princess Leia had pitched it perfectly in her Bespin number, which worked particularly well for her exploring the pottery markets during the day and the balmy wine bars of a Med package holiday at night. However, Han Solo in his Hoth parka and Bib Fortuna and the Emperor's Guard in their heavy felt robes were all perhaps a bit overdressed for the Hersonissos sun. Yet, sporting a recently purchased and rather dashing traditional Greek cap, complete with tassel, I managed to get my founding figures together for a group photo. And a good one at that. The AT-AT Commander kept his tan lines hidden, no one clocked R2-D2's horrendous Babycham hangover from the night before, and Darth didn't neck-choke the slightly incredulous honeymooning couple watching on from the next balcony.

And with a bunch of memories and my twelve *Star Wars* figures packaged away into a new Snoopy backpack I had found on a Crete market stall, my parents, Galactic and Rebel friends and I bid *ya soo* to Hersonissos and Crete. After a long flight delay and a quick bag check at Heraklion Airport, where I really expected the security officer to be more impressed with my *Return of the Jedi* photo storybook than she was, we finally boarded the plane. Hoping to avoid any Imperial entanglements on the flight home, we did however receive midflight news that instead of continuing as planned to our Gatwick rendezvous, our flight would be detoured to the Luton Airport system and its hive of duty-free villainy and emergency landing strip potential. Bespin Luke observed the touchdown from his window seat vantage point and Bib Fortuna made the most of Monarch Airline's complimentary tomato juice and Viscount bar. Once finally landed in Luton during the early hours, we collected our bags and realised the only way home was a minicab all the way. With my founding figures sat tight in my Snoopy backpack I slept most of the journey and was only too glad to get back to Cranleigh and our new home. We bid goodbye to the minicab and trundled indoors. As my stepdad got the power back on and the minicab disappeared into the night, I looked to my *Star Wars* figures and my Snoopy backpack. It was gone. They were gone. In all our early-hour and airport-transfer exhaustion, I had left the bag in a North London minicab we would never be able to trace. My entire collection of *Star Wars* figures was lost forever. To say I was bereft was an understatement. It was like Emperor Palpatine had just executed Order 66 and my whole family of Jedi, Princesses, Rebels and dodgy aliens was wiped out, never to be seen again. And they weren't. With me anxiously at her side, Mum phoned the lost property departments of Luton and Gatwick airports more than once. But it was to no avail. The cab could never be traced. There were tears. Lots of them. Less of a disturbance in the Force, more of an all-out emotional meltdown. All I had left was that slightly blurred photo of my plastic clan on holiday in Crete – like a tour of duty-free that not all of us came back from.

Having my *Star Wars* toys reputation reset in such a cruel way was harsh. They had been key plastic pals in a reset year of new hope and a change of base. I was distraught, ready to hide away like a veteran British actor on the desert planet of Tatooine and to never again speak of Jedi, Jawas, androids and princesses in Cloud City kaftans. Maybe it was a sign. Maybe I should put away such childish things. Later this year I was 8 years old, and there were never going to be any more new *Star Wars* films anyway. However, we are told rebellions – and franchises – are built on hope. If General Leia can survive the death of Han Solo and Luke Skywalker, and Harrison Ford can survive the death of Carrie Fisher, then who am I to go into exiled mourning on some distant swamp planet whilst looking to Zoids and He-Man as my thing now? So, the following weekend I went to the only place that could possibly lend me some of that there *hope* – the first-floor toy department at Guildford Tesco. My sympathetic mum had kindly given me more pocket money than usual and I set about reassembling my *Star Wars* figure family. Would it be the same? Would I get into some rebound spiral of replacement figures not being nearly the same as the real thing? Amongst the first I found were Bespin Luke and Vader, and of course R2-D2 and C-3PO. For mass-produced plastic people, the new Bespin Luke had no recollections of our time in Crete and didn't quite look the same as my previous one. His eyes looked glazed – like he'd spent too long with the stoners and fairies in Golden Gate Park before leaving California for London. And there was no Bespin Leia. Or 4-LOM, my firstborn that once greeted me into my new home. They would never be replaced. Yet soon enough others came along in their stead. It wasn't the same, but it worked, and my founding fathers of twelve became a renewed fifteen, then twenty, then twenty-seven. The ships grew around them, as did the Palitoy packaging I cut out and kept. Every now and then I would pause and wonder what happened to that glorious original dozen of lost figures. Hoping they didn't all end up stuck in the boot of a minicab forever circling the Outer Rim of the M25 or for sale alongside battered Kerplunk boxes at some Sunday car boot sale off the M25, I half-imagined Bespin Princess Leia and some of the others found their way back to Hersonissos. Perhaps they met some unsavoury types in the Luton Airport bar and eventually chartered a cut-price smuggler's transport back to Crete? Maybe Leia opened a wine bar of her own with Bib Fortuna as her door whore, and 4-LOM was tasked with flyering each week's new tourist arrivals as they queued up to check into their rooms by that Space Invaders table. And perhaps that first Bespin Luke I ever had got the coach back to Knossos and set up home there, only to be found later and really confuse archeologists thousands of years from now.

THE FIRST LAST JEDI

RETURN OF THE JEDI

1983. With blue skies meeting the golden sands of a desert planet, a gangster's sail barge cruises over the dunes and its own shadows as a watching princess is tugged by her chains back to her vile captor.

One person who I did not expect to help my *Star Wars* figure recruitment drive was Lord Vader himself. My 3¾-inch Darth with his retractable arm saber was also lost in the Great Luton *Star Wars* Figurine Massacre of 1983. A much-needed clone replacement of said plastic Sith Lord was now not easy to find. The Guildford Tesco just had swarms of red Imperial Guards, yet more Chief Chirpa Ewoks and enough Snowtroopers to handcuff the whole of Surrey. What good was an Empire of malleable troops and ships if there was no Vader?! The Darth figure was a Palitoy stalwart. It was impossible for him to not look like a shrunken version of the real thing. It was only around the release of *Return of the Jedi* that the Luke Skywalker

figures actually started to resemble Mark Hamill. But Vader looked
like Vader – even if he should not really have been as short as the
other figurines. But there is no way the Vader I soon encountered
one Saturday afternoon in Guildford could be classed as 'a little
short for a Stormtrooper'. The local branch of department store
Debenhams was having a *Star Wars* toy promotion day. Not only
would figures and ships be slightly reduced in price, but Lord Vader
was arriving by Imperial Shuttle to inspect the toy department
himself. Cue some of the nervous Lindas from haberdashery having
a Moff Jerjerrod panic – 'but he asks the impossible – we need
more men … and Saturday girls!' It was the real deal. Palitoy and
20th Century Fox had wrangled the Sith Lord to promote their
new *Return of the Jedi* range. As new Saturday girls go, that is not
a bad coup. Vader couldn't be any surlier than the usual weekend
staff. For the first time ever, I was actually excited about going to
Debenhams. Usually it meant school clothes shopping or being
mortified and stuck with your mum in the Ladies department.
But this Saturday I was extra early. Too early. There was no sign
of our man Darth. But something was definitely afoot. The toy
department at Debenhams was not very large, so some older ladies
from the neighbouring soft furnishing department were clearing
away towels, duvet sets and toilet seat covers to make room for the
Imperial visit. They missed a good sales opportunity, as Darth Vader
may well have leaped at the chance to stock up on charcoal-grey
Egyptian cotton hand towels. Who's to say that Throne Room of
his could not have benefited from a few scatter cushions and some
new pencil pleat drapes?

The 'mall appearances' of comic book and sci-fi staples were
common in the States in the 1970s and 1980s. Less so in Britain.
We'd have Ruth Madoc from sitcom *Hi-De-Hi!* opening the new
Bejam, or two kids from *Grange Hill* cutting the ribbon on a new
Tammy Girl clothing store. Or at best, local cockney-drummer

An original Vader costume cuts an ominous sight in the Lucasfilm Ltd lobby, San Francisco.

Phil Collins, who would do his local celeb fete-opening duty should Penelope Keith be unavailable. Though we did once have Ringo Starr light our village bonfire as Cranleigh tried to turn the fireworks night into some Olympics opening ceremony cauldron moment. But it had never before had a visit from the villainous figurehead of the biggest movie in the world. As kids my age started to gather coyly with one already bored parent in tow, we all knew something was afoot as it was our turn to bore and humiliate our parents in Debenhams. Some of us were going through the replenished toy stocks to look for untold finds. I'd already had a quick scout for Bespin Leia. Nothing. Others like myself were quietly rolling our eyes at kids lower down on the *Star Wars* toy owners pecking order getting excited by figures the rest of us had owned for months. Suddenly the Clannad hits on the store tannoy stopped to make way for the rather incongruous 'Imperial March'. And then wending a careful path through the pleated quilts and wicker bathroom baskets was the Sith Lord himself, Darth Vader. Not that his black frame was hard to miss against the sea of chintz and roses that was the palette of the early-1980s retail outpost we all found ourselves in that day. But we never saw him coming. Maybe he had got the escalator up from the glassware and crystal department. This was not a fake-alike or a cosplay gesture, this was the genuine thing – a rather tall Darth in the authentic Vader costume, moving with that slow intent and a black cape that seemed to take forever to finish swishing round his body when one defiant kid kept pulling at it. He didn't talk, nor did he have the breathing apparatus turned up, but Vader was all-out terrifying. The first thing to strike all us gathered sky kids was the height and mighty size of the Galactic Empire's most fearsome of black knights. The chest plate with the detail of lights and switches, the contours of the legs, the foreboding boots, the heavy gloves that audibly crunched every time those heavy digits moved, the suffocating might of the mask and that triangular jaw piece complete with a chain and painful-looking bolts – it's a magnificent piece of movie costume design by John Mollo and *Star Wars* conceptual artist Ralph McQuarrie. The mask alone has a profile like an Imperial or bounty hunter ship of its own. We knew it was a man in a costume. But unlike our home-made attempts to be Vader or that excellent Darth costume that somewhat stole my glory at that fancy dress pageant, no person inside was detectable. In our heads, we had already worked out the

The pen is mightier than the Sith – a Lord Vader autograph on 1980s
Debenhams notepaper.

backstory and prequel to Anakin Skywalker two decades before
George Lucas gave us *Revenge of the Sith* (2005). And it was not a
happy one. It all added to the quiet horror of the character and its
mix of danger and tragedy. My mum instantly took a cautious step
back, younger siblings didn't want to know and few nans were happy
to let their kids step forward. It was a gloriously sinister flipside of a
department store Santa's Grotto. Only, we didn't get to sit on Vader's
lap and profess how much we had stepped into the Dark Side this
year in this strange sort of *Miracle on Sith Street* moment.

It was an incongruous sight – Darth Vader surrounded by
denim-clad kids and floral home furnishing solutions. Then there
was the rather curious beat of a permed member of Debenhams
staff handing Lord Vader a biro. Admittedly it was just about
to get awkward, because what can a Sith Lord actually do on a

Saturday afternoon in Debenhams? Neck-choke the sportswear guy in a tache? Hurl a grizzly toddler down the reactor shaft escalators? And with that biro in hand, our man Darth was handed some Debenhams *Return of the Jedi* cards, instantly betraying the real reason there was an Imperial Shuttle taking up three disabled parking spaces in the nearby multistorey car park – a sales drive. 'See the full range of *Star Wars* toys, books and stationary at your local Debenhams,' proclaimed the card with a publicity photo of Luke Skywalker waving his blaster at the creatures of Jabba's Palace. That was not wholly true. Debenhams did not quite stock the full range. Tesco was always better. But Tesco did not have the real Darth Vader about to sign autographs for the kids. Nor did it have a cannily timed batch of new Vader figurines on special offer. Result. Two decades before Emperor Palpatine tells Anakin Skywalker he has a way of cheating death in *Revenge of the Sith*, my lost Vader figurine had already done it via a Palitoy promotional event and a tall bloke in a Darth Vader costume. It was certainly not a bad way of replacing lost Star Wars figurines. If only Carrie Fisher was at Timothy White's flogging Bespin Leias …

It was Friday, 3 June 1983. Margaret Thatcher was less than a week away from winning her second term as British Prime Minister, the new pound coin was a pocket money novelty, New Edition's 'Candy Girl' was at number 1 in the UK charts, Irene Carr's Oscar-winning song 'Flashdance … What a Feeling' had welded itself to the top of the US charts, and I was hoping my imminent First Holy Communion would see me have more luck with God than my Catholic cosplay attempts to be Luke Skywalker. First Holy Communion did have one benefit. I could pick a First Holy Communion present. I chose a 'battle damaged' Palitoy X-Wing ship complete with a glossy pull-out photo poster of other *Return of the Jedi* ships coming up on the horizon. It's what Jesus would have wanted.

Just over a week after it had opened in the States, my stepdad Rob was taking me to the opening night of *Episode VI* at the Regal Cinema just down the road from our new house in Cranleigh. We were now much nearer to the cinema, and in the summer months of the years that followed I would walk there following the distant yellow gleam of the marquee lights, pushing many a title that would skip the heart upon first sight – *A View to a Kill, The Living Daylights, Jurassic Park, Short Circuit, Ghostbusters, Police Academy 4: Citizens on Patrol, Star Trek IV: The Voyage Home, The Witches* and *Memphis Belle. Return of the Jedi* was the first movie event of my childhood that I was old enough to fully grasp and revel in. *Episode VI* was everywhere in the early summer of 1983. As Palitoy naturally upped its merchandise siege on our toy boxes and parents' good will, the television commercials were awash with mini film trailers, exclusive clips and stilted promotional interviews. And if it wasn't the quick ads forever revelling in the Speeder Bike chase, it was *Return of the Jedi* competitions to win exclusive tickets for London screenings in those mystery 'selected cinemas', T-shirts, yet more toys and soundtrack albums. Putting my search for Bespin Leia to one side, I saved a couple of weekends' allowances – 'pocket money' to us Brits – and bought the cassette of John Williams' soaring soundtrack score. I played it over and over and over, relishing the sleeve notes and the striking image of Luke Skywalker's two somewhat fetching hands holding that lightsaber aloft to the skies in a haze of blue. I pored over every detail of the sleeve notes, quietly fascinated by the names of trumpeters, the recording studios of the London Symphony Orchestra and the track listings that would give some things away – but not nearly as much as *The Phantom Menace*'s soundtrack album listing famously did with 'Qui-Gon's Noble End' and 'Qui-Gon's Funeral' in 1999.

'The Saga Continues …' promised the very red teaser poster featuring the dark silhouette of a duelling Vader and Luke overseen by that menacing Sith Lord mask, '… in your galaxy soon'. That was all very fortunate, as my movie galaxy was the Regal. The excitement of seeing 'RETURN OF THE JEDI' on the 1936 cinema's marquee frontage lettering against its yellow background, complete with film times and a 'U' for its 'Universal' rating, was more than palpable. It dominated the night sky for all passing 7-year-olds – as did the sight of the final UK poster for *Return of the Jedi*, whose blue sweeping heroics and sense of sci-fi montage yielded further cinema lobby radiance to us British sky kids of 1983. Unlike a great many of this American era's movie posters, the UK poster for *Jedi* was designed by a British science fiction artist, Josh Kirby. Kirby had extensive experience drawing cover art for the works of Ian Fleming, Alfred Hitchcock, Ray Bradbury, Jack Kerouac, Richard Matheson and, most notably, Terry Pratchett. He also designed one of the posters for the same year's *Krull* (1983). We pored over Kirby's *Jedi* work like fine art specialists, taking in all the graphical swagger of his twirling vortex of adventure, character heads and oncoming TIE fighters. The widescreen magic of those posters was nearly as cinematic and thrilling as the films themselves. Although Friday, 3 June 1983 was already more than special. Here I was seeing a new *Star Wars* film on its first Friday in a proper cinema. No borrowed VHS copy. No commercial breaks. No more having to lie to school mates that I had seen all the *Star Wars* movies – even the ones they hadn't made yet (making up episodes that didn't exist for playground mystery and one-upmanship was not uncommon). Two films changed my life in the June of 1983: *Return of the Jedi* and *Octopussy*. Who knows what sort of person I would be had *Porky's II: The Next Day* completed the hat-trick.

As soon as Darth Vader's shuttle glides into a newborn, half-finished Death Star – which like all early-1980s new builds was having construction woes – and the Sith Lord himself sashays out to inspect its progress with his nervous commanding officer Moff Jerjerrod, director Richard Marquand restores the sense of expanse to *Star Wars*. For all the correct reasoning, the preceding *The Empire Strikes Back* (1980) kept the internal anguish of the characters and plot to a constricted production design. Here, the confines of *Empire's* visual palette are immediately opened out from the get-go to a gargantuan shuttle bay set housed at Elstree Studios, no doubt using a bit of literal smoke, mirrors and matte drawing trickery. And with a Vader warning about the soft launches of new businesses and one of George Lucas's trademark screen wipes in-between, we zip from the Death Star to Death Valley as C-3PO and R2-D2 negotiate the simmering and expansive sands of Tatooine, California with a willful reminder of how events kicked off six years previously. *Jedi* is the original trilogy's most exterior-heavy *Star Wars* film, and the one which used the state of California the most – be it the sands of Death Valley, the redwood forests, the Buttercup Valley or a bit of neighbouring Arizona for good measure.

Before 2016's *Rogue One: A Star Wars Story* and the Citadel Tower siege on the tropical planet of Scarif, the Galactic Empire did not go in for flora and fauna. Admittedly, in *Return of the Jedi* they do have their Forest of Endor outpost – no doubt a useful pad for all those Imperial team-building weekend retreats, with lovely views of the surrounding trees. I could just see the Emperor guest-speaking to a team of IT support staff from Mustafar with some dull management talk – 'there is no "I" in Jedi'. And pity the poor Biker Scout who slowly raises his hand with an, 'er, yes there is, sir …'.

The Death Star is a good analogy for the *Star Wars* films themselves. The franchise's most recognisable production design motif, the spherical temple of doom is prone to being attacked from all sides, it comes back as a sequel more than once, it helps kill the Emperor, the very mention of it wakes up the prequels, its first destruction gets the special addition of a 1997 CGI shock wave which echoes the non-CGI shock wave fans had over that, it rises again in a new prequel which fills in its backstory, and its offspring gets enhanced and repurposed in *Episode VII*.

The visual demarcations of *Star Wars* are most apparent in *Return of the Jedi*. The Empire, its Star Destroyers and outposts continue their metallic purge of the galaxy as the Rebel Alliance surround themselves in greens, browns and khaki ponchos. The Star Destroyers float like alligators in space waiting to attack, whilst the quilted design of the Rebel Alliance's frigates and cruisers are visually softer and kinder looking. The Rebellion is all about diversity. Lone aliens pilot fighter ships alongside human counterparts of differing ethnic backgrounds, whilst all being led into battle by a middle-aged woman and a benevolent giant prawn in a tabard. The Empire is about uniformity. Until the third trilogy and 2015's *The Force Awakens*, the Imperial forces have no women, no employees of colour, their uniforms are unchanging and the only aliens they let in are deceitful bounty hunters they scorn behind their backs. The diversity of *Rogue One: A Star Wars Story* (2016) is testament to *Return of the Jedi* with its mélange of characters and backgrounds forming a keen and effective assortment of heroes. The whole Battle of Endor is a knowing comment on the industrialisation of man versus the might of nature in good folk's hands. From the sands and Death Star of 1977 via the snow, swamp vegetation and weather systems of 1980 to the forests of Endor here in 1983 — the *Star Wars* trilogy has been going back to nature since it started. Cue the greenery and woodland motifs of 2015's *The Force* and the salt plains and rocky crags of *The Last Jedi* (2017). The forests and trees of *Jedi '83* all felt very familiar to us kids from England and became a crucial factor in our engagement with the film. We only had to pilot our plastic Speeder Bikes and Millennium Falcons out the back door and into the garden to be amongst the greenery of *Return of the Jedi*. One tree branch could be a whole Ewok stronghold and any wild bracken will always mentally have Han Solo pushing through it with a camouflaged overcoat and a stick-breaking panache. Kids at our junior school would pretend the gnarled stump of a tree with its lone bough was a Speeder Bike seat, and there is a whole generation who cannot look at a redwood tree without thinking Endor. In hundreds of years' time, tiny plastic Ewok spears, staffs and catapults will be unearthed in the gardens of Britain and no one will be quite sure why.

The visual palette of each *Star Wars* film tends to operate in threes. The gold sands of Tatooine, the shiny charcoal-grey of the Death Star and the green vegetation of Yavin IV for *A New Hope*. The white snows of Hoth, the murky greys of Dagobah and the terracotta of Cloud City for *The Empire Strikes Back*. Whilst the gold sands of Tatooine, the greens of Endor and the charcoal greys of *Jedi* are not wholly new on the third time round, *Return of the Jedi* is possibly the best shot of all the original *Star Wars* trilogy. A veteran of the *Carry On* films, Hammer Horror, Bond and soon-to-be *Supergirl*, the British cinematographer Alan Hume was responsible for shooting *Episode VI*. A typical British director of photography who worked his post-Second World War way up the ranks throughout the English Home Counties movie studios, Hume was more familiar with lighting Joan Sims, Sid James and the great Roger Moore than Gamorrean Guards, Rancor Monsters and Ewoks. However, as the frosty blues of *The Empire Strikes Back* thaw away, there is a rich polish to the look of *Episode VI* – with the crucial Death Star scenes deliciously crisp with their rich blacks, reds and those trademark white lozenge-shaped lights, the Jabba's Palace sequence is a detailed hive of bounty hunter raggedness and smoky archways, the exterior Endor scenes never lose their Californian daylight, and every X-Wing back-burner and Imperial Shuttle glows the reddest of reds and the bluest of blues.

The whole production of *Return of the Jedi* exudes confidence. Two episodes in and no doubt hundreds of arduous production days on the Land Speeder clock now lend *Episode VI* a notable production poise and assurance. Under the eye of British designer Norman Reynolds (*The Empire Strikes Back, Raiders of the Lost Ark*), the corridors, blast doors and garbage chutes of *A New Hope* now become a cathedral-like Throne Room for the Palpatine administration – complete with wide temple steps and a viewing platform to see the stars and battle raging outside a window that was not wholly dissimilar to the front of Palitoy's TIE fighter ship. The trench battle of *Episode IV* is now a cascading fantastic voyage into the inner workings and main reactor of the Death Star (an action motif echoed in 2017's *The Last Jedi* as the Millennium Falcon barrels through the underground crimson stalagmites and stalactites of Crait as if the planet has a human circulatory system of its own). A trash compactor sequence is now opened out and evolves into the Great Pit of Carkoon – re-staged on many a household staircase, where the Sarlaac Pit's lethal tentacles could be recreated with dressing-gown cords and any old 1980s chintz curtains a mum was stupid enough to leave lying around. The cantina bar ensemble motif is now Jabba the Hutt's gangster's paradise of baroque chambers, alien opium dens, boneyard dungeons and a floating cocktail lounge that can cruise the dunes whilst serving two-for-one Mojitos (a design tic later echoed in the equally shady casino skiffs of Canto Bight in *The Last Jedi*). This sky watcher's greatest shot in any *Star Wars* film is possibly the original 1983 sight of Jabba's Skiff sailing over the sands of Tatooine with the Max Rebo

Band's funk soul beats. Like no other, it encapsulates the movement, extra-terrestrial life and day-to-day vehicular world of *Star Wars*.

The film's whole first act is a great apex and testament to all those crafts which this era of sky watching pushed, evolved and transformed – the make-up designs and work of the Freeborn family and others, the puppetry of the Jim Henson Creature Workshop (fresh off 1982's *The Dark Crystal*, produced by *Star Wars'* Gary Kurtz), Norman Reynolds' monastic art direction, the layers of Ben Burtt's sound design and alien dialects (that familiar subtitles font is back!), the model work and motion control progressions made by Industrial Light & Magic, the barbarian-chic from costume designers Aggie Guerard Rodgers (*Cocoon*, *The Witches of Eastwick*) and Nilo Rodis-Jamero (*Star Trek V: The Final Frontier*) and the baton of composer John Williams tasked with the baroque-synth hits of a jobbing alien lounge music act. And none of that has even factored in the movie elation of witnessing Mark Hamill, Harrison Ford, Carrie Fisher and Billy Dee Williams midway through a long-game operation to rescue a frozen Han Solo from one of the most dispiriting endnotes of 1980s cinema. It still unnerves the hell out of me when Leia has freed Han only for that palace curtain to peel back to reveal Jabba and company were holding a precautionary all-nighter all along. Although, *who* hangs wind-chimes in an alien fortress?!

Alongside the production thinking and photography, *Jedi* is arguably the best edited of all *Star Wars* films. It is certainly the best paced. The final act particularly is a tight, operatic montage of story and action, proving that three-act rule of *Star Wars* again with the Ewok-led fisticuffs on Endor, the Rebel Fleet's Dunkirk attack on the Death Star and the Skywalkers' personal conflicts all expertly juggled by director Marquand and editors Sean Barton (*Quadrophenia*, *Jagged Edge*), Duwayne Dunham (*Twin Peaks*) and original trilogy regular, Marcia Lucas. The editing and production riches certainly compensate for some of the slighter weaknesses in the screenplay. Han and Leia's story is only ever as strong as that Jabba's Palace rescue, where Solo literally melts into his princess's arms and − despite the Leia Boussh disguise figurine giving that twist away on the toy packets before we even saw the film − it still packs a cool punch today. There is a slight passivity to Han and Leia in *Return of the Jedi*. That underlying romantic sparring from *The Empire Strikes Back* has gone. Leia does not disagree with anyone or anything in *Jedi*. She doesn't fight or answer back. Likewise, Han. It is more *Hart to Hart* here than Bogart and Bacall. Maybe it is a side effect of Luke's severing himself from the trio. The last-act revelations of *Empire* have taken a toll on the tone and drive of the trio. Luke has gone off to his solo album and the band takes a bit of a break in *Jedi*. The Emperor barks how Luke's 'faith in your friends' is his weakness. Perhaps it is the dynamic of *Star Wars* itself too. Separate the trio and it makes them narratively vulnerable. *Empire* got that balance spot-on. But then Leia was sparkier, Han was pluckier and Luke was naïver. A certain weakness of fandom is certainly hindsight. This fan's hindsight would have kept Luke facing Palpatine and liberating Anakin, but tried putting the marooned and not-so-cuddly Han Solo encountering and recruiting the Ewoks first, and somehow saved featuring Leia in the space battle above Endor until the last act. That way Han can be the boss on the ground but is fighting for Leia's safety before that of the Rebel mission, she is hanging out with Lando Calrissian and playing with Han's jealousy, and getting the trio back together in one piece is as pressing as defeating the Empire. Maybe. Perhaps this is why 7-year-old *Star Wars* fans do not get to make *Star Wars* movies.

Luke Skywalker is certainly a changed man in *Return of the Jedi*. That naïve, bounding and romantic farm boy from Tatooine is long gone as Lawrence Kasdan and George Lucas's screenplay presents him with greater maturity, responsibility and a growing distance from his core friends. Whilst the deliberately isolated Luke of *The Last Jedi* has become a disillusioned and neurotic Jedi Master lurking around the ancient stone hives and over-lit precipices of Ahch-To, that distance and need for seclusion already began in 1983. Dressed throughout in black robes that deliberately leave his final act allegiances up for question, Luke's Jedi convictions now weigh heavily on the character. He has already adopted the loner lifestyle, is no longer the romantic lead and clearly the revelations of *Episode V* have knocked his soul. There is the suggestion that Vader wants him to join the Dark Side as a way of protecting him. It is about keeping his son alive, regardless of his allegiances. The worst-case scenario for Luke is also Anakin Skywalker's most fatherly gesture. He wants to ensure his safety. If *A New Hope* and *The Empire Strikes Back* are Luke's stories, then *Return of the Jedi* is very much both their films. One could argue that the titular Jedi that returns is indeed Anakin, not Luke. *Episode VI* is as much about Vader reaching breaking point as it is Luke Skywalker becoming a fully-fledged Jedi. Way before it forms the core of the prequel trilogy, here it is already very much a matter of wife and Darth for Anakin. The light in his soul went out a long time ago and he does not want that for his son – the only relationship of note he has left. Very few third acts and movie trilogies get away with twisting their most famous villain towards the good side. Not even Anakin's old pal Obi-Wan Kenobi has time for him any more – 'he's more machine now than man'. But Vader does hold a humanity. And whilst the vocal work by James Earl Jones of course carries the Darth scenes in all the *Star Wars* films, credit must also go to director Marquand and David Prowse here for all those Sith Lord hesitations and lingering looks of doubt. For a film that famously shows us behind the mask with Sebastian Shaw's endnote scene as a dying Anakin, Vader has shown his true, more compassionate colours already. It makes the sight of

The Guildford Odeon circa 1991, and the local picture house base of too many *Star Wars* movie near-misses for this sky kid.

that burnt and distorted Vader mask in *The Force Awakens* that bit more tragic, as its new, proud owner Kylo Ren (Adam Driver) is oblivious to the reconciliation and contrition the cremated Darth Vader represents at the close of *Return of the Jedi*.

Many an expensive folly of a blockbuster has tried to emulate the sense of event, spectacle and personal stake of the *Star Wars* films. Yet, when stripped bare they are particularly pared-down movies with a narrative simplicity and purity. That is no more apparent than in Richard Marquand's *Return of the Jedi*. With the two further trilogies that followed in its wake, *Jedi* is now the first *Star Wars* movie to suggest that a wider, glossier, more adventure-packed template can still work alongside that of the personal, familial soul as cultivated by the previous *The Empire Strikes Back*. Its story successes, visual palette, sense of colour and the urgency of the ongoing battle is all over 2005's prequel, *Revenge of the Sith*. The very wars in *Star Wars* and that Agincourt sense of final combat, flotilla panic and armada artillery all come from *Return of the Jedi*. As does the pace and sense of movement of 2018's *Solo* with its kinetic car chases echoing both the Speeder bikes and Ford Falcon (yep) of George Lucas and Ron Howard's automobile-heavy youth. When the final act of *Rogue One: A Star Wars Story* (2016) is so grandly executed, it is surely *Jedi* that director Gareth Edwards and his editors John Gilroy, Colin Goudie and Jabez Olssen have all kept an eye on the most. The everything-or-nothing momentum of *Jedi* is all over the dual Scarif and space battle finale as force-shields go up and down, our heroes scramble desperately to accomplish their piece of the victory puzzle, X-Wings piloted by diverse heroes, aliens and English actors from across the galaxy spitfire their successes and sacrifices with equal bravado, the battle-crying Mon Calamari boss Admiral Raddus sits on a funky gimbal captain's chair keeping his panic to a minimum and his orders to a maximum, and the slo-mo majesty of a Star Destroyer nudged into a mesmerizing, yet deathly destruction.

These key and buoyant beats of the new wave of *Star Wars* on screen owe a great debt to Richard Marquand's *Episode VI*. It is curious how the 1983 film, which was meant to end the *Star Wars* movie cycle, now holds out a helping hand to furthering the saga more than any princess, paternal confession or smuggler's popularity.

Barely half an hour into *Return of the Jedi*, and with my Dr Pepper consumption at the Regal Cinema at a nervous high, I was soon trying to gauge when was a quiet moment to nip off to the Gents for a very quick pit stop. Praying I could get to the end of the first act shenanigans of the Sarlaac Pit brawl – although R2-D2 and his on-screen drinks service didn't help – as soon as Luke flew to Dagobah I made a mad dash for it along with all the other 7-year-olds maxing out on fizzy sodas. The Gents at the Regal were always a freezing interlude in a dripping, 1940s tiled urinal with poor lighting. As I finish up I hear Alec Guinness's deep, theatrical tones echoing through the walls, and Obi-Wan's attempts at explaining why he wasn't wholly honest to Luke years before. I panic and return hastily to my seat to see the cigarette smoke of the theatre trapping his Force ghost face like a blue information hologram projected from a robot at the back of the cinema. To this day, I recall the sounds and smells of that cinema and that night with nothing but vivid fondness. I remember that first-time elation of seeing the expanses of space flecked with new ships, sounds and scene dissolves. I can remember the brass shell ashtrays between every seat, the older kids in front of us lighting their cigarettes with a boastful bravado and hoping when the opening crawl starts they will calm down and not ruin it for everyone. They did calm down. I remember how the drums of the Ewok Village resounded off both speakers and the art deco bas-relief panels either side of the screen.

And I can recall the unending tension of the Emperor scenes and just how black and dark the last act was to a 7-year-old.

I wanted to see it again immediately, and assumed I was when my dad took me a week later to the Odeon Guildford on the Sunday. I was quite taken aback – and demonstrated as much – when it transpired a great familial reason meant we were there to see some man called Roger Moore in some film called *Octopussy*. That film changed a lot of my life, and all for the good. But when I was 7 years old, *Return of the Jedi* made my life. Curiously, both films are shot by the same cinematographer on post-war British sound stages close to London at a time when homegrown production and movie investment was dropping fast. And both films feature a quick in-joke to Tarzan. I did eventually watch *Jedi* again with my stepdad in a bizarre Odeon double-bill alongside Kirk Douglas's Australian outback drama *The Man from Snowy River* (1982).

On any viewing, and for someone who had not long seen the 6-year-old *Star Wars* and nothing of *The Empire Strikes Back*, *Return of the Jedi* was immediately a much more contemporary, bigger and slicker movie. It is not the best *Star Wars* film. That was yet to come. But it is easily my favourite.

THAT'S CLARK, NICE

SUPERMAN: THE MOVIE

1978. The golden fields of the Kansas Corn Belt sway with a yesteryear majesty as a kind and humble silver-haired mother watches the dawn skies with her adopted son. Both know it is time to say goodbye.

It was Christmas 1983 when the nuns got me into hot American men in tight pants. All Catholic primary schools in Britain of the early 1980s were fitted out with their own set of 1950s Irish nuns. Fortunately, one of our teachers was a less austere model – and it was she who curiously mentioned to us 7-year-olds that *Superman: The Movie* was on television that very Christmas Day. It was a repeat showing following its January 1983 UK television debut, which I had not even been aware of. You'd think *King of Kings* or *The Ten Commandments* would be a more Catholically-apt recommendation from a nun bidding her flock some festive goodwill? Maybe Sister Anne-Marie saw religious parallels in the man from Krypton's story.

Superman can walk on water, is meant to be the same 33 years old as Jesus himself allegedly was, is relatively chaste – until 1983's *Superman III* required him to suddenly notice dangerous woman and flick peanuts at bartenders in drunken anger – his origin story is all but Moses in the reeds, and his dad was played by an acting god (Marlon Brando) trying to actually *be* God. In the later *Man of Steel* (2013), Superman's Earth and star fathers are played by mere earthling Robin Hoods (Kevin Costner and Russell Crowe).

When we were required to talk to the other God via prayer at primary school, it was Brando's Jor-El who I imagined having a conversation with – 'Forgive me Father, for I have sinned … I quite enjoyed parts of *Superman III*, even though I know you weren't in it.' It was a sort of *On the (Holy) Waterfront*. And no one can convince me that if Jesus himself came back, he wouldn't demand the same record-breaking appearance fee Marlon Brando got out of director Richard Donner and Warner Brothers in the late 1970s for *Superman: The Movie*.

Aside from the later sight of Luke Skywalker in his Hoth underwear in that Echo Base recovery water tank in *The Empire Strikes Back*, it was Christopher Reeve who was my first inkling of abs, thighs, pecs and everything in-between. I am not so sure Sister Anne-Marie had that in mind when she mentioned *Superman: The Movie* to us kids packing our home-made advent cards into our satchels for the Christmas break. Before I even knew why, I had a thing for Clark Kent. I desperately wanted my perfect vision to deteriorate enough to warrant a pair of his thick-rimmed black glasses, to not be blonde and to become a *Daily Planet* intern forced to share a desk and a sidewalk lunch with Clark. I so craved a walk and talk with Clark round that *Daily Planet* lobby globe and out across the street together clutching polystyrene cups of coffee, whilst that lone blonde dude in the plaid shirt and tight denim crotch-bombed every *Daily Planet* establishing shot of the

Reeve era. Maybe it was that Aladdin-produced *Superman: The Movie* school flask that accompanied me on that very first day to school in September 1980, with its *Daily Planet* tableaus and Clark in various stages of shirt-opening undress. It was certainly a brave statement starting my Catholic primary school education with luncheonware emblazoned with Christ-like imagery of what resembled a hot and clean-shirted Mormon guy getting his pecs out for the boys. Throw in a ripped guy in a crisp white shirt and black-rimmed glasses battling a jet-black cowlick, and I will kneel before Zod and anything else he wants me to.

Years later my future husband and I made a birthday trip to New York. Whilst spending the requisite tourist time at the Empire State Building, Central Park, Macys and humming Carly Simon's 'Let the River Run' on the Staten Island ferry, my real Manhattan goal was a pilgrimage to the *Daily Planet*, those slightly vexed, big-haired Metropolis pedestrians and one of the key location homes of 1978's *Superman*. After hailing a yellow cab for the first time in the States ever – well, after mounting the Limey courage to hail a yellow cab for the first time in the States ever – we were soon riding down East 42nd Street towards the *Daily Planet* and its real-life Daily News Building counterpart. In a Krypton second we were instantly in a Donner *Superman* movie. Those busy lanes of traffic, the horizon of encroaching granite, the manhole cover steam clouds, the disgruntled cabbies, the phone booths, the news vendors, hot dog stands and the 'Don't Walk' pedestrian signals. And the film crews. More than many an American city, New York is a living, breathing movie set. When we arrived at our midtown hotel in the early hours one weekend, Harvey Keitel was shooting a movie in the bar. He was playing a Manhattan taxi driver in the film, *A Crime* (2006). Naturally. New York is of course the movie backdrop to many cinematic skies – the Tribeca firehouse and New York Public Library statue lions from *Ghostbusters* (1984), Tootsie preening her hair in the commuter rush, the Times Square of *Taxi Driver* (1976), Dustin Hoffman jogging around the reservoir in *Marathon Man* (1976), *Splash*'s Daryl Hannah contemplating the waters of the Hudson at Cadman Plaza, and Justin Henry learning to ride a bike down the Central Park mall path from *Kramer Vs Kramer* (1979). But the 1970s, Richard Donner and one of the most

Superman: The Movie's Daily Planet stunt double – The Daily News Building on East 42nd Street, New York.

expensive movie projects of the decade put New York back on the fantasy movie map it once helped nurture with *King Kong* (1933).

And with a slow, skywards stare people only do as they get out of cabs in American movies, we alighted from our gloriously surly medallion cab at the 1930 art deco behemoth that is the very real Daily News Building. Immediately I squinted at the top of the marble edifice to exactly where that red helicopter dropped Margot Kidder's Lois Lane onto a marvellous Pinewood Studios back-projection of a Metropolis sidewalk. I remembered that toy helicopter I had as a kid, and how it spent all its time just hanging off the edge of our dining table. I would say aloud, 'You've got me, but who's got you?!' with a Kidder rasp and an added, 'Stand back everyone, stand back,' which got the attention of at least one Manhattan pantsuit owner on her lunch break who did not stand back. And yes, I might have even been in a deliberately Krypton green 1970s leather jacket and 1970s-minded bootcut jeans as I strutted along said *Daily Planet* sidewalk. I insisted my man Elliot take some photographs of my super-fly attempts to duplicate those *Superman* movie extras wandering nonchalantly past the *Planet*'s art deco brass frontage – especially that cute blonde dude in the plaid shirt who seemed to get into at least three opening shots in as many Superman movies. The Salkinds were masters of repurposing unused takes and coverage – the original 1976 plan to shoot *Superman* and *Superman II* back to back was a cost-cutting, studio appeasing measure they had learnt from their *Musketeer* movie days.

And with a bit of faux Miss Lane intent, Elliot and I pushed through the *Planet*'s brassy revolving door doing that walking and chatting Kidder thing as a decoy. Very soon we had bypassed the security guards as easily as Terence Stamp in *Superman II* (and without devastating the chief editor's easily breakable desk) before pausing to marvel at how the sizeable, rotating and beautifully art deco *Daily Planet* lobby globe from *Superman: The Movie* has actually been a real News Building fixture since 1930 – complete with compass-point tiled floor flourishes which remind of Kal-El's Star Pod escape ship.

I don't know whether it is serendipity or luck or some Kryptonian spin of the dice, but when Elliot and I later got married at Pinewood Studios, it turned out our head table was on the same spot where a lunching Christopher Reeve and Margot Kidder would often sit during the *Superman: The Movie* shoot.

It is impossible to overestimate the cinematic importance of Richard Donner's *Superman: The Movie* (1978). The end result of many attempts to bring DC comic book writers Jerry Siegel and Joe Shuster's 1930s icon onto and through the big screen, Richard Donner's late-1970s American classic is the very template every comic book or superhero franchise overlooks at its peril. From a heady mix of mid-century Americana married up to a contemporary East Coast city rife with crime pickings, to veteran stalwart casting, barbed wit, grand orchestral movements, Boy Scout heroism devoid of political colour and a through line of humanity over spectacle – 1978's *Superman: The Movie* is a vital Kryptonian memory crystal all superhero moviemakers must keep safe in their barn at all costs. When Zach Snyder's *Batman v Superman: Dawn of Justice* (2016) starts as a Caped Crusader movie with a fated Wayne family montage straight out of Tim Burton's *Batman* (1989), and ends as a Man of Steel movie with a sense of funereal tragedy straight out of *Star Trek II: The Wrath of Khan* (1982), it is still *Superman: The Movie* which is influencing them all. When Henry Cavill crops up in *Justice League* (2017) it is as much to bring some Christopher Reeve humility and balance as it is Kal-El and Superman.

Despite Marvel Studios' superhero movie world dominating the box office, cosplay wardrobes and toy boxes of the twenty-first century's first two cinematic decades, Marvel's moviemaking machine (under its then name 'Timely Comics') dates back to 1944 and Republic Pictures' *Captain America* serial. But DC Comics and Clark Kent's own on-screen history had already started with Max Fleischer's 1941 cartoon film series *Superman* (the first of which was nominated for the 1942 Best Animated Short Academy Award). Very soon, DC Comics and Columbia Pictures had their 1943 *Batman* serial starring Lewis Wilson (the father of Bond producer Michael G. Wilson) as the first on-screen Bruce Wayne. DC and Columbia followed that with their own live-action 1948 serial *Superman* – starring Kirk Alyn as the first on-screen Clark Kent with Noel Neill as his Lois Lane. Neill then later joined George Reeves as his second Lois in Warner Bros' TV series, *Adventures of Superman* (1952). Later still, Neill joined Kirk Alyn as the young Lois Lane's parents in Richard Donner's *Superman: The Movie*, continued to appear in the various TV incarnations that followed (*Superboy*, *Lois & Clark: The New Adventures of Superman*) and finally played Mrs Lex Luthor in 2006's *Superman Returns*.

The serial nature of the comic strip world of Superman, Batman, Doctor Strange, Wonder Woman, Captain America, Spider-Man, Thor, Iron Man and The Incredible Hulk is a natural fit for the episodic nature of television. The trick was to translate that onto the big screen. Whilst 1978's *Superman* was in production in the studio belt of London's Home Counties, back in America the superhero movie world was very much a TV one. It was one possibly stymied by only having that 1960s Batman TV show template to follow – with broadcasters vying for a series commission via feature-length pilots, crude production ethics, leading men from the Adam West school of superhero physique, and a recurring, budget-beating urge to forever shoot round the back of warehouses and at abandoned dockyards. A decade that had seen the might of the disaster movie juggernaut wanted some of that for new, younger audiences who craved more than golden age Hollywood stars fighting fires and egos, Oscar-winning names their parents remembered drowning in their Edith Head jackets and visual effects which had pretty much stood still since, well, 1951's *The Day the Earth Stood Still*. Stanley Kubrick's *2001: A Space Odyssey* may have accelerated the physics of movie visuals out of a B-movie wormhole, but the philosophical proclamations – or lack of them – of Kubrick's 1968 masterwork were never going to be filling bedroom wall poster space or toy boxes the world over. The same year's *Planet of the Apes* may have been a popular turning point for younger audiences embracing more serious sci-fi with a commercial slant. Yet it still featured our parents' Moses (Charlton Heston) in the lead role, and a Californian studio backlot ethic straight from the era of biblical blockbusters.

One could argue Franklin J. Schaffner's *Planet of the Apes* (1968) is almost more of a familiar sword-and-sandal epic than a sci-fi game-changer. It certainly has its own curious place in both American movie and political history. In the 1970s, the pioneering *Apes* make-up designer John Chambers (who also worked on the original TV series of *Star Trek* and *The Munsters*) was enlisted by the CIA to assist with prosthetic make-up disguise kits for various covert operations. Chambers was also involved in the elaborate January 1980 rescue of six American hostages stranded in Tehran since the Iran hostage crisis the previous December. In order to provide an elaborate and working Hollywood cover for the escaping hostages, that real-life hostage drama tapped into a very *Watching Skies* era of movies and production contexts to fake a wooden horse of a *Star Wars* sci-fi blockbuster by the name of '*Argo*'. This, and Chambers' involvement, later formed the basis for 2012's Best Picture Oscar-winning *Argo* directed by and starring Ben Affleck – who incidentally played Superman and his TV alter-ego George Reeves in 2006's *Hollywoodland*. The initial rescue plan of *Argo* springs from Affleck's Tony Mendez catching *Battle of the Planet of the Apes* on TV one night, and ends on a visual beat straight from Elliott's bedroom in *E.T.* with a kid's toy shelf brimming with *Planet of the Apes* dolls, a Muffit figurine from *Battlestar Galactica*, *Star Trek*'s Kirk and Spock and Kenner's Millennium Falcon, 1979 Boba Fett doll and 1978 mail-order '*Star Wars* Action Display Stand'. To compound the pop-cultural irony, *Argo*'s Academy Award-winning screenwriter Chris Terrio later becomes one of the writers tasked with penning *Star Wars: Episode IX* alongside director J.J. Abrams. Whilst there was a historical, international and dangerous reality to the fake '*Argo*' production, Affleck's *Argo* presents the Hollywood pecking order, sense of gossip and box office one-upmanship that was very much the Salkinds' reality when prepping and shooting *Superman*. Despite the phony sci-fi blockbuster being obviously sanctioned by the successes of a galaxy far, far away, the fake '*Argo*' logo, trade paper announcements and script declarations are now very reminiscent of the *Superman* production and publicity machines. Those fake production notes and script for '*Argo*' are now on display at Washington DC's International Spy Museum alongside John Chambers' prosthetic mask for *Planet of the Apes*' Dr Zaius. Christopher Reeve's *Superman III* costume and George Reeves's TV Superman costume now reside across town in the Smithsonian Museum of American History. As does an example of my all-important first ever *Superma*n school flask. America has a lot of histories. None more so than that of its entertainment industries.

Political history aside, the legacy that *Planet of the Apes* left on the new wave of American cinema was how it ultimately lent 20th Century Fox the production confidence to make a sequel or four – albeit of diminishing returns – and turn one film's shrewdly timed apocalyptic message into a five-movie franchise, complete with a spin-off cartoon show, a live-action TV series, merchandise and one of composer Jerry Goldsmith's finest moments (the score to 1971's *Escape from Planet of the Apes*). The next time 20th Century Fox had a sci-fi franchise to play with on that scale was a movie called *Star Wars*.

As father and son producing duo Alexander and Ilya Salkind were using some of their ever-notorious Russian-Jewish chutzpah to get their big blue Boy Scout onto the cinematic skies of the late 1970s – and before *Star Wars* had taken its globe-conquering flight – various writers had endeavoured to put some narrative steel in the Man of Steel's planned movie debut. Robert Benton (*Bonnie and Clyde, Kramer Vs Kramer*), Mario Puzo (*The Godfather, Earthquake*) and the spousal pairing of Leslie and David Newman (*Santa Claus: The Movie, Superman II* and *Superman III*) all tried to believe a superhero script could fly. But it was Californian 'Creative Consultant' Tom Mankiewicz who more than rose to Richard Donner's eleventh-hour challenge to condense a purportedly mammoth tome of a two-film script into something physically workable, more romantic, less camp and more of an American hero – no mean feat when you remember the post-Watergate, post-Nixon and post-Vietnam malaise of a bruised America in the late 1970s that left the country's psyche hanging precariously off a metaphorical bridge like a packed school bus. As the nephew of screenwriter Herman J. Mankiewicz (co-writer of *Citizen Kane* and *The Wizard of Oz*) and son of writer-director Joseph L. Mankiewicz (*All About Eve, Suddenly Last Summer, Cleopatra* and *Sleuth*), Tom Mankiewicz's movie-thinking DNA was pure California, pure cinema. Not only was he too from that baby boomer generation of Spielberg, Coppola, Lucas and Scorsese, he was furthermore gaining a Hollywood reputation as an astute script renovator steeped in the idioms of both sides of the Atlantic's moviemaking machines.

As evident in the Bond bullets *Diamonds Are Forever* (1971), *Live and Let Die* (1973) and *The Man with the Golden Gun* (1974), *Superman: The Movie* sees Mankiewicz as the master of cutting to the chase, affording tight exposition to otherwise sprawling capers and the barbed retort – 'Do you know why the number 200 is so vitally descriptive to both you and me? It's your weight and my IQ.' Not only did his credited – and uncredited – work help re-point and maintain the fortunes of the Bond series throughout the 1970s with an entertaining precision and clear hold of the idiom of the on-screen 007 at that time, Mankiewicz was also a valued script surgeon on some key *Watching Skies*-era titles. John Badham's *WarGames* (1983), Joe Dante's *Gremlins* (1984), Richard Donner's *The Goonies* and *Ladyhawke* (both 1985) and Tim Burton's *Batman* (1989) can all quietly claim Mankiewicz's pen and fingerprints on their end result.

In the wake of *Star Wars* and its younger audiences and kids-skewed merchandising world, *Superman* opens with a coy 'June 1938' curtains-up of an overture as a boy narrator turns the pages of a 1930s Action Comic with the voiceover innocence of Charlie Brown from a 1970s *Peanuts* cartoon. A film projector soon flickers out black and white footage of the *Daily Planet*'s iconic rooftop globe and composer John Williams' cub reporter of an opening motif floats ever higher to reach the kettle drums and low strings momentum of the 'Superman Theme'. And we're off – flown into our first taste of the United States, corn fields, impatient cabbies, chunky Studebakers, preppy high school cardigans, skyscrapers, busy press rooms, subways, hot dog stands, Marlboro billboards, steamy manhole covers and yellow school buses.

For a long movie with three very tonally different acts, *Superman* is succinctly told. Clark Kent's Smallville youth is almost voiced in comic strip panels – the star boy lands on Earth, the star boy is very quickly a high school football-playing senior who can run faster than a speeding train, the star boy receives valuable wisdom from a father who then tragically dies, the star boy accompanies his Earth mother to the funeral and the star boy tells his mother he is leaving home. Done. It is an origin sequence made up of emotive beats rather than an origin trilogy made up of reboots, knee-jerk recasting and post-credits codas forcing movie fans to trudge that movie fan walk of shame out of movie theatres with disappointment. Franchise cinema – particularly that with a comic book slant – appears now to almost have shifted its commerce to the online clamouring for that first glimpse of a logo, the fever of a teaser date announcement or the teaser for a teaser and the emoji-strewn damnation of a casting decision, rather than making an end product that works as a movie in its own right. The pre-release fever is almost about the click rate and not the dollars. And it can all be traced back to 1999 and the first teaser trailer for *The Phantom Menace*. But more of that later.

There is a curious intersection of stylings going on in *Superman* – with the British artistry of production designer John Barry (*Star Wars: A New Hope*) and the diffused visions of director of photography Geoffrey Unsworth (*2001: A Space Odyssey*, *Murder on the Orient Express*) meeting at a heady crossroads of American influences. In one beat the news desks, police precincts, detective trilbies, creaking fly-screen doors, bowties, pigtails and a mother's apron are pure Norman Rockwell – the classic twentieth-century American painter and illustrator who died just as *Superman* was first released in late 1978. Geoffrey Unsworth's poignant warm hues, farm truck running boards, the family dog and father/son goodbyes of Rockwell's *Breaking Home Ties* (1954) are all there in the Kent Farm scenes as a fatal heart attack claims Jonathan (Glenn Ford) and Martha (Phyllis Thaxter) soon bids a dawn goodbye to her son Clark (Jeff East). Sadly, Unsworth himself died of a heart attack not long after completing *Superman* and the film is rightly dedicated to him.

Steven Spielberg and George Lucas are both noted fans of Norman Rockwell's illustrative work. The River Phoenix overture of *Indiana Jones and the Last Crusade* (1989) is straight out of Rockwell's famed khaki-clad scouting paintings (*All Together* and *The Scoutmaster*) and the blue-collar everyman hero of *Freedom of Speech* (1943) is easily Richard Dreyfuss's anorak-clad soul in *Close Encounters of the Third Kind*. That sense of home and the homestead is vital to Donner and *Superman*. The first act of *Superman: The Movie* is marked by both Kal-El and his older, earthly alias Clark Kent having to leave home not just once, but twice. Cue one of the most affecting scenes of late-1970s American cinema – the teenage Clark Kent watching the skies and cornfields of Smallville and bidding goodbye to his Earth mother, Martha. Played with a temperate and Rockwellian brilliance by Phyllis Thaxter (producer Ilya Salkind's then mother-in-law) it is an emotional baton and grounding that Christopher Reeve's subsequent films try to emulate, and one which both Eva Marie Saint and Diane Lane take on when continuing the role in the subsequent *Superman Returns* (2006), *Man of Steel* (2013), *Batman v Superman: Dawn of Justice* (2016) and *Justice League* (2017).

As a kid, I would roam the barley fields surrounding my childhood home in that home-made cape humming John Williams' 'Superman Theme' whilst imagining *Superman III* inspired dramas involving picnics gone wrong and the combine harvesters we had to keep the dogs away from. These films, their defining scenes and single frames seared themselves onto our own narratives in a way adulthood never allows. Something particularly stirring, poignant and noble remains about the early *Superman* films' motifs of growing up and moving on. When my own parents later moved out of that childhood home, the adult me had a final tour of the very garden and neighbouring fields that were often my own leafy Fortress of Solitude, Endor, Death Star, Octopussy's Palace and Temple of

Doom. The beginnings of a soulless Home Counties housing estate had replaced the combine harvesters and the remaining fields were suddenly never, ever Kansas-sized. Yet it was still John Williams' soul-stirring 'Leaving Home' I remembered as my hands sailed a field of *Superman* dreams through the barley crops – no doubt somewhat spurred on by my Celtic romanticism and only-child nostalgia. Life will always have mental crane shots straight from *Superman: The Movie* when the first inkling we have as kids that our adult selves will have to both leave home and eventually lose our parents comes from the movie likes of Donner's 1978 caped fable, *E. T. the Extra-Terrestrial* and *Star Wars: A New Hope*. The emotional power these films have on generations of filmgoers is not just because of the audience's nostalgia for our movie-blessed childhoods. It is also because of the nostalgic pushes of those characters within these films themselves.

Whilst we rarely see Clark Kent's Metropolis apartment home on-screen (apart from a brief appearance in 1987's sloppy *Superman IV: The Quest for Peace*), Kal-El has an altogether different fixer-upper in the form of the Fortress of Solitude. An icy and remote (super) man cave of peace and instruction – or what *Superman II*'s General Zod calls 'a sentimental replica from a planet long since vanished' – the Fortress is not just one of the most majestic sets to grace both Shepperton Studios' 'H' Stage and Pinewood Studios' 007 Stage – *Superman* was one of the first non-Bond productions to shoot on Albert R. Broccoli's new 007 Studio after 1977's *The Spy Who Loved Me* completed photography. It is also perhaps the most visually striking vista to the Man of Steel's on-screen lore. Not only is it the frozen backdrop for the very first time we see Christopher Reeve in the role in *Superman: The Movie* and the vital hall of learning that allows the outer-wordly wise Jor-El (Marlon Brando) to educate his son on Krypton etiquette, humanity and sciences (and allow the Salkinds to get their dollars' worth from the famously overpaid Brando), the key romance and dramatic beats of *Superman II* are predicated on this crystalline bachelor pad. The subsequent *Superman III* (1983) sorely misses the production statement and sense of home that the Fortress represents and its depiction in *Superman IV: The Quest for Peace* (1987) is yet another victim of that movie's famed (lack of) budget, which downgrades it to a melted emerald-green popsicle of a set populated with cameos from Krypton elders the big screen does not even recognise.

On the flip of *Superman*'s mid-twentieth-century Rockwellian influence, there is very much a Studio 54 clubland era New York – a Metropolis of super-fly bystanders commending Superman on his 'bad outfit', bosomy hookers in low-cut tops, Supertramp playing on a gas station radio, those flared extras strutting past the *Daily Planet*'s marble entrance on East 42nd Street, harassed Brooklyn lady commuters berating cabbies and a *Daily Planet* newsroom that is itself a filter-coffee-fuelled hub of Woodward and Bernstein multi-tasking, breaking TV news, tight-fitting Castro Street tees, panicking typesetters, smoking ashtrays and the now antiquated chorus of typewriters. For years as a kid I genuinely thought New York was also called Metropolis. Again, that comic book pace comes into its own as Donner and Mankiewicz switch the tone to a quicker comedy and sense of movement. Gone are Unsworth's tableau frames, and in come roaming cameras soaring like Superman himself through glass side doors and Lois Lane's splintered work chat and attentions. That Studio 54 era notion of celebrity, notoriety for notoriety's sake and that urge to publish the one image that trends around the world is still prescient stuff. The villainous narcissus that is Lex Luthor is not just preempting Donald Trump with his planned Lex Springs, Luthorville, Lexington and Marina Del Lex resorts and hotels. He is an East Coaster wanting to destroy the West Coast. But as Luthor boasts it will allow him to create the New West Coast, he would ostensibly be killing the moviemaking belt of Lucas, Spielberg, Coppola, Williams, Donner and friends. Not just the greatest criminal mind of our time, but ultimately the cruellest to us sky kids.

Lorenzo Semple's *Batman* TV series had of course helped set an earlier precedent for big name casting of comic book villains (Vincent Price, Liberace, Otto Preminger, Joan Collins, Shelley Winters), the disaster movies of the 1970s loved old Hollywood (Gloria Swanson in *Airport '75*, Olivia De Havilland in *Airport '77*, Fred Astaire in *The Towering Inferno*) and *Star Wars* featured Alec Guinness and Peter Cushing. But – again – these were the stars and names of our parents' and even grandparents' cinemagoing. Marlon Brando may well have been a casting coup from an older generation's moviegoing, but he was also a twentieth-century movie icon – and one who could have even played Superman had the timings, production capabilities and movie tastes of the 1950s been different. With 1970s credentials like *The Poseidon Adventure*, *French Connection II*, *Young Frankenstein* and *The Conversation*, Gene Hackman added a savvy, contemporary zeal to *Superman*. Playing his bewigged scoundrel as a vainglorious cad and showman ('I want my Liberace record back tonight' – *Superman II*), Hackman is deliciously cushioned by Tom Mankiewicz's caustic dialogue. 'There's a strong streak of good in you, Superman,' he asserts, 'but then nobody's perfect … almost nobody.' With his canary-yellow lapels, matching buttonhole and jaunty cravat, Hackman doesn't just chew the Pinewood scenery. He fillets it, grills it and flambés it to death in nearly every scene. As Brando's pricey attendance is all but consigned to that grand first act overture, it is Hackman who lends *Superman* its gravitas, its humour and its spite. He grins throughout at the gross fun of Luthor and the comic book pantomime at play. Yet he never mocks it. If anything, by the time of *Superman II*, when Clark and Lois's romantic sabbatical becomes an irreversible(ish) foray into superpower-surrendering mortality for Kal-El, we are glad that Hackman's Luthor is around. He is almost the eyes of the audience as he privately rolls his at the heinous conduct and lack of grace of his interstellar cohorts Zod, Ursa and Non. And the *Superman II* beat of Lex and his peroxide moll Miss Teschmacher (Valerie Perrine) heading north on a skidoo in costume designer Yvonne Blake's furs crackles with back projection fun, Edith Head glamour and Tom Mankiewicz's verbal trappings – 'North Miss Teschmacher, north!' By the time of 1987's *Superman IV: The Quest for Peace* and its budget and script's uncanny ability to literally fall apart before the audience's eyes, there is still a joy in seeing Reeve and Hackman's verbal jousting. That film only just about works because of Reeve and Hackman. When the Luthor (Jesse Eisenberg) of *Batman v Superman: Dawn of Justice* (2016) makes the mistake of being younger than Henry Cavill's Kal-El and sneering at the audience as much as the protagonists he is pitched against, it reminds us just how vital Hackman was to the *Superman* movies of the late 1970s and 1980s. He certainly helped open up a Pandora's box of American cinema to this underage kid, as I later and secretly devoured late-night Friday TV screenings of seminal titles like *The Conversation* and *The French Connection*. Just as Bruce Wayne must have his Joker and 007 must have his SPECTRE foe, when a *Superman* film diverts totally from Luthor it struggles. Without Gene Hackman's triple movie-stealing turn as 'the greatest criminal mind of our time', it is questionable whether 1980s cinema would have even had Jack Nicholson's Joker in *Batman* (1989). And had we not had *Batman*, it is equally questionable whether or not we would have had the timeline of Marvel Studios titles that now so dominate our movie skies.

But it was Christopher Reeve in that red and blue suit that adorned many a bedroom wall, 1970s montage, school flask and Catholic gay kid's confessional box confusions. The star-billing around the lesser-known lead is very much a Salkind trope. Raquel Welch (*The Three Musketeers*), Dudley Moore (*Santa Claus: The Movie*), Faye Dunaway (*Supergirl*) and Marlon Brando (*Christopher Columbus: The Discovery*) were never the leads in their respective Salkind productions. Likewise, Christopher Reeve was wisely not meant to be a name when cast in 1977. But what was it that got me into *Superman*, that got me spinning in my phone box in the first place? Clark Kent. That's who. He is the nine-to-five, the working day of the Man of Steel. A *Superman* movie progresses and evolves through Clark Kent. *Superman II* is as much predicated on Clark and his story as it is Superman's. And just like the on-screen Bruce Wayne in a *Batman* movie, how the everyman Clark is played always frames these movies more than the titular hero. Whilst the heroics and vital energies of the *Superman* movies take to the skies when we watch the skies for all that cat-rescuing, missile-kicking and earthquake-reversing heroism, it is the bespectacled Clark who is on the audience's street level. There is some sort of calm transcendence surrounding Reeve as both roles are lent a soul, dignity and on-screen diplomacy. He is impulsive and angry when justice is stretched ('Luthor, you poisonous snake!'). Yet he is always that cute and deliciously polite country boy who does not know he is cute, as Clark is pitched as a bumbling yet wholly fetching Cary Grant in *Bringing Up Baby Kal-El*. Throw in Margot Kidder's definitive and vice-heavy Lois Lane and the end result is a sort of comic book, East Coast echo of Mona and Mouse from Armistead Maupin's *Tales of the City* (1978).

As much as the subsequent Kal-Els have tried – Dean Cain (*Lois & Clark: The New Adventures of Superman*, 1993–97), Tom Welling (*Smallville*, 2001–11), Brandon Routh (*Superman Returns*, 2006) and Tyler Hoechlin (*Supergirl*, 2016) – it is still Reeve's humanity in the role they are circling. Three decades on from the last time Reeve played the role in *Superman IV: The Quest for Peace* (1987), it is still that speeding bullet momentum and emotional verisimilitude he gave the role and franchise that is the founding DNA of contemporary on-screen superheroes. When the film incarnations of Iron Man, Spider-Man, Thor, Wolverine, Wonder Woman, Ant-Man and The Flash work, it is because they remember that strategy set by Reeve, Donner and *Superman: The Movie* – a domestic hero rather than corporate deity. And now we have Henry Cavill and a truly British Man of Steel. Once again, it's not the suit that everything hangs on, but rather what Richard Donner would always reference as that 'verisimilitude' – how a film handles the reality of an outer-worldly superhero in present-day America.

Cavill is a particularly super Superman. He has the kind Clark Kent eyes and that beard and ripped chest make most previous incumbents of the cape look like Supergirl. Or Faye Dunaway. With the cynicism of modern-day superhero movies removed, *Man of Steel* is successful because it is not an over-reverential nod to Donner's 1978 interpretation – despite school teachers being seen in flashback with big 1970s lapels and hair, the *Daily Planet's* newsrooms returning to a busy Woodward and Bernstein press room glory and Metropolis is New York again rather than the downtown Sydney, Toronto, Calgary or Milton Keynes stand-ins of before. Hans Zimmer's score is often majestic stuff, as are the urgent, discordant Bernard Herrmann strings and the hellish bombast of his brass which soon scatters into the homespun lyricism of Smallville. To not use John Williams' famed 'Superman Theme' and get away with it is one of *Man of Steel's* unspoken triumphs.

The crystalline imaginings of the Krypton of *Superman: The Movie* still hold more sense for what is meant to be a dignified and scientifically-minded planet rather than Snyder's stitch-punk Gallifrey. And since 1980's *Superman II*, the New York superhero bitch-fight has become a horrendous cliché. With scant finesse, the likes of *The Avengers* (2012), *The Amazing Spider-Man* (2012),

The Man of Steel (Magnolias) begins construction on the Mattress of Solitude, January 1984.

Pacific Rim (2013) and *Transformers* all clearly hope and pray the canvas of New York will somehow add story gravitas to these comic book cage-fights. They don't. The falling masonry merely fills out the teaser trailers a year before and loses the audience on the night. Snyder is ever so guilty of that here – with a tad too much of Michael Shannon's Zod and Kal-El bitch-slapping their way through various tower blocks, apartments, more tower blocks and a Sears' coupon day. Yet – for the most part – *Man of Steel* is an Americana-minded tale about destroyed gas stations, Midwest agriculture and interrupted museum tours, where a shop owner locking his store is more pressing than the Statue of Liberty face down in the Hudson.

And whilst Henry Cavill may well surpass Reeve's four-film tally, when his Kal-El finally comes out as the Man of Steel to the baying press and army officials Cavill echoes that wit, diplomacy, another planet's – or even era's – sense of virtue and the gift of calm dignity that Christopher Reeve bestowed on the role for evermore.

Back in the January of 1984, and with the heavy snows filling our back garden with that wintry silence and sparkling silver hue, I felt inspired by that recent Christmas Day viewing of *Superman*. Without a magic crystal bequeathed to me at birth by Marlon Brando but very much with the experience of building an igloo in our last house already under my Krypton belt, I picked my perfect spot, got the wheelbarrow and singlehandedly set about building my own recreation of Kal-El's icy bachelor-pad, the Fortress of Solitude. Of course, the snow quantities, freezing temperatures and lack of the 007 Stage at Pinewood Studios and a Warner Bros budget somewhat hampered the final dimensions and wow factor of said Fortress of Solitude. I purposely donned a red tracksuit and wellington boots and eventually fashioned my very own couture Superman cape out of a black trash bag. We will brush over the comic book law that says the black cape was normally reserved for villains. Using my old *Superman* school flask as a reference, I spent ages recreating that triangular chest 'S' before finally Sellotaping it onto the trash bag cape. Sadly, my snowy headquarters were less a fortress and more of a Mattress of Solitude – a sort of snowy chaise longue our Golden Retrievers soon left their yellow marks on. Not that this hampered this fledgling Krypton star child from asking my stepdad Rob to become Jimmy Olsen to my Clark Kent and help me with my very own Superman photo shoot. With said cape billowing loftily in the cold breeze, I knelt dramatically down, clutching aloft an icicle off the shed as if it was some wintry shard of Kryptonian knowledge. And then, as I endeavoured desperately to look all DC Comics butch with my wrists perched firmly on my Christmas chocolate pumped hips, I stood aloft the *Daily Planet* rooftop – or the top of our brick sewerage outhouse, where you could do a dramatic Margot Kidder hang-off with only about three inches to fall. Less Man of Steel. More Man of Steel Magnolias.

A week or two later, after the spring sun has melted both my Fortress of Solitude and my *Superman* fantasies, my yearnings to one day share a sidewalk with Christopher Reeve and Clark Kent were oddly realised. And not in Metropolis or Smallville, but my home town. It was a Saturday afternoon. I was no doubt avoiding another school-shoe-buying trip to Freeman, Hardy & Willis by spending my week's pocket money on yet another Biker Scout figure in Tesco, rather than that ever-elusive Bespin Leia figure, and then – as if Metropolis had been twinned with Guildford and no one told us – there was Superman himself wandering down the cobbled high street. It was not a man in a costume or Saturday staff trying to promote movie toys to the kids. It was Christopher Reeve in all his humbly paced, unnoticed glory. It transpired he was playing at our local theatre opposite Vanessa Redgrave in a London-bound production of Henry James's *The Aspern Papers*. No one else had seen him. What should I do? I was 8 years old and didn't go up to strangers – even a Kryptonian one a Catholic nun recommended I spend Christmas Day with. I was so match-ready with my perfected Superman ankle twist when launching into flight, clearly had my portfolio of cosplay photographs, and had wasted many a swimming lesson doing the chest-fist flying pose instead of the backstroke my 200-metre swimming badge desperately required. And then Clark Kent was gone. Superman was gone – like he had just rescued my cat from a tree, flown into the sky, and no one would believe me as soon as I ran inside to try to tell the world what had happened. Reeve must have just carried on walking. Maybe he failed to recognise me because he was Clark Kent and couldn't blow his Krypton cover? I understand. I now know how Lois Lane later felt when she was so rudely snubbed by Superman in the subway scene from *Superman IV: The Quest for Peace* and for most of the previous *Superman III*.

Flash-forward two and a half decades and the same thing happened again. My mum and I were Christmas shopping around London's Oxford Circus when I collided straight into Henry Cavill. For the briefest of moments and with a pair of contrite hands on my rather un-Kryptonian biceps, Superman immediately apologised. As did I. And at the moment I mentally fell into those baby blues of his and he slipped into the night leaving me in a sort of 'that's Clark, nice' Lois Lane confusion, I suddenly realised: That was two Clark Kents my mum had now blatantly failed to invite back to ours for supper.

COUSINS OF STEEL

SUPERGIRL

1984. An ethereal girl from another world stretches her cape and arms and learns to fly, amidst the sun-flecked trees and skies of a glistening lake in the summer.

○————————○

1984. The year of *Indiana Jones and the Temple of Doom, Star Trek III: The Search for Spock, Beverly Hills Cop, Romancing the Stone, Starman, The Terminator, A Nightmare on Elm Street, Repo Man, Police Academy, Footloose, 2010, The NeverEnding Story, Dune, The Last Starfighter,* and of course, *The Muppets Take Manhattan.* It even had a *Star Wars* movie. The first *Episode VII,* no less. It was a forest moon of Endor spin-off called *Caravan of Courage: An Ewok Adventure* and started life as a Lucasfilm-produced feature-length television movie on American TV. With a story by George Lucas, *Caravan of Courage* was directed by John Korty – one of the original Folsom Street American Zoetrope clan. It had a theatrical release in some parts of

Europe, including Britain in the May of 1985. But to many British sky kids, the film and its quick sequel were forever bottom-row relics of the wall of VHS movies at our local rental stores. We all naturally believed it was the sequel to *Return of the Jedi*. But *Caravan of Courage* was set before 1983's *Episode VI*. Technically, it is the first *Star Wars* prequel, predating *The Phantom Menace* by a good fifteen years.

Yet despite this impressive roll call of this year's movies and still somewhat motivated by seeing Christopher Reeve out shopping when I was on the prowl for *Star Wars* figures, in July 1984 this super sky kid was having another brand-new, hands-on-hips, yellow-booted summer fixation. And it wasn't Ewoks. Or Indiana Jones. Or even Steve Guttenberg's pecs in *Police Academy*. It was over a girl. A real girl. Well, a real girl from Argo City. As if my Man of Steel (Magnolias) hang-ups could not really get any worse – in the summer of 1984 along comes one big summer pageant of superhero kitsch with Jeannot Szwarc's *Supergirl*. Ever since I had seen Alexander Salkind's *Supergirl: The Making of the Movie* one Saturday morning on British TV – complete with an introduction by a magnificently lit Faye Dunaway and a focus on the Pinewood Studios shoot and production – I was transfixed by all things related to this *Superman* spin-off adventure featuring Clark Kent's cousin, Linda Lee. I wondered if my obsessions over Supergirl's alter-ego Helen Slater were the beginnings of a path to an altogether straighter side. Perhaps my Christopher Reeve infatuations had been kissed away by one of those Kal-El memory wipe kisses he uses so willingly on poor unsuspecting Margot Kidder whenever she must totally forget her recent green-screen flying date. Already my *Look-In* magazine *Supergirl* pull-out-and-keep centre-spread was taking pride of place on my wardrobe door, and I would stop everything when this new hot blonde film sensation from Argo City was doing the British TV interview circuit. Not only did

Supergirl's hair go from Kara blonde to Linda Lee brunette as the Skywalker locks of my junior years began darkening, I too had an Omegahedron. Okay, my all-important spherical Argo City power source was in fact a hand-crafted, less-important air freshener ball I tried to colour up with a felt-tip to look like said Omegahedron. I had form at the time for trying to home-make a lot of early-1980s merchandise and cultural favourites. There was one week when I got quite gripped by the *BBC News*'s constant reports of the Cabbage Patch Kid craze sweeping America. Another one was Frank Oz's *Little Shop of Horrors* (1986). 007 and my lifelong obsessions with all things Commander Bond could not really come along soon enough.

In hindsight, it was never a fixation for *Supergirl*, Linda Lee or Helen Slater when it came to the Salkinds' 1984 ex-super-ganza. As *Midnight Cowboy* stalwart Brenda Vaccaro mentions in the movie to her villainous pal Faye Dunaway – 'You know, I think I recognise the costume' – it was very much the costume. The red vinyl boots, the arrow yellow belt and glow in the dark wrist bracelet. And the shorter and tidy waist-length cape. Definitely the shorter and tidy waist-length cape. Not only was this movie about a super girl with a super woman villain, a super hench-bitch, a super-hot, fuzzy-chested super love interest and a super score by Jerry Goldsmith (*Planet of the Apes*, *Chinatown*, *Alien*), *Supergirl* was ultimately the only American summer camp I was ever going to experience. And it was a caped caper that Britain was getting in the July of 1984, whilst the States had to wait until at least late November 1984.

A week or two into its UK release, I was in Glasgow for part of the summer school holidays. Maureen, the McGintys cousins and I were having a *Supergirl* day in town. It was all very exciting. The hottest Glasgow afternoon I can remember to this day and my pasty Celtic soul went to another art deco behemoth that was the Odeon

Renfield Street to see the fourth DC Comics super adaptation in six years, in what soon became a Salkind double-bill day.

For all its million-dollar hopes, big branding, hype, cutting-edge and costly opening titles, expansive Midwest town set on the backlot of Pinewood Studios, and the no doubt big pay cheques for the likes of Faye Dunaway, Mia Farrow and Peter O'Toole, critically and commercially *Supergirl* did not so much watch the skies as fall out of them from a great height. It is nevertheless – like all camp follies worth celebrating after time – movie matinee brilliance, and marks the point where the worlds of *Superman* met *Jaws*, as *Supergirl* director Jeannot Szwarc previously helmed *Jaws 2* (1978).

Just like all the Reeve *Superman* movies, there is a British production context and sensibility on show in *Supergirl*. The

Supergirl and *Superman III* proudly flank the corridors of G Block, Pinewood Studios, 2008.

yellow school buses, Popeyes fried chicken diners, chunky wide cars, those high-school bench stands on the pitch and frat-house fonts have been gloriously shipped into London's Pinewood and the surrounding countryside all doubling up for Midvale, America. And the cast is scattered with UK stalwarts, trying in valiant vain to lend some Brando-style marquee billing to proceedings. The most memorable of which are the two Peters – Cook and O'Toole. The former turns in a fascinating performance as emaciated and self-made necromancer Nigel, whose fetishes for spells, silver anoraks and the random ingredients of a warlock oddly end up creating a character more like a recovering swinger from Surrey suffering from the detox sweats than any wand-waving fearsome warlock. Pitching for that Gene Hackman sense of societal one-upmanship and clearly gearing up director Szwarc for a Pete & Dud reunion – Cook's comedy partner Dudley Moore in the director's next, *Santa Claus: The Movie* – the pallid Nigel works hard to try to give Hackman's Lex Luthor a run for his scene-stealing money. There is some delicious, yet ever strange witching bitching by Cook's Nigel – causing Dunaway's gauze-lit villain Selena at one point to rather curiously proclaim, 'I am the ultimate siren of Endor!' If only *Supergirl vs the Ewoks* was actually a 1984 thing. I would have gone. And you would have too.

The decision to pitch Peter Cook as a bitter maths-teaching warlock stuck in a school for girls he cannot stand whilst trying to woo the ladies at witchcraft gatherings in abandoned ghost trains soundtracked by Howard Jones is not just delicious. It is a glorious sign of this film's banquet of low, bitter camp. It shouldn't work. It doesn't work. But in a movie era of boy-skewed narratives and male leads, this film is garish, camp and all sorts of fun the masculine world of Christopher Reeve and Metropolis cannot warrant. The skies of *Supergirl* are less about the homely nostalgias, city aggression and arch-villainy of *Superman*, and more about the kitsch currency of *The Four Musketeers* (1974), *Mommie Dearest* (1981) and Cannon Films' *The Wicked Lady* (1983) – all of course starring a pre-*Supergirl* Faye Dunaway. Despite her cracked turn as Joan Crawford in Paramount's *Mommie Dearest* already gaining bad movie immortality, here Dunaway ironically plays it more as a brunette Bette Davis, complete with the cat's eye glasses and Rita Hayworth hair. Dunaway's eyes and distinctive cheekbones are forever over-lit, her tiger-print world is matched in her tiger-skin picnic and homeware, her wardrobe goes from Dietrich Berlin via Japanese kimonos to *Dynasty* quarterback chic in barely five minutes, and she has an unorthodox ability to turn herself into multiple Kate Bushes when trying to surround and defeat our hero, Kara (Helen Slater). Add Selina's cigarette-sucking, champagne-pouring, husky-throated ally Bianca (Brenda Vaccaro) and the end result would not be out of place at one of Peaches Christ's drag tribute shows at San Francisco's Castro Theatre. It is certainly very much now the territory of Ryan Murphy and his television projects (*American Horror Story*, *Feud*). There is also something particularly Pedro Almodóvar about these two middle-aged women and amateur occultists losing grip on reality, their home, wardrobe and looks as the tale of plucky hockey girls being taught in mid-America by hungover Londoner Peter Cook unfurls all around them. The upshot of *Supergirl* is not one of villainy or beating the superhero. Selina and Bianca are just bitter at the attractive young blonde girl stealing all their glories, hot gardeners and fairground cars. It's the classic trope of backstage backstabbing. *All About Weave* maybe. Or *Super Showgirls*. There is certainly a better barbed wit in the dialogue than the film possibly deserves – 'without me you'd still be reading tea leaves in Lake Tahoe' snaps a dismissed O'Toole as chief bitch Selina suddenly has no plans for Nigel.

Supergirl is not just a *Superman* film for the girls and boys. It is a *Superman* film for queer kids too. One reading of the Superman and Supergirl worlds is, of course, one of being the outsider with personal secrets who must keep real identities hidden in a closet alongside the blue and red costume. The villains of the Salkinds' super-movie world are themselves always hiding away from society in rather theatrical abodes, such as disused 1930s subway stations, abandoned fairgrounds and penthouse apartments with their own ski slopes. And predating the Diet Coke break commercials by years, Hart Bochner's hot blue-eyed, air-head and often topless gardener Ethan was a hairy-chested revelation for this sky kid and his later VHS pause button. I was about to enter an American television era of scruff-chested Colby, Carrington and Ewing boys and Bochner was a great foundation course. Richard MacDonald's production design is often deliriously Liberace with its Vegas lobby zebra prints, candelabras, mirror mirrors on the wall and extravagant *Octopussy* beds. Maureen Teefy's Lucy Lane (younger sister of Lois) is possibly just that bit too butch with her baseball caps, Castro Street sense of 1970s protest and bedroom posters of Superman fooling no one. And the conjuring cougar Selina and her attempts to secretly ply hot gardener Ethan with a witch's version of Rohypnol is all kinds of brilliant wrong. Whether producers Alexander and Ilya Salkind and Timothy Burrill wholly planned all this is debatable. Of course they didn't. But hindsight now makes this particular piece of sky watching a glitteringly camp, red and blue gem. Well, some red and blue fake costume jewellery gathering dust in a Pinewood Studios shoebox. The end result is exactly what shrewd screenwriter Tom Mankiewicz lent his first, multi-owned *Superman* script – careful slivers of wit threaded with a certain dignity into the adventure of the piece. Not that the Christopher Reeve *Superman* films are themselves devoid of all camp. Lex Luthor and his platinum moll Miss Teschmacher, General Zod, Ursa, Pamela Stephenson and her Norma Jean shtick, Nuclear Man's fiery leather-harness look, Marlon Brando in a cream vanilla wig and intergalactic jumpsuit and the hot Clark Kent with his cute cowlick and a close-fitting bodysuit are also all up for other interpretations too. You'll believe a man can fly *and* bring in new audiences. You'll certainly believe that other readings and experiences watching the skies of 1970s and early-1980s fantasy cinema are just as valid as the expected mainstream ones.

And all this is before mention of Laurence of Argo City herself, Peter O'Toole. In the Salkinds' attempts to inject some British theatrical gravitas along the lines of *Superman: The Movie*'s Trevor Howard, Susannah York and Harry Andrews, O'Toole's academic exile Zaltar mostly succeeds in the few scenes he has with Helen Slater's Kara. Fresh off a couple of Academy Award nominations for Best Actor, it is worth remembering that Peter O'Toole was nearly as big a deal as Faye Dunaway circa *Supergirl* and its 1983 Pinewood shoot. Like all *Superman* films, *Supergirl* starts with a veritable who's who of late-1970s cinema, as Argo City elders Mia Farrow, Simon Ward and O'Toole muse upon creationism and trees amidst some Haight-Ashbury idyll in the stars … which is underwater. Right. With a script penned by Jim Henson alumnus David Odell (*The Dark Crystal, The Muppet Show*), O'Toole's washed-up, alcoholic Zaltar finally allows the audience to witness the oft-mentioned shadowy purgatory that is the Phantom Zone. 'Your suffering will be short, mine will be –' he laments with a Beckett pause for proper O'Toole effect – 'forever.'

Not only is Helen Slater in the shadow of Christopher Reeve, his Clark Kent and Kal-El, the relative unknown is also up against Faye Dunaway on full take-the-cheque-and-run crazy. Whilst she is not the strongest of performers and just about holds her own in the hand-on-hip moral and patriotic posturing of the piece, Slater certainly earns kudos in a lot of the flying sequences – lent greater balletic elegance than before as she trails high above Pinewood Studios' neighbouring Black Park on mostly undetectable wires.

And the unspoken, but time-honoured tradition of actors in DC Comic adaptations later returning to play their character's parents or family members has of course continued, with Helen Slater going on to play the Earth mother Eliza Danvers in Warner Bros' newest television relaunch of *Supergirl* (2015) alongside Melissa Benoist's Lara and the totally apt Tyler Hoechlin as her Cousin of Steel. And Slater had already played Clark Kent's Krypton mother, Lara, in the long-running *Smallville* television series.

As a Salkind superhero pic, *Supergirl* is possibly more disciplined than its immediate cousin, *Superman III* (1983). It certainly holds more worth and creative successes than the next and final entry in the Man of Steel's first wave of movies, *Superman IV: The Quest for Peace* (1987). *Supergirl* is a puberty superhero film – with adolescent preoccupations about bras, boys, school rivals and stolen kisses. The bitchy school girls and sabotaged showers are straight out of *Carrie* (1976) or even *Porky's* (1981). There is almost a *St Trinian's* vibe with Peter Cook all but clutching his Miss Fritton pearls as he berates the younger generation. And that vintage *American Graffiti* world of cars, main streets, diners, root beer and jukebox pop hits – in this case British popster Howard Jones – are all still influential beats of American youth cinema. Director Szwarc just about maintains that Richard Donner sense of verisimilitude and reality as Midvale School is all desks and chat, Lucy Lane reads Marvel comics with a mini poster of Britain's Prince Andrew by her bed, various billboards and blue-collar advertising vie for attention, TWA advertise on the radio waves and Supergirl flies over a midnight drive-in playing *Psycho II* (1982). There is never any sense in this film that we will have more Helen Slater *Supergirl* films. And it didn't feel so at the time either – which makes it even more of a curious Salkind folly of the *Watching Skies* era. Rumours and suggestions point to how the Salkinds purportedly burnt their finances and enthusiasms out on *Supergirl*. It is often alleged as a key reason why they had to then sell on their interests in *Superman* movies to Cannon Films and the movie carnival showmen that were Israeli Cousins of Steel, Menahem Golan and Yoram Globus. The Golan/Globus partnership then notoriously scaled back the already frugal budget for *Superman IV*, and the rest is a rather undistinguished eighty-nine minutes of movie history that will forever remind how the previous *Supergirl* was not that bad after all.

As the fourth spin of the Krypton dice in less than six years, *Supergirl* was never going to match the box office, timings and impact of *Superman: The Movie*. In America, the film was denied the summer window slot taken by *Ghostbusters* and *Gremlins* and was only finally released in late November 1984, where it was soon rubbing box office shoulders with *Beverly Hills Cop* and later *Dune* and *Starman*. As a film, it is a great tribute to that short-lived genre of the Home Counties of England doubling up for Metropolis and Midvale, before Britain's pallid grey Milton Keynes fooled no one in *The Quest for Peace*. All the greatest Salkind Supermovie hits are on display: Kara's near-biblical arrival on Earth via a Buckinghamshire fishing lake – looking vaguely like the same lake that General Zod walked on back in *Superman II* – back-projection cityscape flying scenes, the fun foundation years at school, sexist and naïve truckers coming unstuck against superhero brawn, the tilting camera proving just how wonderful it is to be hung from a Pinewood wire with a back projection of wild caribou running amok beneath you, a big orchestral theme tune by a movie composer legend, the vertical take-offs we all thought we could do with a skip and a jump in the school yard, the resourceful costume changes, the nods to the respectability of the *Daily Planet* and the A-list villainy.

And as *Supergirl's* rather lengthy end credits continued rolling at the Odeon Renfield Street until at least February 1987, my cousins and I emerged blinking into Glasgow's summer of 1984. We wended our way back to Clydebank and the McGintys' home. It must be an only-child thing, but I was fascinated by the size of their house, the multiple levels and the fact that – yes – they too had a video player. Having no access to the world of VHS was an increasingly open wound for me. I can only liken it today to realising you have no cell phone and are not sure where or how to even procure one. To keep the day's super theme going, Margaret McGinty offered me a seat at the table for tea if I would stay and watch *Superman III*, which the McGinty boys could easily rent from the local video store. With the life impact of *Octopussy* and *Return of the Jedi* spending my summer movie allowance in 1983, *Superman III* totally bypassed me when it flew onto British cinema screens in July 1983. Naturally, I said a big 'yes' to Margaret and her *Superman* tea.

Two years later, that particular title flew down again and saved me as the curriculum and sports teacher's enthusiasm could no longer stop this delicate sky kid from something he had long dreaded – playing football in school. In the early fall of 1985, the beginning of my first – and last – hellish tour of school soccer duty was made slightly more bearable by the kind scheduling of ITV to screen a barely two-year-old *Superman III* that very night. It was a welcome red and blue light at the end of a very dull, muddy and cold football tunnel. It was one ITV had clearly got the broadcast rights to early – the then unspoken ritual was a five-year wait between cinema and television. But now their autumn schedule was commencing with the 'network premiere' of *Superman III* and every ounce of airtime and commercial space was reminding us as much, via oft-repeated clips of the chemical factory fire rescue and plenty of notice for 'Thursday 5 September at 8 p.m.' sharp. Apparently enthusing about how good tonight's TV premiere of *Superman III* is going to be because I had watched it in Glasgow two years ago is not a good enough excuse to explain letting in a least three goals whilst chatting on the sidelines like a distracted Lana Lang.

SUPERMAN III

1983. In a Metropolis scrapyard, a beleaguered hero finally stands tall after a vicious brawl with a malicious version of his alter-ego. He slowly looks to the skies, and with battered hope he peels open his white shirt with renewed resolution and a need to fly.

By the time of *Superman III* and 1983, the on-screen fortunes of the Man of Steel and the political skies of America had shifted. Whilst the Salkind family's very own Jor-El and Kal-El are still on producing duties with a decent sense of Pinewood Studios production, as backup there is a swing from the American folklore of the first two movies towards *Superman* as consumer commodity with a comedic slant. Gone is the majesty of Richard Donner's Krypton fairy tale, the stately John Williams motifs, that stifling and petty crime-ridden Metropolis, the narrative grounding that is the Fortress of Solitude and the romantic hooks and East Coast impudence of Margot Kidder's Lois Lane. In *Superman III* that painterly and Rockwellian grandeur of before becomes a sort of *Happy Days* nostalgia or a *Back to the Future* rehearsal – with Clark returning to Smallville, his high-school sweetheart and football field bully with the added confusion of realising he was suddenly from the 'Class of 1965' and not the mid-1950s as 1978's *Superman* depicted.

It is especially apparent in *Superman III* that the Salkinds' moviemaking drives are possibly now less the Man of Steel and more balls of brass when it comes to box office prowess. In *Superman III*, Superman himself is almost a side character to a slapstick, consumerist satire on the computer age guided by an incompatible need to cash in on stand-up comedian Richard Pryor's rising star in Hollywood at the time. The film opens on Pryor's hapless Gus Gorman signing on for job benefits in a grimy employment bureau. Whilst it totally ignores the events of *Superman II* and the life sacrifices the two key leads Kal-El and Lois Lane made for love, it is a very Donner overture with gum-chewing clerks, grubby employment lines, litter-strewn floors, multiple ringing phones and a correct amount of disillusioned and tired Manhattan sass. Cue the main titles, an unthreading of John Williams' anthemic overture and a peculiar decision to switch the comic book lore of the previous two Reeve films into *Superman Three Stooges* with a jarringly comedic tone that the film does not arguably recover from. It is not just an opening titles bystander who gets a cream pie in the face as the somewhat telling 'Directed by Richard Lester' title card nosedives through the rather incongruous knockabout chaos. Lester's famed sense of clowning holds a damaging Krypton rock up to the verisimilitude of *Superman*, *Superman II* and all that Brando/Hackman gravitas. With a clear lack of New York doubling up as Metropolis and a *Pink Panther* sense of slapstick, *Superman III* is peppered with faces, comics and actors from Richard Lester's late-1960s swinging heyday (Bob Todd, Graham Stark, Ronnie Brody, Henry Woolf). For British audiences – even young ones like us at the time – it forever broke the fourth American wall seeing these comedy stalwarts fooling about with a 1960s moddy swagger in alleged downtown Metropolis. The valuable lessons of the Donner original to not spoof or mock pretty much fly out the *Daily Planet* window here, quicker than it takes a flaming toy penguin to be extinguished by Clark Kent's breath.

The first two *Superman* movies' delicious mix of Americana mythology and urban modernity here becomes the modernity of consumerism and a mythologising of computer technology. This is no longer an America with the White House at its proud core. Faceless computer banks and satellites now govern the land and skies. Robbing a bank with glass cutters and ropes is now less pressing than transferring funds digitally – which never makes for good cinema. Cue an over-elongated scene between Pryor's Gorman and Gavan O'Herlihy's Brad labouring to drunkenly turn on a computer system simultaneously. 'Couldn't we get a computer to do this?' barks the *Daily Planet's* Perry White (Jackie Cooper) as the new witchery and fears of the computer age take hold, glossy sneakers are bandied about an IT office like sporting contraband, the film has a constant obsession with bank statements and what people earn and Robert Vaughn's heinous Ross Webster lives a gauche Gatsby penthouse lifestyle with his own Atari-designed missile system for killing superheroes.

The movie America of *Superman III* emerges here as a cynical beast – one already very much in the grip of a consumerist and progressively hi-tech Reaganite era – with perhaps its simpler, more domesticated times behind it. The *Daily Planet* is now depicted as running sham prize holidays. You'll believe a man can be a barfly as Superman himself can only be narratively interesting if he is a bad Kal-El, drinking hard liquor and flicking nuts like bullets. Alcohol seems to be everywhere as Brad is a raging, easily fooled alcoholic and Pamela Stephenson's Lorelei resorts to drunk floozy anytime she wants to woo the red outside pants off of Superman. The Fortress of Solitude, Marlon Brando and Kal-El's Krypton elders are all but absent. Martha Kent has died, but son Clark forgets to visit her Smallville grave when back home for a high school reunion.

Superman: The Movie made sure that hillside graveyard is quite key to Clark and his sense of home. Computers and technology are both feared and deified in equal measure. Boozy local Gavan O'Herlihy almost plays an identical patsy role to that he does in the same year's unofficial Bond film, *Never Say Never Again* – which also has a similar tendency to play Atari-like wargames with computer systems and missile with a youth-reaching intent. Some of Richard Pryor's clearly improvised comedic scenes fall flat with a sense that the Salkinds are trying to get the most out their new star's fee, regardless of the narrative imbalance that ensues between Reeve and Pryor here. A long-winded rant about moulded and high-grade plastics to the Smallville populace cannot hide that it is yet another spin of the 'Kryptonite will kill him' trope. And it is not just Lois Lane who has had her memory wiped by a Clark Kent kiss at the close of 1980's *Superman II*. The Salkinds are hoping it worked on the audiences too, as Margot Kidder's Lois Lane is sidelined almost entirely and replaced by Annette O'Toole's single mum Lana Lang. Granted, Lang is a *Superman* comic book stalwart and ably played here by Annette O'Toole as a sort of anti-Spielberg mum bedecked in 1950s housewife whimsy and without a life vice in the world. But without that vital Lois and Clark dynamic, the emotions of *Superman III* feel more 1980s soap than honouring that once carefully curated love story between Kidder and Reeve. When *Superman IV: The Quest for Peace* debuts in 1987, Lang is then herself totally forgotten in favour of Mariel Hemingway's awkward daddy's girl, Lacy Warfield, and a criminally underused Lois Lane.

The more cynical world of *Superman III* is not wholly wrong, however. Villain Ross Webster (Robert Vaughn) plays it like a gauche Republican senator holidaying in Aspen. The fruitier language and lapsed morals of Metropolis are exactly the city Lex Luthor left behind. And this is a 1980s *Superman* movie with songs especially produced by Italian synth legend Giorgio Moroder

The cousins of steel's famed factory of movie dreams and magic – Pinewood Studios.

(*Midnight Express, The NeverEnding Story*). The tonal shifts aside, *Superman III* is still a grand old Pinewood Studios production with a 007 Stage-sized finale set, enough homespun jeopardy and set pieces that still haunt to this day. *Jaws* and its water scenes was not the only one to burn itself onto our perceptions of hidden dangers for evermore. *Superman III* made a whole generation of kids terrified of combine harvesters and falling unconscious in a cornfield. Oh, and wearing skis and a pink tablecloth when atop a Calgary penthouse doubling up as one in Metropolis. *Superman III* still has that late-1970s, Cinzano billboard sense of Europe, the sub-text of *Superman: The Movie*'s crucial leaving home motif is explored again with Lana Lang's inert life in Smallville, jazz singer Annie Ross is a butch-femme delight as Webster's ball-breaking sister-in-crime Vera, dangerous missiles are still back-projected at breakneck speed against the canyons of Arizona, the thumbprints of Tom Mankiewicz's caustic wit is still prevalent – 'Vera, get a hold of yourself, no one else ever will' – and the super-computer final-act battle with Vera getting robotomised is oddly chilling. And of course, only Christopher Reeve can make that maroon Smallville high school jumper with the canary-yellow 'S' look some damn sexy when knotted across Clark's shoulders with a proper 1983, yuppie yachtsman panache. I tried the same with my Catholic grey V-neck at school. I just looked like a chubby, faggy Simon Le Bon.

Years later I found myself at the Grand Canyon, Arizona. As my science teacher partner marvelled at the physics and geology of what is indeed a breathtakingly expansive and alien place on Earth, without thinking this sky kid blurted out to a band of Russian tourists, 'Yes, never mind how the Colorado River has created this canyon over millions of years – it was around here that Richard Pryor went to battle with Superman on the back of a donkey.' It turns out Russian tourists are not *Superman* fans. But I was. And in 1983 I was a more forgiving fan of *Superman III* because I was 8 years old and this was the film that was all over the Cranleigh Regal's confectionary counter, TV ad breaks and soon the VHS carousels of our local garages and video stores. It was typical of many a *Watching Skies* title. Because of timings especially, the latter sequels – *Return of the Jedi, Jaws 3-D, Star Trek III: The Search for Spock* and *Superman III* – become the ones a lot of us grew up with, and sometimes experienced more of a personal dialogue with than the landmark originals. As I later discovered with the Bond films, everyone's entry point into a particular franchise or saga is different. As many *Superman* fans came to the Man of Steel via first seeing *Superman III* and *Supergirl* as were the first in line on the release day of *Superman: The Movie*. Both entry points are ultimately Salkinds of wonderful.

IF YOU'VE GOT IT, HAUNT IT

GHOSTBUSTERS

1984. A wraithlike rollercoaster of purple phantasms rises from a Tribeca firehouse into the blue skies of Manhattan, only to cascade and dance with ghostly menace onto the streets, subways, and people below.

2005. New York. The Tribeca district. On the wall of the Hook & Ladder Company 8 Firehouse on North Moore Street is a white 'Entrance' arrow pointing away from a familiar red garage door. As you follow the arrow around the corner of the station, some over-keen movie fan has confirmed your familiarity with the firehouse by scrawling 'Ghostbusters live here' near a buzzer on the ivory wall. Although the interiors were shot in a downtown Los Angeles firehouse on the other side of the country, Tribeca's Hook & Ladder Company 8 station is of course the very real New York face of *Ghostbusters*, with its pillar-box red door and terracotta brickwork.

'They're here to believe you' at Tribeca's Hook & Ladder Company 8 Firehouse, New York.

Like all firehouses in central New York post–September 2001, a certain silence and a gap of sadness befalls a building otherwise known for its comedy chaos and 1980s movie deity. It crosses your mind as you stand waiting for your other half to cross the Tribeca traffic to get the all-important full impact Ghostbusters HQ photo. And it crosses your mind for evermore when you return to Ivan Reitman's 1984 movie - where watching the skies and populace of a Manhattan in jeopardy is a bit less comic book easy than it once was. We'd already tried to explain to a kind, scholarly passer-by why the photo she offered to get of us both outside the

New York Public Library had to be one of us running in a panic down the stone steps and past the stone lions and pigeons in the style of *Ghostbusters'* opening gambit. But even that didn't quite feel appropriate in a city that was still in its infancy of recuperation after 11 September 2001. But one October afternoon in 2005 on the west side of Central Park, we'd stopped on the Bow Bridge to try to work out which sizeable Manhattan edifice on the west side of Central Park might have been Sigourney Weaver's apartment building from *Ghostbusters*. A kind, but gruff-looking older guy stopped and could sense Elliot and I scanning the skyline before us with newbie uncertainty. 'The *Ghostbusters* building?!' he correctly assumed. I nodded sheepishly. 'That one, sir.' And with a kind nod and a quick pointed finger clarifying it for more silently unsure visitors poised on the bridge, he wandered off. Sometimes the movies we have in common are all people need. New York is certainly proud of its joint history with the movies and American cinema's insistence on using it on-screen as the embodiment of contemporary life and contemporary America.

Ghostbusters was the first all-out horror movie many of our generation saw at the cinema. Still too young to understand or even find the then-banned *The Exorcist*, and not brave enough to bring in a pirated VHS copy of *The Driller Killer* to play during a wet lunch break at school, we were barely aware of the American-owned traditions of Halloween, let alone John Carpenter's famed 1978 movie chiller of the same name. When E.T., Elliott and the kids of Tujunga, California go trick-or-treating in *E.T. the Extra-Terrestrial*, it was something us early-1980s British kids couldn't quite fathom. The only *Carrie* we knew played Princess Leia. The only *Wicker Man* we knew was TV travel host Alan Whicker and his penchant for using Concorde to nip over and interview Joan Collins on the *QE2*. The nearest we got to all-out chillers was the creepy and white-masked Mr Noseybonk on kids' TV show

Jigsaw and the teatime drama encounters of a science fiction kind that was *Chocky* and its unnerving ability to be deathly dull, very Surrey and sinister all at the same time. However, a group of us kids did once also ask the teachers and nuns if it would be okay to write to TV show *Jim'll Fix It* to request that a whole class of us could experience the bumps and scares of a real haunted house. As hindsight has now woefully proved, maybe going to BBC Television Centre circa 1984 to get involved in that particular kids' programme had the potential of being one ghost ride too many.

However, I had seen some of *Omen III: The Final Conflict* on VHS. I was barely 9 and my friend Mark's older brother had rented it from their local video store. We had an odd affinity with the original *The Omen* in Guildford. Director Richard Donner shot a large proportion of the film in the Surrey towns, roads, cemeteries, churches and even safari parks we were locally familiar with. One of our old school buses is even visible in one shot. The scene with Gregory Peck and Lee Remick abandoning a wedding as young Damien has an anti-God outburst at a church was filmed at Guildford Cathedral. And none of us to this day forget that if we ever pass by. I once had a similar emotional flare-up when us Cub Scouts were driven the same route in the back of a Bedford van to attend a whole obligatory seven hours of Scouts Day with flags, salutes, dry sandwiches and hymns. Having Gregory Peck burst in to try to stab me with an ancient Roman dagger was actually preferable to this annual pageant to Lord Baden-Powell. As it was, *Omen III: The Final Conflict* scared both the bejesus and the bedamien out of my 9-year-old self and gave me a fear of prams, fox hunts and priests being shrouded in plastic sheets and set alight on national television ever since.

The release of *Ghostbusters* was a happening. Not quite on a par with the Jedi mind tricks played on the box office and audience psyches in the wake of *Star Wars*, *Jaws*, *The Empire Strikes Back* or

E. T., the momentum of *Ghostbusters* however was still sizeable – perhaps the last genuine hurrah alongside *Gremlins* (1984) of an era that properly launched with that shark movie. But its success was almost as much about television and satire as it was cinema. Initially exorcised from the paranormal occupations of actor and writer Dan Aykroyd and his pal and comedy partner John Belushi, the DNA of *Ghostbusters* traces back to American television's satirical bastion *Saturday Night Live*, the magazine pages and radio shows of *National Lampoon* and the various comedy clubs, revue projects and TV sketch shows of *The Second City*. *The Second City* was – and still is – an improvisational comedy troupe based out of Toronto, Chicago and Los Angeles. By the late 1970s and early 1980s it had already boasted an influential sketch show *SCTV* and past and present alumni that included John Belushi, Martin Short, Gilda Radner, Jim Belushi, Andrea Martin, Eugene Levy, Catherine O'Hara, John Candy, Shelley Long, George Wendt, and *Police Academy* stalwarts Lance Kinsey (Proctor) and Tim Kazurinsky (Sweetchuck). Add to that Harold Ramis, Rick Moranis, Bill Murray and Dan Aykroyd. Whilst this particular quartet may not have instantly crossed each other's comedy streams to begin with, the performers, writers and general zest of *The Second City* and *The National Lampoon Radio Show* would feed into the subsequent *Saturday Night Live*. Very soon the triangle of American comedy houses secured the fortunes and futures of all three stables, including their forays into motion pictures.

The Second City had already dipped its toes into cinema with 1964's *Goldstein* (co-directed by Philip Kaufman, who later wrote and directed 1978's *Invasion of the Body Snatchers* and co-wrote the story for *Raiders of the Lost Ark* with George Lucas). *National Lampoon* followed suit with 1978's *National Lampoon's Animal House* (co-written by Harold Ramis and produced by Ivan Reitman) and 1983's Griswold-tastic *National Lampoon's Vacation* (directed by Ramis). *SNL* meanwhile spawned 1980's *The Blues Brothers* (directed by John Landis, co-written with Dan Aykroyd and with a score by Elmer Bernstein). Its success came at the key comedy time of 1979's *Meatballs* (directed by Reitman, co-written by Ramis and with a score by Bernstein), 1980's *Caddyshack* (directed and co-written by Ramis) and 1981's *Stripes* (directed by Reitman, co-written by Ramis and with a score by Bernstein). All three films also starred Bill Murray.

Aykroyd and Belushi were already Steven Spielberg veterans, having completed a wartime tour of duty in his post-*Close Encounters* folly, *1941* (1979). A rare dud for Spielberg in a comedy genre he has yet to return to as director, *1941* did at least further showcase the talents of John Belushi, Dan Aykroyd, John Candy (an original casting thought for *Ghostbusters*) and Michael McKean (*This is Spinal Tap*). Whilst the bearded, long-haired geeks working out of various late-1970s lock-ups and warehouses in California's Van Nuys, San Rafael and San Francisco were rewriting the movie rules of visual effects on the West Coast, these various comedians, writers, directors and actors were tearing up the comedy rule books on the East Coast. With shared anti-establishment pulses and counterculture drives it was inevitable that the physical new world order of American movie visual effects would someday marry up with the new world order of American comedy. And with a script purportedly rewritten by Dan Aykroyd and Harold Ramis on a writing trip to Martha's Vineyard – or Amity Island, as it is known in *Jaws* – the best and first result of those new wave worlds colliding is easily 1984's *Ghostbusters*.

Ghostbusters opened in America on 8 June 1984. Yet again it took a whole six months for Columbia Pictures to row those film reels across the Atlantic in time for the British release on 7 December. It was also the same day that *Gremlins* was released in the UK. In any other universe, that early December weekend represented perhaps the best example of 1980s *Watching Skies* movie nirvana. Assuming you weren't 9 years old. The British Board of Film Classification was to slap a '15' rating on Joe Dante's Christmas caper, thus putting it out of reach to any 9-year-olds without an older brother with a magical age-increasing, leatherette bomber jacket on hand to borrow. To be fair, the BBC's annual Christmas six-part teatime drama *The Box of Delights* (based on the novel by John Masefield – an author Kirk is keen to quote in *Star Trek*) had already spooked the hell out of me that December with its creepy wolves, predatory vicars and nostalgic obsessions over buttered eggs.

So, it was all arranged. Inigo and I would be going to the Cranleigh Regal to see *Ghostbusters* on its opening Saturday. We had lobbied to make the trip on our own, as going to see *Ghostbusters* or any PG-rated film with your mum was now about as cool as a Louis Tully accountant party. Although I saw a lot of Spielberg films with my mum in school holidays. As the new Bond films became a key family tradition with my dad, any new Spielberg output was always something Mum and I did. It of course started in late 1982 with *E.T.* and continued with the likes of *An American Tail* (1986), *Who Framed Roger Rabbit* (1988) and later *Schindler's List* (1993), *The Lost World: Jurassic Park* (1997) and *Saving Private Ryan* (1998). In the end, there was a compromise with *Ghostbusters*. Inigo's visiting older cousin accompanied us. As was my seat-panicking wont, I suggested a stupidly early time to meet outside the glittering monoplex that was the Regal – despite the December climate, which Inigo was still getting used since his recent move from Madrid. But it did mean more time to savour the cinema's posters. For a cute rural-deco 1936 cinema with only one screen and often just one film showing during the week, at any time the Regal's entrance windows still had eight posters of upcoming movies to scrutinise, as well as others in the front foyer alongside that old-school movie house magnificence that were the lobby cards. I remember Eddie Murphy perched on the bonnet of that red Mercedes in the *Beverly Hills Cop*, the bare chest of Schwarzenegger teasing *The Terminator* and the burnt orange skies of Kyle MacLachlan in *Dune*. But I was always much more interested in the 'STEVEN SPIELBERG presents' promise and a partly concealed Mogwai in a cardboard box on the *Gremlins* poster. Not all the films touted would ultimately play at the Regal but it didn't matter. Here was a so-far-unseen *Gremlins* poster by the artist who painted the neon blues and deep browns and purples of posters like *E.T. the Extra-Terrestrial*, *The Color Purple*, *Cocoon* and the *Blade Runner* artwork the Regal kept on proud display by its vintage confectionary counter for years. The Californian artist John Alvin later went on to design other key quad posters that I would glimpse in the windows of the Regal for the first time ever from our passing school bus with a bump of excitement – titles like *Short Circuit*, *Innerspace*, *The Princess Bride*, *Spies Like Us*, *The Lost Boys*, *Empire of the Sun*, *The Golden Child*, *Hook*, *Willow*, *Always*, *Arachnophobia* and *Jurassic Park*. Apart from half hoping to glimpse a teaser poster for *A View to a Kill* to satiate my growing hunger for all things Bond, I would scour the credits on, below and to the side of the designs for the pecking order, soundtrack guest stars, unannounced cast members and the studio logo.

Talking of black, white and red cinematic graphics, the archetypal 'no ghosts' *Ghostbusters* logo was of course a 1980s staple – as key to the decade as the MTV logo, the *Back to the Future* title shield, the mighty yellow lettering of *Dallas*, the Atari moniker, the *TV-AM* banner, the *He-Man and the Masters of the Universe* font, the Apple apple, the *BAD* album font and the Cannon Group insignia. It was designed by one of *Ghostbusters'* associate producers, Michael C. Gross – an artist who also drew for *National Lampoon* magazine. Clean, ubiquitous, playful and globally translatable, the ghost icon was not just in the glass poster booths of the Regal (with a mirrored reverse of the famed graphic which none of us noticed on the British posters). It was also a call to arms that features throughout the film itself – on car doors, TV commercials, the characters' uniforms and on signage hanging from that Tribeca firehouse HQ.

To an audience hungry for another American movie event after 1983 and *Return of the Jedi*, *Ghostbusters* was it. But it was not just a movie event. It was a keynote pop *and* pop cultural notch on the 1980s movie bedpost. And another vital way in which TV fed into the momentum of *Ghostbusters* was Ray Parker Jr.'s title track. Parker Jr. followed up three weeks of being number 1 in America's Billboard Hot 100 in August 1984 by haunting radio playlists the world over, and a British chart tenure that lasted eleven weeks in the Top Ten (with three weeks at number 2) and forty weeks in the Top 100. But it was no longer just radio playlists where a movie could lay out its stall. The age of MTV was at its zenith. And with that, so too was the era of the pop video and, in turn, the movie song pop video.

Showcasing a movie with a song was nothing new. Distributing sheet music and phonograph records to accompany and promote a film goes back to the dawn of early cinema itself. The contemporary multi-artist soundtrack LP was merely the 1980s equivalent of the golden age movie musical album. The sales impact of a 1970s movie composer like John Williams just evolved into more youth-orientated pop collections that were more in tune with younger tastes, spending habits and technology. If anything, the *Watching Skies* titles like *Jaws*, *E. T.*, *Close Encounters*, *Superman* and *Raiders* are glorious, classical exceptions to the pop movie soundtrack development of the late 1970s onwards – one that can be traced back to the chart-based, vinyl bestsellers from movies like *Jailhouse Rock*, *Goldfinger*, *Help!*, *Easy Rider*, *American Graffiti* and *Saturday Night Fever*. The classical orchestral score was now being usurped by

Symmetrical book stacking and the lions at the New York Public Library.

ensemble soundtracks to films such as *Beverly Hills Cop, Flashdance, Footloose, Purple Rain* and *Rocky IV*. Here was a film that did have an orchestral score by Elmer Bernstein – the movie-composing royalty responsible for the sounds of *The Magnificent Seven, To Kill a Mockingbird, The Ten Commandments, The Great Escape* and *Cape Fear*. But it was Ray Parker Jr. us kids were buying the seven-inch vinyl singles for. Well, I wasn't. My one-title vinyl collection had only just started with Band Aid's 'Do They Know It's Christmas?' – which came out the week of *Ghostbusters* in the UK. I had been given some Bond score cassettes from EON Productions via my grandfather, but this was the first ever piece of vinyl music I bought. And with the *Ghostbusters* single came the omnipresent curio that is Ivan Reitman's own directed video. Not only is a young lady being held against her will in a haunted neon house and having to endure both Ray Parker Jr. doing his stalking-at-a-foot-away dancing, and that 1980s movie song pop video trope of dropping incongruous movie clips in at total random, the video also stars *Fame's* Irene Cara, Carly Simon, John Candy, Danny DeVito, Chevy Chase, *Columbo's* Peter Falk and *Close Encounters'* Ronny Neary (Teri Garr). Who you gonna call? Everyone it seems. And with that video and track, *Ghostbusters* haunted our movie minds for about half a year before the film was actually released in the UK.

Ghostbusters is that rare thing – a movie that almost knows its place in pop culture before the end credits roll. Bystanders are familiar with Parker Jr.'s anthem as they chant 'Ghostbusters!', the morning news shows echo the same reports they no doubt had for real when Murray and co. promoted the film, talk show deity Larry King cameos as himself, as does radio and cartoon voice legend Casey Kasem. And yes, we all memorised the *Ghostbusters* phone number so we could try it out when we got home to see if they really were ready to believe us. They weren't. Firmly pinned to the story world of the movie, the celebrity fever within the film seemed to be echoed outside of it in movie theatres. The box office ascendency of Bill Murray, Dan Aykroyd, Sigourney Weaver, Rick Moranis and Harold Ramis was rising fast in the wake of *SNL, Trading Places, The Blues Brothers, Tootsie, National Lampoon's Vacation, Alien* and *Caddyshack.* This may partly account for why 1989's *Ghostbusters II* had such an uphill struggle amongst audiences. Released in a sequel-heavy summer of 1989, its apparition apparatus felt a beat too late and less of an organic caper than before. What originally felt like a burst of pop culture zeitgeist perfectly poised alongside Michael Jackson's *Thriller* video, the Los Angeles Olympic Games, *Indiana Jones and the Temple of Doom* and another quartet mucking about in the back of the van in *The A-Team*, did not transplant so well in a harrying tale of society's ills mutating into phantasms. And nothing gets the kids cheering in the aisles more than a sixteenth-century Carpathian villain from Moldovia. As a spooky and fun summer caper, *Ghostbusters: Answer the Call* (2016) is strangely

A 35mm reel of *Rosemary's Baby*, one of the starting pistols to *Ghostbuster's* sense of New York horror, waits for collection in California.

maybe more of a 1980s frolic than *Ghostbusters II*. It is about as successful at hiding that it is ultimately *Ghostbusters III* as a kid under a white ghost sheet on Halloween, but it is also an ensemble pantomime with a gloss, a pace, likeable characters and not quite the childhood-destroying proton beam the cackling dead of the online movie fan community needed it to be. In an age when the gatekeepers of summer cinema are comic book movies obsessed with endless teaser-y teasing to movies not yet made, it is refreshing to just have a self-contained film that has a confidence in itself. That is more 1980s cinema and *Ghostbusters* than not.

Whilst *The Empire Strikes Back*, *Superman II* and *Poltergeist* are undeniably cool to us sky kids with a bit of justifiable and misty-eyed hindsight, *Ghostbusters* was the first movie that took over our lives that was adult cool. We may not have got the more mature-skewed gags. The rather suggestive lady ghost unfastening Ray Spengler's trouser belt and some of the verbal jests were often exorcised from television and video versions quicker than it took a rosary-clutching Father Karras to launch himself down those Georgetown steps. *Meatballs*, *Trading Places* and *Saturday Night Live* were not quite aimed at us British kids raised on *The Two Ronnies* and eagerly awaiting ownership of our first Millennium Falcon that forthcoming Christmas. But here was a film with four not-gym-honed thirtysomethings scrabbling around New York for ghosts, work and love. It is not a perfect film, but our memories of it are. Aykroyd is clearly on the verge of corpsing with laughter at Bill Murray's improv too much of the time, and some of the script's historical convolutions and references take the momentum away from the ghost ride at play. But *Ghostbusters* is one of those valuable conduit films that leads us to others. We didn't know who Bill Murray or the curiously-named Sigourney Weaver were. But we did afterwards. And before long our older, 14-year-old selves were getting our mums to rent out *Aliens* and then *Alien* on our behalf and do what a lot of us sky kids did with our movies – start with the most recent and work backwards. Continuity was always less important than content.

Ghostbusters was a film that was pinned to a New York still reeling from its 1970s financial and social slumps. Despite the new sideshow of office computers, this is very much a turn of the century Manhattan with its ornate firehouses, slightly tired grand hotels straight out of Dan Aykroyd's previous *Trading Places* and the old guard taking the elevator with a cigar-chomping curiosity – 'What are you supposed to be – some kind of cosmonaut?' Admittedly, New York was good for 1970s American cinema. The decade's big movie strides were often made with New York as their co-star – from the starting pistols of *Rosemary's Baby* (1968) and *Midnight Cowboy* (1969) to *The French Connection* (1971), *Klute* (1971), *The Godfather* (1972), *Mean Streets* (1973), *Serpico* (1973), *The Taking of Pelham One Two Three* (1974), *The Prisoner of Second Avenue* (1975), *Marathon Man* (1976), *Annie Hall* (1977), *Saturday Night Fever* (1977), *Manhattan* (1979), *The Warriors* (1979), *Cruising* (1980) and of course *Superman: The Movie* (1978). The New York of *Ghostbusters* is still the 1970s cinema America of *All the President's Men*, *The Conversation*, *Dog Day Afternoon* and *Network*. It is the cluttered walkways, dicey subways, filthy cabs, rain macs, wooden police cordons in the streets, meeting by the fountain, baying crowds, burning oil cans, homeless folk in fingerless mittens and police precinct front desks that can be lifted with a petulant sigh from the chief. Upper West Side diners ignore passers-by as they are attacked by hellhounds at the windows, and the city has that orange dawn glow that quietly sticks in the mind of anyone who has visited New York.

The skies we watch here may be full of the architectural, corporate and housing might of one of the greatest cities on earth – but these New York tropes all contain their own movie grammar and are as key to non-Americans' sense of the United States as the medallion cabs, yellow school buses and Rockwellian fields of *Superman*. *Ghostbusters* has all those New York tropes caught firmly in its proton beams – the dramas of apartment life, hunched hot dog vendors, pen-pushing pencil-necked officials, prissy hoteliers, gum-chewing real estate agents, rotund cops on the eve of retirement and wailing sirens. Sigourney Weaver's Dana even has one of those gargantuan refrigerators (it's not a fridge) that not only holds enough food to be thrown out onto the floor for dramatic *Watching Skies*-era effect, it also houses some 1980s silver leotarded villainy in the form of Gozer the Gozerian – a punk, red-eyed Sheena Easton dominatrix stuck on the roof of a west Central Park apartment block with two hellhounds for company. Naturally.

Ghostbusters is also a movie where the drives and societal hustles of Ronald Reagan's America are unescapable. The film was released in Britain a month after a landslide second-term Presidential victory for the former movie actor who had once been the Governor of California and – by default – Hollywood throughout the early rise of American cinema's 1970s new wave. The naïve officials and gaudy mayors of *The Sugarland Express*, *Jaws* and *Close Encounters* are now politicised city chiefs worrying about voting figures, business regulators and environmental protection agencies. It is around the time of *Ghostbusters* that those Reaganite – and Trump – tenets of house prices, wealth and property deals begin threading themselves into the fabric of mainstream 1980s cinema. Suddenly the simpler adventures and narrative spirits of *Duel*, *Jaws*, *Star Wars* and *Superman* have become the kids in *The Goonies* (1985) facing separation when lead adventurer Mikey (Sean Astin) and his family face foreclosure, the Christmas Scrooge that is Mrs Deagle and her rent rises and Judge Reinhold's Republican yuppie pretensions in *Gremlins*, the building permit hell of *The Money Pit* (1985), and the corporate development might and menaces of *Batteries Not Included* (1987).

Despite the presence of two cutesy television movies centred around the Ewoks and Endor – 1984's *Caravan of Courage* and 1985's *Ewoks: The Battle for Endor* – the *Watching Skies* era of cinema is beginning to miss those far, far away galaxies. Without perhaps the fantasy flag-bearing might of *Star Wars*, our sci-fi movies begin to modify themselves as they evolve with the zeitgeist and original audiences become older. They become grounded in a sort of NASA, tech and data-based reality and often with a military edge that yields such 1980s stalwarts as *D.A.R.Y.L.* (1985), *Explorers* (1985), *Spacecamp* (1986), *Aliens* (1986), *Short Circuit* (1986), *Flight of the Navigator* (1986), *Innerspace* (1987), *Robocop* (1987) and *Predator* (1987). The domestic mystery and cinematic fantasy of what is out there in the skies and imagination shifts to the dramas of takeovers, eviction, money, development and the might of big cities. The Cold War was somehow never quite a part of *Star Wars*, *Superman*, *E.T.* and *Jaws*. Those counterculture working and creative visions of George Lucas, Francis Ford Coppola and that first American Zoetrope collective had no enemy other than decaying Hollywood hierarchies, creativity, time and budgets. As the contradictory bedfellows of nuclear proliferation and détente make real-life marquee names of East and West, cinema ultimately reflects that. Dan Aykroyd's very own *Spies Like Us* (directed by John Landis) gets a bit glasnost lost in its attempts to try to catch a bit of *Ghostbusters'* lightning in its vodka bottle, and Sylvester Stallone's *Rocky* (1976) has gone from a blue-collar Philadelphian to an inadvertent Reagan poster boy punching above his weight on the streets of Moscow in *Rocky IV* (1985). With this uglier Reaganite – and Thatcherite – push for profit and progress over people, the movie world eventually echoes that like the litmus paper it quietly is. The Americana of *Blue Velvet* (1986), *Platoon* (1986), *Top Gun* (1986), *Wall Street* (1987), *The Lost Boys* (1987), *The Witches of Eastwick* (1987) and even Spielberg's own *The Color Purple* (1985) has a very different cynicism compared to *Jaws* and the 1970s.

With its trippy gobo patterns gyrating around the flood-stained stage curtains soundtracked by Limahl's 'The NeverEnding Story' and Queen's 'I Want to Break Free', Inigo, his cousin and I took our front row seats that cold December Saturday. As a 9-year-old who had seen at least half of *Omen III: The Final Conflict*, I assumed I was ready for Bill Murray and his hot dog chomping spectres. The TV clips we'd been fed on a loop were the cuddly, fun ones with the cool orange proton beam, Annie Potts manning the phones with her Brooklyn sass and Slimer's green chaos. Inigo had the *Ghostbusters* photo storybook and all we saw was the Stay Puft Marshmallow Man, the cool orange beams of the Neutrona wands and Sigourney in her winter knits. Cue the library ghost fiasco and a childhood touchstone of utter terror. Ten or so minutes into *Ghostbusters* and some floating books, skittish library cards and Bill Murray quips have created a false sense of security for all us 9-year-olds sugared to the eyeballs on *He-Man* jellies in the Regal. Yet when Raymond Stanz pushes his opening act luck with a floating schoolmarm apparition quietly perusing the dusty volumes of the New York Public Library, the resulting skeletal-zombie jolt didn't so much turn the air blue, but the 466 seats of the Regal somewhat brown. Crash cut to thirty-one years later, and the next time I am watching the skies of *Ghostbusters* on the big screen with a crew of twenty or so mates I am still cagey of that sodding library ghost. With our aptly-sited wedding only a month away, my man Elliot and I were not so much having a shared stag night, but a fully-fledged Uncle-Sam-inspired Bachelor Party … in London. Our two Best Men, Greg and Alex, have astutely booked an independent cinema, pizza and beer. And in a movie programming coup our 9-year-old minds could not have handled – imagine being able to book a cinema and movie of your choice in 1984?! – the guys have procured a generation-baiting copy of *Ghostbusters* as our movie matinee. I've seen behind-the-scenes production stills and plenty of gorier and crueller tics in many a horror movie since. But the languid, flowing *Little House on the Prairie* spectre of that opening act of *Ghostbusters* still has that childhood-seared power to scare the ectoplasm out of me. It was partly the real reason I didn't want to go into the New York Public Library that day. Oh well. If you've got it, haunt it.

THE TV PEOPLE

Saturday 15 December 1984. That was when my world changed for evermore. That was the day I was liberated. That was the day I was emancipated from a world of enforced closedown, suspended television services in the afternoon and constant war films on a Sunday. That was when my four TV channel existence ended. That was when I no longer had to watch the skies of *Star Wars* or *Jaws* at a preordained time set by someone else, with commercial breaks and ads for Rumbelows, those Natwest pigs and Tefal toasters somewhat ruining the moment. For Saturday 15 December 1984 was the day our house got its very first video recorder. And a new television to match. I think my parents' pal Dave had sensed my only-child isolation and a lack of *Star Wars* home video access and had quietly worked on them both for months. Dave would often come round on a Friday night, nod politely at my new karate club moves and talk movies and TV over fish and chips. He was the first adult and family pal I could talk cinema with. He would bring round his player so my parents and I could have a test run to see if they liked the idea. Yes, some video players in 1980s Britain were like the school rabbit – there to take home and have a trial run before you made that commitment to house one for life. Dave's dummy runs of *Airplane* and episodes of *Auf Wiedersehen, Pet* may well have done the trick on my parents. And the fact my mum could not buy petrol or a garage bottle of Black Tower for her Sunday roast without an hour of grief from me about why we had not yet joined the Gaston Gate Garage's video club when everyone else had. Gaston Gate was a utopic VHS membership world of overnight rentals, reserving a film in their special leatherbound booking diary and plastic display carousels that would proudly display lone and sun-worn copies of not just *Raiders of the Lost Ark*, but *The Entity, Dressed to Kill, Under the Rainbow, 48 Hrs, The Fog, The Howling, Time Bandits, V: The Original Series, Grease 2, The Man with Two Brains* and *Octopussy* – the film I ended up renting the most as my Bond fan trajectory took hold.

My mum led the research process, asking around for recommendations from the many folk who were already VHS savvy and scouring the white goods catalogues that were plentiful in the Britain of 1984. She also led the charge in the television store that Saturday afternoon to the tune of a new front-loading Hitachi VT-33A video recorder, a new and much bigger Hitachi television set, a pack of three Polaroid 180-minute blank video cassettes and a faux mahogany television cabinet to house it all. Everything in British homes of the 1980s had to be housed in a faux mahogany or beech veneer something else. You have a new hi-fi stereo system? Hide it from immediate sight in this half-sized mahogany coffin with pull-out drawer space to house all those cassette-tape albums. You have a new beige push-button trimphone? Marvel at this beech veneer telephone table complete with a wipe-screen, pull-out A–Z contacts board and a resting slot for a biro on a wire. You have too many films on video? Ditch the original covers and their beautiful poster art for these faux navy-blue video covers that cannily double up as rare seventeenth-century books.

And like proud parents bringing baby home for the first time, we carefully lifted the cardboard Hitachi boxes into the lounge, fished out the service manuals and set about connecting the whole revolution together. Of course, this was before easy-to-connect thinking and self-tuning divination. In 1984, you had to manually tune in each channel and look for two white bars on the screen that would indicate your television and video recorder had found each other's signal. It took Mum hours of patient knob-turning to finally find those elusive white bars. But she did it. And from that point on, those two alien-looking lines were the starting pistol to a life of movies, television and lovingly archived film libraries. The following morning, I taped the entire breakfast slot on *TV-AM* for no other reason than I could. And over the following days I taped, erased and then taped again all manner of titles. *Scrooge, Benji, Russ Abbot's Christmas Madhouse, Return of the Pink Panther, Scarecrow and Mrs King, Fraggle Rock* Christmas specials and episodes of *Muppet Babies* were all lovingly recorded, joyously watched at random times because that was now possible, then erased for something else. It took me ages to just chill out and keep a movie or show rather than impulsively tape over it. How to use the video recorder soon became useful domestic currency. Mum wanted a show taped, so I would ask for her knowledge in how the timer record option worked. I had the blank cassettes and could indeed tape *All Creatures Great and Small* for her, and the Brazilian Grand Prix for my stepdad, but some more blank VHS tapes would be needed – ones that I will knowingly use more than they ever will. Eventually the three of us had individually labelled cassettes like milk in a student fridge. As the collection grew, I had ten blank tapes from BASF, Sony and Polaroid to my mum's lone 'Crufts '85' cassette. Within a year that had doubled again.

For those who back up their movies, jpegs and files on invisible clouds and virtual safe boxes, the very first incarnation of such protective measures started with VHS video cassettes. Safeguarding your films would involve a highly technical manoeuvre of taking a flat screwdriver from the garage and carefully prising off a black plastic tab the size of a tiny stamp in the bottom left corner of the tape. There. Done. Your special ITV copy of *Jaws 2* was saved for all time because a small black piece of excess plastic was now lost in your carpet. Knowing how to reverse such tab removal to make the cassette recordable again also became a bargaining chip. The person who demonstrated how an inch-long piece of Sellotape over the hole did the trick without getting something in return was a fool. And there will forever be whole generations that say 'tape' rather than 'record', 'buffer' or 'download', and anachronistic sentiments like 'I have the whole new season of *Stranger Things* taped and ready to go on Netflix.' When a hard drive or DVD recorder declares 'memory full', I still instinctively wonder if I deleted out all the adverts. And whilst the emancipation to watch the skies of whatever movies we wanted was more than welcome, it was the beginning of fragmented audiences, of people not watching broadcasts at the same time and of not having those shared film experiences to chat about on the school bus in the morning.

And what was the first film we rented from the Gaston Gate Garage with our new video club membership? *Star Wars* of course. Which we didn't really get to watch until about midnight that first night due to our technical learning curve. But when it did happen, it was the best thing in the world ever for a 9-year-old obsessed with *Star Wars*, *Superman* and *Octopussy*. Being able to watch *Star Wars* or any film of my choosing in my own lounge, at my own time and with my own volume levels and toilet breaks was akin to sending one's first email or using Wi-Fi on a plane. It very nearly made up for how *Star Wars* and all future video rentals would have to be returned like Cinderella before midday the next day. Yet, such movie confines made us kids resourceful. Repeat breakfast screenings were a must and I would watch many a title again in the early, quiet hours of dawn when it was still just dark enough to pretend our lounge was a cinema. This was what the 1970s American blockbusters gave the kids of the world. It emancipated us from movie houses and television broadcasters. *Star Wars, Close Encounters, Superman* and *Raiders* were key and vital reasons why so many households caved and joined the VHS uprising. It was the idea of having those movies in your possession that converted so many lounges into proud home cinemas. *Star Wars* was not just a movie. It was a household name. Owning a home copy was akin to social mobility – to having a cordless phone, a car with a sunroof, a barbecue set or a microwave. And just like those British households that bought or borrowed their first television sets to watch the 1953 coronation or the 1969 Moon landing, or those bedrooms that suddenly got new turnstiles to play the latest Rolling Stones album or their first CD deck to play Springsteen's *Born in the USA*, movies like *Star Wars* and *Superman* compelled households to gain their first video players and make that crucial first step away from the movie skies other theatre or TV station owners wanted them to watch. The natural, most vivid and current evolution of that can be seen in the likes of Netflix, box-set bingeing and catch-up TV. And yet – none of these *Watching Skies* titles ever feature characters using a video player. Or even allude to one.

Very soon our 1984 movie theatres would also be our curved analogue television screens, the theatre drapes would be the hinged mahogany doors on our TV storage units, and the *TV Times* would be our 'Coming Soon' lobby boards. To this day, a great many people upgrade their flat-screens, movie systems and surround-sound units, and the first litmus test they put on to trial it all is *A New Hope* or *Close Encounters*. With their inaugural films of the 1970s and early 1980s, Steven Spielberg and George Lucas almost singlehandedly changed the consumption of cinema. *Ownership* was becoming as key an audience drive as *spectatorship*. That ownership in turn evolved fandom. Aficionados became scholars, professors and staunch deans of Lucas's many worlds. The waiting time between theatrical release and the home markets began to inch nearer and nearer each other, and today – with the likes of *The Force Awakens*, *Rogue One* and *The Last Jedi* brilliantly leaping their way through the box office's blast doors the world over – the expectancy of seeing a new *Star Wars* movie on the big screen on its opening weekend is now matched by owning it on DVD or Blu-ray four months later. However, a side effect of that is where ownership can evolve into proprietorship. Lucas particularly has received fan criticism for the sheer volume of the ongoing new editions, directors' cuts and repurposed tinkering of – yes – his *Star Wars* saga. Firstly, *A New Hope* was a work in progress from the get-go. The later addition of the very title *A New Hope* is symptomatic of that. Barely weeks after the May 1977 US release, new prints would emerge featuring fresh shots, different frames, renewed sound effects and image rendering. Back in the late 1970s and early 1980s the theatrical re-release and double-bill programming of the time – an exhibition trend that has all but disappeared nowadays – was soon enabling Lucas to further carve, heighten and fine tune his work.

Secondly – and putting fan-led notions of sanctity aside – it is arguable that the very reason we still have new *Star Wars* films is because George Lucas continued to recondition those original films for new technologies, new ways of theatrical presentation and new ways of enhancing the home cinema experience. More vital even than all that was how he did it for new generations. Watching the fantasy skies of Lucas's universe at home has done more for the future of all the *Star Wars* sagas than any flared-jean nostalgias about queueing outside the Grauman's Chinese Theatre in Hollywood or the Regal Cinema in Cranleigh. The 1997 theatrical reissues not only stoked the fires of anticipation for the announced prequel trilogy and allowed the new and old visual effects boys and girls to cut their *Star Wars* teeth by renovating the company's vintage car before starting to drive a new set of wheels. They also scooped up new sky kids, new audiences and new *Star Wars* fans who had as much right to be at the fan table as those who had queued in the Californian sun of 1977. Christmas 1988 saw me become the proud parent of the original CBS/Fox 'All Time Great' VHS releases of *Star Wars*, *The Empire Strikes Back* and *Return of the Jedi*. At the time, these early VHS releases genuinely felt like the ultimate memento and commemoration of those films – the last word in owning these stories physically and mentally. As did the 'widescreen' VHS editions that emerged a few years later. And the initial DVD boxsets. And then the ultimate, documentary-loaded Blu-rays. What George Lucas was cannily doing more than anything was keeping these films current. He was keeping them relevant. Lucasfilm Ltd never simply continued to rework and maintain the original trilogy to make a quick buck every three or so years. Without wanting to burst some bubbles of fan-hate, George Lucas and the company coffers probably haven't had a cash-flow issue since the 1980s. This is where the commerce of Lucas and *Star Wars* wrongly overshadows the mythology and storytelling might of the saga. It is one of the key twentieth-century fairy tales. Just because the creator wants to evolve and have his work seen, it does not always boil down to dollars and pound signs. As home cinema audiences, we now all care greatly about HD, hi-res and Blu-ray. These days, watching a standard DVD is almost akin to VHS. Even our online trailers have to be seen in full HD or what is the point!? We care about our movies looking and sounding sharp because people like George Lucas care about their movies looking and sounding sharp. *Star Wars* didn't just change cinema in 1977. It continued on a path to focus it, clean it up, get rid of the scratches, improve the sound and keep the widescreen wide.

RAIDERS OF THE LOST MOVIE ART

RAIDERS OF THE LOST ARK

1981. The silhouettes of a rogue archaeologist from Connecticut and his local diggers toil against the orange skies of an Egyptian dawn. As the archaeologist doctor adjusts his fedora, the Tanis sand is tossed into the air amidst the screeching of the winds above and the snakes beneath.

And on the same December 1984 weekend that we entered a new age of magnetic tape, breakable tabs, sticky labels and extended-play wizardry, I experienced the downside of VHS in the 1980s – having to return *Star Wars* to its video store home the next day. After Sunday Mass, we dropped responsibly into Gaston Gate Garage with the outsized black plastic VHS cover emblazoned with some faded and numbered sticker. It was like saying goodbye to a new date you don't really want to leave at the bus stop because you've only just got to know them and kind of like their company. Fortunately for me, I was just about to get another hot movie date to shamelessly take home for a one-night wonder. It was probably Mum's way of apologising for the technical delays the night before. Not that I minded. And I knew exactly what my second piece of VHS trade would be. With a flying whip in his hand, an open-shirted torso, a creased fedora and that glorious jungle B-movie sensibility of snakes, feisty brunettes in distress and chiselled-jawed Nazis, that CIC Video sleeve was of course for Steven Spielberg's first movie foot in the 1980s, *Raiders of the Lost Ark* (1981).

The poster on that rectangular cover had long been staring at me from the bottom of one of the video store's rental carousels. Even when we did not have our own video player yet, I would pore over those VHS covers and sleeves every time Mum would be in the queue waiting to pay for fuel. All those studio logos, corporate branding, fonts, boxes, rating stamps, classification buzz words that would entice more than warn and all those frozen graphical promises of the movie journeys within. A particular favourite of mine was the simple three-part 'W' of the Warner Communications logo designed by movie graphical design god Saul Bass (famed title designer for Alfred Hitchcock, Otto Preminger and Martin Scorsese). It was somehow a stamp of both cinema and graphical perfection – so much so that Ben Affleck opens Warner Brothers' *Argo* with the vintage, era-savvy black, white and red Bass Warners' logo. It wasn't just American cinema of the 1970s and 1980s that was having a new golden age. The marketing drives and visual impulses for these films, their imitators, and the movie floodgates they inspired and opened were experiencing a zenith of mainstream cinema art. The film did not have to be good or even one you would ever watch, but the stamps it made on our childhoods and the hours spent cruising the plastic-boxed world of our video stores and cinema foyers were vital. The artwork for middling rubbish was nearly as key to the sky kids generation as the better titles we rented first. I would run my fingers along the spine imagery and font choices on so many a VHS box. How long a film was in minutes, its cast, who did the score, the rating and chosen stills were vital to know. We would hold those little anti-piracy hologram labels up to the light to see the letters WB, CIC, UA, EMI or CBS Fox glistening like the Sankara Stones from *Indiana Jones and the Temple of Doom*.

A severed hand pressing a doorbell in *House* (1986), the clawed cover for *The Howling* (1981), the confusingly ripped torso of Chevy Chase on the cover of *National Lampoon's Vacation* (1983), Bo Derek running along a beach in *10* (1979), the college boys of *Chariots of Fire* (1981) running along another beach two years later, the fleshy shower play of *Porky's* (1981), the hanging family heads of *On Golden Pond* (1980), the stiff screaming of *Scanners* (1981) and the abundant Richard Pryor and Eddie Murphy stand-up concert tapes. This was always the sea of imagery surrounding our *Star Wars* and *Superman* VHS tapes. Bloody hands and daggers were as ubiquitous as curvy-thighed denim, every other video cover had to feature the lead actor cowering on all fours and surrounded by leggy cheerleaders and horror reigned supreme.

The reputation of *Raiders of the Lost Ark* had long proceeded it with its cover art. Not only was the *Raiders* artwork a marvellous summons into the fresh adventure of Spielberg and Lucas's homage to 1930s serials and the episodic swagger and story licence of James Bond, it was also one of the first instances where a flash of male flesh – even in graphical form, told in the brushstrokes of yesteryear marquee traditions on the worn cover of a VHS cassette box – stopped me in my tracks like a killer dart in a booby-trapped Peruvian cave. None of the other men in my movie life – James Bond, Luke Skywalker, Han Solo, Clark Kent and Kal-El – flashed flesh on their posters like Indiana Jones did for *Raiders* and later *Temple of Doom*. But then, these films were not just made for straight boys. They were made for all walks of life. And all walks of life left their mark on these films – including gay American poster illustrator Richard Amsel.

Perhaps now lesser-known than key poster wizards of the era Bob Peak (*Rollerball, Superman: The Movie, The Spy Who Loved Me, Star Trek: The Motion Picture*) and Drew Struzan (*Back to the Future, Police Academy 3: Back in Training, Indiana Jones and the Last Crusade, Revenge of the Sith*), Richard Amsel designed the poster graphics for *Hello, Dolly!* (1969), *Woodstock* (1970), *McCabe and Mrs Miller* (1971), *The Sting* (1973), *Murder on the Orient Express* (1974), *Chinatown* (1974), *Flash Gordon* (1980) and *The Dark Crystal* (1982). He also produced various Bette Midler album covers and promotional artwork and many a magazine front page. Arguably, Amsel's most famous work is the artistry and chest hair he gave *Raiders of the Lost Ark*, video stores and bedroom walls the world over with its memorable burnt-sand-tinged billboard art and fetching leading man. Like all the *Watching Skies* movies, the accompanying artwork campaign and cultural presence was as key to *Raiders*' success as ILM, John Williams or editing by Michael Kahn.

With its 'return of the great adventure' promise, clear thinking and painted character vignettes, Richard Amsel was easily the forerunner for the slightly later likes of Drew Struzan and his iconic painterly ethics and visual placements. Amsel's parchment-like *Raiders* influence is all over the sense of poster adventure of Struzan's lush work on *The Goonies* (1985), *Hook* (1991), *Big Trouble in Little China* (1986) and *Harry Potter and the Sorcerer's Stone* (2001). Richard Amsel died in 1985 of an AIDS-related illness. He was only 37 years old. It reminds us how during the initial glory days of *Star Wars* and *Indiana Jones*, an epidemic was taking a growing toll on America – especially in San Francisco and New York. As Lucasfilm, its artists and technicians laboured throughout San Francisco on the likes of *Return of the Jedi* and *Indiana Jones and the Temple of Doom*, down in Eureka Valley and its Castro neighbourhoods an altogether darker force was claiming the lives of countless men, women, artists and creatives. It all quietly underlines how San Francisco's moviemaking and queer communities no doubt converged during these *Watching Skies* years. Lucasfilm Ltd's former head of licensing and now franchise manager Howard Roffman is not only a local LGBT advocate and photographer, he was a donor producer on the striking San Francisco AIDS documentary, *We Were Here* (2011). And Lucasfilm itself has not only built up a committed history of HIV/AIDS charity work and fundraising and now takes part in the San Francisco Pride March and various benefit events, it also pushes a wholly inclusive community mantra where LGBT Lucasfilm employees make a point of reaching out to gay folk the world over – including taking part in the *It Gets Better* project that reaches out to gay kids and adults who maybe don't have a galaxy of inclusivity surrounding them. To be fair, it is near impossible to have both creative and tech-based interests in San Francisco without being inclusively minded. But George Lucas, his peers and pals were in town doing just that, way before the big tech boys set up home. When *Star Wars Celebration 2017* has the first dedicated and energetically attended LGBT panel discussion that celebrates Lucas's world, its queer fans, pink sci-fi and how the franchise could expand its rainbow galaxy of fans and representations, it sends out an R2 message more crucial than just good cinema and our love of it.

As that first *Indiana Jones* movie plane was circumnavigating the globe, I was five and half thousand miles from the Golden Gate Bridge and where Harrison Ford first sets off on his red-lined global trajectory in *Raiders*. But already I was quite the Indy boy. Not only did I too have a fear of snakes and own the mandatory kids' Read-Along cassette tape of *Raiders of the Lost Ark* – complete with a square book of photos and a patronising American narrator urging how 'you will know it is time to turn the page when you hear the bullwhip crack like this ...' – I also had the BBC Records cassette story of *Temple of Doom*. Unlike the amateur dramatics and sound-alikes of the Read-Along books, this lengthy double-sided BBC cassette featured the real audio soundtrack, dialogue, sound effects and John Williams score. There would be many a night where Mum wondered why she could hear a Pankot Palace dinner party in full flow as she went to bed hearing the screams and gunshots of *Indiana Jones and the Temple of Doom* coming from my bedroom.

Wearing an old fedora my stepdad had found in a charity shop, this 8-year-old only child would pop on a black waistcoat and brown slacks and scurry about the woodland and bushes in our back garden singlehandedly doubling up for every Thugee assailant, Gestapo stooge and Peruvian tribesman on my own. The same brick outhouse that was my *Daily Planet* HQ and Octopussy's Palace would also become my Pankot Palace, Temple of Doom, South American treasure cave, Nazi island, and Well of the Souls. It even had a small cupboard alcove inside covered in spiderwebs that I was too much of a Willie Scott to go anywhere near. My stepdad Rob was an aviation and military connoisseur and collector. Our house would be dotted with all sorts of old pistols, ancient rifles, Zulu shields, WWI German helmets, chainmail headpieces, wooden plane propellers, parts of old aircraft steering units, a leather racing helmet once belonging to the Prince of Siam, tribal spears, decommissioned cartridges, vintage racing car gears, aeroplane canopies and a piece of dinosaur vertebrae. Our house was already quite the Last Ark of Doom. Although I was surrounded by all manner of real-life treasures and military leftovers, my main Dr Jones obsessions were not about the pistols and relics, but that

I knew most of the words to Kate Capshaw's opening number from *Indiana Jones and the Temple of Doom*.

Before we had that all-important video player, I would tape the audio of vital broadcasts and films by positioning a 1970s tape recorder near the mono speaker on our television. In the summer of 1984 Lucasfilm released a *Making of Indiana Jones and the Temple of Doom* documentary, produced and directed by Frank Marshall (co-founder of Amblin Entertainment, producer, director and husband of Kathleen Kennedy). Shown on Saturday morning ITV – as all good things were in the 1980s – I could not 'tape' the documentary itself. But our movie fan resourcefulness compelled me to the next best thing – I could record the documentary's audio onto a cassette. 1984 seemed to be a golden time for these 'Making of …' documentaries. It seemed all the big releases had their own hour-long special produced by the filmmakers themselves. The sort of access and sense of production opinion on offer is a rarity today, as that genuine insight and reasoning have made way for teasers, neutrality and hype. One of the highlights of this *Temple of Doom* documentary was a look at how they choreographed, rehearsed and shot the opening overture of 'Anything Goes'. I lost count of how many times I would listen to that sequence being produced on the soundstages of Elstree Studios. I still want to wear a silver sparkly top hat and tails and tap in time with those backing dancers on that polished black studio floor. And own a Lazy Susan. Ever since *Temple of Doom*'s opening Shanghai club scene, I have wanted a revolving Lazy Susan-style dining table so I can flaunt my stolen diamonds for all to see. Whilst other kids were all about the boulder sequence from *Raiders*, the Hitler-saluting monkey in a waistcoat or the melting Nazi faces, this sky kid was marvelling at Anthony Powell's dragon-embellished red and gold sequinned dress for Steven Spielberg's future wife, Kate Capshaw.

Looking back, that opening titles nod to musical choreography legend Busby Berkeley is an amazing work of camp drag, with all these Home Counties dancers in black Chinese wigs tapdancing around Capshaw's club singer Willie as she stumbles and smiles her way through the routine like a misguided cabaret act at a bad Asian restaurant for tourists. Through that 'Making of …' documentary, a pen and paper and copious usage of the pause button, I phonetically learnt 'Anything Goes' in Mandarin without once looking at the English lyrics. And then after that, and with the lounge curtains firmly shut, I tried my hand at some of Kate Capshaw's hand on hip, fan-flicking choreography – including all the glorious styled-out, fourth-wall breaking glitches she carefully drops in. Very soon my visiting grandmother Chrissie was regretting swapping her Glasgow home for a Southern England vacation of Cole Porter, Indiana Jones and Shanghai cabaret. She not only had the patience of a saint, but the lifelong burden of severe, debilitating arthritis and loved nothing more than enduring her dumpy grandson's regular cabaret spots in *Mark O'Connell's Lounge of Doom* without being able to walk away politely. Chrissie liked a cigarette, so I was always grateful how her smoke fumes added to my Club Obi-Wan production design as I struggled with that Mandarin in a Kimono dressing gown my dad had found on a work trip to the Far East. I convinced myself that the masculine drives of Indiana Jones and Harrison Ford were a total Benson and Hedges smokescreen to my flamboyant movie whims. A glitterball the size of the *Raiders* boulder crashing through the lounge to the disco sounds of Sylvester would have held more subtlety than my Capshaw obsessions in the lead-up to finally lifting *Raiders of the Lost Ark* from our local VHS well of movie souls.

Whilst these *Watching Skies* films were pushing and utilising new technologies, production thinking, exhibition practices and marketing, *Raiders of the Lost Ark* is a cracking example of how the traditional ways of doing things still have great purpose at the beginning of the 1980s. The technical advancements of *Close Encounters*, *A New Hope* and *The Empire Strikes Back* have now passed on their FX baton, staff, studios and offices to Doctor Indiana Jones. The 1936 story context demands director Steven Spielberg think outside his 1970s box office in similar ways to when he was tackling his previous title, *1941* (1979). But whereas *1941* was a loose caper of a Second World War movie with copious characters and untamed sight gags all vying for attention, here Lawrence Kasdan's screenplay of a *Book of Exodus*-inspired treasure hunt against the rise of the Third Reich is a masterclass in story precision. Whilst it is a step back from the fantasy momentum of *Close Encounters* and very much a step aside from the cacophony of chaos that is *1941*, *Raiders* marks the first in a rich, but infrequent pedigree of Spielberg movies that are not strictly tied to explorations of the human spirit. *Raiders* is less concerned with the darker foibles of human history than it is the gleaming Hollywood searchlights of homage and entertainment. It is arguable no other story world allows Spielberg the director that sense of adventure and liberation from both the moral conscience of history and the boundaries of genre. Possibly only *Jurassic Park* (1993), *The Lost World: Jurassic Park* (1997) and *The Adventures of Tintin* (2011) echo the Indiana Jones series and its licence for unattached adventure over profound statements on human history.

In coyly pitching a 1930s-era American hero in that matinee serial world of cliffhangers, *Casablanca*, Peter Lorre villainy and Hedy Lamarr damsels in distress, Lucas and Spielberg do not just allow themselves a classic jaunt in the pulp movie sandpit. They create an ongoing franchise that can celebrate the B-movies and world politics of many a subsequent story era since. In *Raiders* (1981), *Temple of Doom* (1984) and *The Last Crusade* (1989) it is all about the black and white serials of derring-do, jungle skirmishes, snake pits, truck chases and Nazi caricatures. By the time of *Temple of Doom* a bit of Kipling-skewed, colonial British B-movie bluster and Charlie Chan shenanigans come in to the mix. And *The Last Crusade* opens on the Boy Scout Americana of Norman Rockwell's paintings, tips its brief fedora to Errol Flynn storming many a blazing movie castle, and closes on the knights, swords and sorcery of countless British support features circling the King Arthur legend. By the time of 2008's *Indiana Jones and the Kingdom of the Crystal Skull*, the 1957 caper – whilst dedicating a great deal of screen time to hiding itself in Conquistador lore – is ultimately a saucer-shaped UFO B-movie by way of the Nuclear Age, Marlon Brando, *The Wild One* and the rise of rebel teen cinema without a cause. Twelve or so years later the options for the touted fifth movie in the summer of 2020 are potentially delicious. Late 1960s America, Vietnam, Nixon, the summer of love, student protests, the Space Race, the rise of television, the Moon landings and the B-movie world of the living dead and body horror are rich pickings for our man Henry Jr. It is curious how a possible fifth Indiana Jones movie could now be nearer in era to the 1970s birth of the character than any 1930s B-movies that inspired it. How fitting would it be to see the veteran Indiana Jones wander idly past a young George Lucas and Francis Ford Coppola in early-1970s San Francisco? I would learn Mandarin twice over to be a flared Folsom Street extra in that one!

Raiders of the Lost Ark marks the moment when the two giants of the 1970s American blockbuster – Steven Allan Spielberg and George Walton Lucas Jr. – seal their personal friendship by finally marrying their movie worlds and influences together at the altar of Paramount and Britain's Elstree Studios. Starting off as a

Indiana Jones and the Temple of Doom plays at San Francisco's famed Castro Theatre.

mix of high adventure in the Americas and stoical academia in America, the ensuing quest throughout Nepal, Cairo and an island off the Aegean Sea is a tour de force of pacing, characterisation and dialogue. And it is the very antithesis of the two space operas Spielberg and Lucas would almost be defined by, had the Nazis not been digging in the wrong place. Whilst George Lucas is already two *Star Wars* films into changing science fiction cinema forever, here with Philip Kaufman (*The Right Stuff, Invasion of the Body Snatchers*) he crafts a story that is less attempting to beat Hollywood at its own game, more totally embracing the exhilarating freedoms of entertainment that old Hollywood once stood for. *Raiders* is also the first film for both Lucas and Spielberg where neither of them are the only big player on the bill. There is a sense of summer camp freedom to the Indy films, and maybe less to prove for Lucas and Spielberg. After this first instalment – or even before, off the back of Richard Amsel's artistry – it is *Indiana Jones* that becomes the marquee name. Not that this stops the images of Steven and George on-set in their desert flap hats and baseball caps becoming as key to the Indy series and 1980s cinema as any frame of Douglas Slocombe's cinematography. By the time the flyers for *The Last Crusade* filled our cinema lobbies, images of the bearded duo at work on location were as ubiquitous as the stills of Harrison Ford, Sean Connery and John Rhys Davies.

To pitch a mainstream Second World War movie in the early 1980s *and* so soon after the futuristic strides made by *Close Encounters*, *Star Wars* and *Superman* is a bold move. Too many kids of that era –myself included – were still trying the great escape from those black and white, wet Sunday afternoon combat flicks. The Nazis may have lost the war, but for the last forty years American and British cinema kept producing war films just in case. Yet, the 1970s and the new wave movement had now evolved the war movie into the more pertinent Vietnam War movie. Maybe that is one reason why *1941* landed so unfavourably in 1979. Its slapstick patriotism and comic-strip lunacy was too late for the baby boomers and too invasive for the generations still witnessing the cruel vagaries of Vietnam both at home and abroad. There is nothing Sunday afternoon matinee about *The Deer Hunter* (1978), *Coming Home* (1978) and *Apocalypse Now* (1979). Perhaps that is why the winds of success rather than war got under *Raiders'* wings. Despite the shared friendships and working associations of all involved, *Raiders of the Lost Ark* is the utter antithesis of *Apocalypse Now*.

In the wake of Spielberg bolstering the on-screen depictions of American family life, that 1970s domesticity of cinema has subsequently turned a corner. The dinner-table realism of *Jaws* and *Close Encounters* has now become the more marked disintegration of the family as seen in *Interiors* (1978), *Kramer Vs Kramer* (1979) and *Ordinary People* (1980). Spielberg may have one more definitive tale of contemporary family life in him with the following year's *E. T. the Extra-Terrestrial*, but unlike its sequels, *Raiders* has no family dynamic. *Indiana Jones and the Temple of Doom* has the loose beat of the dad, mum and child of Indy, Willie and Short Round. *The Last Crusade's* father and son pairing of Sean Connery and Harrison Ford is now one of the defining beats of Spielberg's career. And *The Kingdom of the Crystal Skull* upgrades Indy and Marion's winning dynamic from *Raiders* to now include their long lost son in the guise of Henry 'Mutt' Williams III (Shia LeBeouf) – who could well have been conceived on that 1936 tramp steamer before a U-boat put the *Das Boot* into his parents' romantic plans.

Instead, *Raiders of the Lost Ark* is about adventure and sheer romance. It is oddly the most romantic of all Spielberg's films. His future directorial work is of course not devoid of it, with strong couples and marriages evident in *Hook*, *Schindler's List*, *The Terminal*, *Munich* and *Lincoln*. *Always* is a nostalgic tale of devotion, but firmly pointed towards the aftermath of love. And Spielberg's subsequent *E. T. the Extra-Terrestrial* is one of the most beautiful love stories ever committed to cinema. But it is still *Raiders* that is about the couple. It is pure classical Hollywood cinema. Not that Karen Allen's Marion Ravenwood is the simpering heroine. Costume designer Deborah Nadoolman's ivory dresses and Cairo slacks may tie her to the railway tracks of 1930s Hollywood traditions, but Marion's resourceful pluck and defensive guile untie such clichés very quickly. When we first encounter Marion she is downing shots of hard liquor in her own Nepalese bar surrounded by mountain men, and eventually Gestapo agents trying to put the *Heil* in happy hour. Very soon she is demonstrating that backbone and nerve last seen with Margot Kidder's Lois Lane, who Marion would no doubt get on with like a Nepalese bar on fire. She certainly brings a bit of Metropolis walk and talk to the streets of Cairo, and gets herself into scrapes others must get her out of nearly as much as Margot Kidder in *Superman II*. 'Don't you touch me!' she snarls with menace as German soldiers steal her away, having earlier played villain René Belloq (Paul Freeman) like a Nazi harp. When she is not playing drinking games with Tibetans, Egyptians or Nazis, Marion is Indy's emotional anchor. She comforts when his body and ego have taken a bash, she is kind to the families of those few he trusts and her absence in subsequent films is marked. When Indy has lost the Ark to Washington bureaucracy at the close of the film, Marion's loving 'come on, buy you a drink' lift of his hat says everything. Again, it is Spielberg ending on a romantic note that only the Indiana Jones films seem to have. And don't think I didn't confuse my future husband by once doing exactly the same gesture on exactly the same steps in San Francisco's City Hall – which had doubled up for a DC government building during the *Raiders* shoot.

Talking of doubles, years later I met the stunt couple Vic Armstrong and Wendy Leech. The married pairing were Ford and Allen's respective stunt doubles and continued through the first three Indiana Jones films, with Armstrong doubling up as Indy and Leech covering various female leads – which they also did on many a 007, *Star Wars* and *Superman* movie. One of my earliest memories of being 'behind the scenes' on any movie was when I caught some *Making of Raiders of the Lost Ark* television special circa 1981. Armstrong and Leech seemed kindly perplexed at how someone would remember a documentary from at least thirty years back detailing the whole Well of the Souls set piece and their stunt-work involved. But I did. Leech taking direction from Steven Spielberg whilst doubling for Marion hanging off that Anubis statue was probably the first time I ever encountered the bearded director. Or even heard his name. Twenty-seven years later both Karen Allen and Marion return for 2008's *Indiana Jones and the Kingdom of the Crystal Skull*. Whilst Allen is on fine fettle, the passage of time has evolved the Marion character away from that quick-witted fortitude of *Raiders* into a slightly spaced-out campus wife. If anything is decided for the fifth Indy instalment, a grand scene with Mrs Ravenwood Jones getting back her drinking game skills is surely a must.

Raiders is a film that forges ahead through its visuals. Everything we need to be told about Marion is there when she lines up the empty shot glasses surrounded by the men and their bets against her. From the South American sun breaking through a silhouetted opening title jungle, a Pan Am Clipper and its red line flying over a map of the world to the shadow a hero and his fedora make at a Nepalese reunion via a thug's blood splattered across a Nazi Flying Wing aircraft, the healing properties of a loved one's kisses to a rat convulsing in the presence of evil and a crated relic disappearing into the anonymity of a government warehouse – *Raiders of the Lost Ark* is forever powered forward by Douglas Slocombe's strident cinematography and Spielberg's sense of story precision. A veteran of the key Ealing Studio comedies (*Kind Hearts and Coronets, The Man in the White Suit* and *The Lavender Hill Mob*), Slocombe had already proved his action acumen by lensing *The Blue Max* (1966), *The Italian Job* (1969) and *Rollerball* (1974). To mount this new and successful take on a very familiar genre, director Spielberg and cinematographer Slocombe strip away that black and white or even faux Technicolor war world for a sharply shot, sand-filled caper punctuated with the golds of Peruvian idols and the Ark of the Covenant, the whites of Cairo and the black and blood-red reminders of the Nazis and their ever-sinister branding. Slocombe's lone shot of Indy, Sallah (John Rhys-Davies) and their helpers digging for the Well of Souls against that burnt orange Egyptian sky is as good as any frame in *Lawrence of Arabia* (1962), *Barry Lyndon* (1975) or *Days of Heaven* (1978).

Some of the most famous, influential movie set pieces of all time are in *Raiders of the Lost Ark*. The truck chases, the market brawls, the marauding felons, the last-minute punch-ups with an impossible heavy, the assault course predicaments and puzzles – they are echoes of a lost age of cinema and matinee serials, but realised here with a new accuracy and physicality many a contemporary action movie has laboured to emulate since. Part of the film's precision ensures that these are not over-elaborate or elongated sequences. The famed boulder chase is comprised of barely eight separate cuts. The final opening of the Ark and the unleashing of literal hell is almost over before it begins. By the time of *Indiana Jones and the Kingdom of the Crystal Skull* (2008), it was notable how even a first-act visit to Marshall College could not just see Indy catching up with colleagues, story exposition and students secretly professing their love for teachers with hidden missives on their eyelids. Now Indy is required to lead an extracurricular action interlude involving son Mutt's Harley Davidson, Russian agents, anti-nuke students, heavy-handed Studebakers and all manner of orchestrated fun that the first *Raiders* film would have held back until the last act. Like the Bond series, the Indiana Jones adventures broke and rewrote the very rules they must now work with.

Spielberg has long mentioned his yearning to direct a James Bond movie. For whatever reasons, that delicious prospect has never happened. Yet. But the Bond tropes are all over *Raiders* and its sequels. Each of them always kicks off by tying up the action-skewed tail-ends of a previous quest. Indy's mission often emerges

After nineteen years the man in the hat is back cracking the whip at London's Odeon Leicester Square, May 2008.

from a first-act explanation of what is at stake from suited experts. Spielberg makes a globetrotting point of depicting Indiana arriving with a movie swagger not unlike those 'Bond Arriving' beats. Indy's romantic leads are mostly one-film wonders. Chief villain Belloq is a French, Nazi-funded playboy and adventurer straight from the villain box marked 'SPECTRE'. *Crystal Skull*'s villain Irina Spalko

(Cate Blanchett) is Rosa Klebb from 1963's *From Russia with Love*. Even Karen Allen's heroine Marion Ravenwood is echoing Roger Moore's Bond films of the 1980s and their predilection for female leads safeguarding their father's legacies.

Yet, unlike a Bond film, the chief antagonist of *Raiders* is firmly out of sight. Lucas and Kasdan's writing pitches an unseen Adolf Hitler who wants to locate and weaponise the Ark of the Covenant to use it against all humanity. The genius of *Raiders'* story, screenplay and final pay-off lies in how this whole caper will go down in history as a localised incident. In fact, it is not even going to go down in history at all. Washington doesn't want that. Faced with the very real, very un-fictional realities of the Third Reich, the global ramifications and fantastical fictions of *Close Encounters* and *E.T.* oddly become more impacting than those of *Raiders*. Maybe Spielberg didn't need or want to stoke the Nazi narrative – even in a comic-strip-skewed swashbuckler like *Raiders*. There are certainly two types of German Nazi in Spielberg's movie world. Those cartoon baddies in an *Indiana Jones* flick and those non-fiction fascists, monsters and dangerous cowards of *Schindler's List* (1993) and *Saving Private Ryan* (1998). Would Spielberg have made *Raiders of the Lost Ark* after *Schindler's List*? Maybe not. Would Spielberg have made *Schindler's List* if he had not tested his own mettle and attitude to on-screen Nazis in the Indy films? Possibly.

Like many a Spielberg title, the opening beats of *Raiders* are told without dialogue. And unlike many a Spielberg movie, it has a relatively small band of main characters. An off-story world of Indy's mentor and Marion's father Abner Ravenwood and of archaeological rival Forrestal sits on the peripheries of conversation. Just like screenwriter Lawrence Kasdan's previous work on *The Empire Strikes Back* a year before, here with George Lucas he assembles a small, ragtag band of heroes. As opposed to the organised might and affluence of Belloq, his Nazis and Gestapo henchmen, here Indy, Marion and Sallah (John Rhys Davies) are often on the run, improvising as they go with Nazi flags as rope, anti-swordfight pistol shoot-outs and canny kids creating well-timed distractions in busy market bars. The German high command sport immaculate suits, stock the best wines, own the newest film cameras and drive the best cars. Indy and his small gang of underdogs are less tailored, rely on the kindnesses of local elders, use scraps of paper and string to make calculations and blag passage at every turn off seadogs and in-laws that owe favours. Arch-villain Belloq is less the goose-stepping Nazi, and more the blazer-over-the-shoulder, Panama-hat-wearing French cad straight from a late-1970s Agatha Christie movie. The echoes of *The Empire Strikes Back* – the mighty resources of the Galactic Empire versus our heroes on the run in old ships from a previous time – is most prescient. And wouldn't Belloq have made a delicious Imperial officer?!

However, Indiana Jones is not Han Solo. Whilst his *Raiders* scrapes and skirmishes are familiar to *Star Wars* fans, Harrison Ford is playing a very different character here to the Kessel Run smuggler. With both roles taking it in turns alongside *Blade Runner's* Deckard to own the American box office over five successive summers, Ford carefully separates each without fanfare. Solo would never have a care for academia, but Indy places great reverence on others' findings and efforts. Solo blags his way around what he doesn't know. Indy thrives on filling those gaps of knowledge. Both are quick thinking, yet Indy is less sure of his luck and exploits than Solo whose cool complacency almost expects it. The second batch of Indiana Jones movies pitches the hero in a family dynamic with a father, son and eventually wife. Han Solo doesn't have any family other than Chewbacca until 2015's *The Force Awakens*. And that brief bout of parenthood hardly ends well. Admittedly, both Indy and Han love wearing the enemy's uniform to work an angle and have a useful rogue pal in every port or spaceport. Indy is certainly more of a leading man. Chivalrous, topless and more physical than Solo, Indy has to carry the film. Solo has only to carry the blaster. But when faced with Belloq in a Cairo cantina, Indy should really have shot first.

In no time at all, the *Raiders* imitators – just like those in the wake of *Jaws* and *Star Wars* – were lining up and jostling for movie theatre space like straw baskets in a Cairo market. As historical artefacts, the movie mimics ranged from the pleasant with good provenance – *Romancing the Stone* (1984), *High Road to China* (1984), *Jewel of the Nile* (1985) and of course Richard Donner's Indy for kids, *The Goonies* (1985) – to the downright fake movie replicas like *Sahara* (1983), *Biggles* (1986), *King Kong Lives* (1986), *King Solomon's Mines* (1985), *Baby: Secret of the Lost Legend* (1985) and *Allan Quatermain and the Lost City of Gold* (1987). British pop act Duran Duran soon got a crack of the Indy whip with their *Hungry Like the Wolf* (1982) pop video, James Bond and EON Productions fed a bit of that exotic *Raiders* swagger into 1983's *Octopussy*, and suddenly Robert Redford was playing the khaki-clad and lion-taming adventurer opposite Meryl Streep in Sydney Pollack's *Out of Africa* (1985).

Richard Amsel didn't just design artwork for a film's promotional campaign. In an immediately recognisable illustration, he captured the essence of a motion picture and left one image to serve as a blueprint for a series. From its matte painting effects, the use of light and brushstrokes of Douglas Slocombe's lens, the painterly detail and uncluttered simplicity of Norman Reynolds' production design, the storyboarding drive of Michael Kahn's editing, the palette of John Williams' romantically pounding score and the sense of story placement of a director at the peak of his game – *Raiders of the Lost Ark* is a living, breathing movie poster.

Whether the man in the hat was looming over the Odeon Leicester Square, the local monoplex that didn't have enough marquee letters to spell the whole title, or the bottom of a plastic

VHS tape carousel in a petrol station – Spielberg and Lucas raided the lost art of movie art, repurposed it, re-orchestrated it, and in making a movie about the might and power of culture and history created a modern movie artefact which achieved both.

Whilst I no longer have the Kimono dressing gown or the ability to perform 'Anything Goes' in perfect Mandarin, one particular relic of that time has lingered. When flying long-haul I am surely not the only one who selects the flight tracker to watch my plane flying over a global map in an Indiana Jones line to my destination. And as I slump into my seat and wonder if a dinghy would indeed be more useful than a parachute in an emergency, I scan the passengers hiding behind their newspapers and mentally pull down that thrift-store fedora which is now as lost to time as an Ark of the Covenant.

A day or so after this first all-important weekend of VHS liberation, marked by a Harrison Ford double-bill of *Star Wars* and *Raiders of the Lost Ark,* I was watching ITV when an exciting montage of their festive movies came on. It was the first year I was really anticipating all of the big Christmas TV movies. Now I could tape them, watch them, keep them and delete them. It was the starter pistol on many a wondrous Christmas where my movie fan traditions became as personally prevalent as turkey, chocolate, fairy lights, the smell of pine trees and enduring Midnight Mass. It would all start with a hopeful teaser glimpse from the main channels – yep, all four them – of their Christmas movie trailers. The very clipped tones of a very well-spoken English man would soon be mustering enthusiasm with boasts like, 'Come and join ITV this Christmas as we take you on an action-packed journey through space and beyond. Get aboard the Nostromo this coming

Sunday night,' he would continue, 'as Sigourney Weaver fights for her life in the horror classic, *Alien.*' This was the beginnings of what would become an annual bonanza of eagerly procuring the double-issue Christmas *Radio Times* and *TV Times* listings mags, circling the must-sees with a marker pen and maybe even organising a schedule of movies. Blank VHS tapes would be lined up and checked thrice and their running time carefully calculated to avoid any recording space crisis. Selection box chocolate would be mindfully allocated and prioritised according to the importance of a film – a *Superman* film was definitely worth a pack of Rolos, whilst a random *Herbie* film could get away with a mini Bounty. An inability to tape two films at one time meant tough *Sophie's Choice*-style decisions would have to be made, and God help any young sky kid whose parents would throw a festive spanner in the sky-watching works by proclaiming, 'We're going to your great-aunt's that afternoon so you'll have to tape it then, won't you?' It was like the Cannes Film Festival for sky kids. *Airplane, Ryan's Daughter, Gallipoli, The Incredible Shrinking Woman* and *Superman II* were all zealously touted. And what was ITV's big Christmas Day 1984 evening premiere? *Raiders of the Lost Ark.*

AT-AT ON A HOTH TIN ROOF

THE EMPIRE STRIKES BACK

1980. Flanked by security fighters, a Corellian freighter ship undulates through the terracotta skies of an alien dawn and heads towards a graceful city hanging in the clouds, unaware that the permission to land comes at a price.

○————————○

Christmas Day, 1984. It is a foolish man, woman or child who underestimates the impact of the Argos catalogue to British kids in the 1980s. It was like a printed, private and free copy of Amazon, or everything you could buy off the Internet – a thick and quarterly New Testament of consumerism, household appliances and futuristic white goods. Tents, sleeping bags, Breville sandwich makers, Rainbow Brite Starlite horses, topless men stood around demonstrating affordable dumb-bells with their permed wives in mirror-tiled bathrooms, *The A-Team* satchels and pencil cases, floral garden furniture flanked by beefy men from the suburbs in their tight

Crete holiday Speedos, Tomy Turnin' Turbo Dashboard playsets and one of my personal favourites that didn't involve tache-wearing hot dads – the faux leather cassette-tape storage solutions. If the straight boys had their mum's Littlewoods catalogue for tear-out-and-keep encounters with the lingerie ads and crop-top silk nightwear, then the girls and queer boys had the suburban machismo of the Argos catalogue. Just as we were the last generation to remember a time when we could not glimpse our upcoming movies online, so too did we only have shopping catalogues to see the flesh that would soon preoccupy our hormone-steered minds gripped by some Jedi mind trick called adolescence. Oh, and *Star Wars* figures. The Argos catalogue always had a new double spread demonstrating that season's *Star Wars* must-haves – usually photographed on plastic rock formations, white polystyrene worlds and sandpits.

The Argos catalogue would be a vital precursor to all Christmas and birthday toy thinking. Next to those first glimpses of the TV ads for the films the BBC and ITV were showing over the festive break, circling and cutting out the *Star Wars* pages in the Argos catalogue was a vital part of the lobbying campaign that would usually start at the end of October and not really end until your parents were spotted loading the car boot with rather large, square-shaped carrier bags with the Palitoy logo visible through them.

An October trip into Guildford had procured the Argos catalogue for the Autumn/Winter 1984 season. But even if you forgot, they were being bandied about like contraband, with family friends often asking, 'have you got yours yet – we picked up four and have a spare.' Us kids knew the drill. Take the Argos catalogue into the lounge on a Sunday afternoon, put on *The Box of Delights* and pore with excruciating detail over the dimensions, costs, what the 3¾-inch figure accessibility was like for each ship and how many AA batteries it required (too many and that was a separate gift request in itself). The ships were always the main deal. Argos had a

Home. My Luke Skywalker figure ponders 827 Folsom Street and the site in San Francisco of a former warehouse that helped propel George Lucas and eventually *Star Wars*.

The canary-yellow road lines of the Pacific Coast Highway stretching into the distance, just like the opening crawl of a *Star Wars* movie.

A Muppetational pose for a 6-year-old Jim Henson fan in sandals.

Atari's 1983 *Star Wars* arcade game on display at San Francisco's eclectic Musée Mécanique, Fisherman's Wharf.

Darth Vader and my Mark Hamill panache meets moisture-farmer chic wowing the nuns and visiting priests.

My founding family of *Star Wars* figures basking in the 1983 Crete sun before being lost forever. Many childhood memories died to bring us this photo.

Our local single-screen movie palace, the Regal Cinema, in 1991.

A Kryptonian lunch box from Aladdin Industries marking 1978's *Superman: The Movie* (The Verasphere Collection).

A superfly Superman fan recreates his own *Daily Planet* establishing shot.

The Man of Steel (Magnolias) promises you'll believe a kid can fly both then and now.

The very real *Daily Planet* lobby globe at the Daily News Building, East 42nd Street, New York.

(Opposite) There's something iconic in the neighbourhood – looking for work at Tribeca's real-life *Ghostbusters* firehouse.

Chewbacca watches over San Francisco's most diverse neighbourhood and a town where the vibrant excesses of sci-fi are celebrated.

Indiana Jones and the Temple of Doom plays at San Francisco's famed Castro Theatre.

With Lucasfilm Ltd in Presidio Park (right) and the production history of *Star Wars* dotted throughout the city, the histories of San Francisco and George Lucas often meet.

The famous Yoda statue welcomes staff and visitors to Lucasfilm Ltd's Presidio Park home, San Francisco.

Saturday morning *Mogwai* pencil art from this 9-year-old *Gremlins* fan.

X-Winging on a prayer during a British snow day.

Edgartown's present day 'Amity Walking Tour' advertises in the film's hardware store window.

'It's going in the pond!' Running in Chief Brody's footsteps on the American Legion Memorial Bridge, Edgartown.

Oak Bluffs locals remember the Kintner boy and why Martha's Vineyard is aligned to cinema forever more

'Figures Set' option which was a lucky dip of four random figures and the caveat of 'collection may vary from the photograph'. I had been burnt by that plastic lottery too many times before – which accounted for why I had a whole chorus line of Stormtroopers, a family of Biker Scouts, three Ewok Chief Chirpas, two Bespin Security Guards with that odd leg-bombing protruding thing going on and still no Princess Leia in her Bespin evening gown! Having duplicates of *Star Wars* toys was no bad thing. Divorcing parents meant both sides would furnish my Palitoy needs when they could, and surprise gifts would often be a Speeder Bike, Scout Walker or X-Wing I already had. It didn't bother me that my only-child status often pitched me as a plastic play advocate of both the Rebellion and the Empire. As much as I cherished flying two X-Wings down the stairs in tight formation, arranging them on my bedroom shelves with the appropriate figures or sides flanking like an Argos catalogue promotional photo was just as important. *Star Wars* toys were like childhood badges of honour – exhibiting them was as important as playing with them. As my Greek photo shoot proved – displaying my *Star Wars* toy world was less about the play and more about honouring the films at stake. That is partly why the *Star Wars* toy industry exploded like it did. It was owning a scaled-down piece of the film itself. We knew these films used models and replicas. The craft of the Lucasfilm artifice was key to the fascination, and these toys were officially sanctioned pieces of that which we could own. That is why many of us photographed our collections … on the balcony of Cretan villas whilst wearing traditional Greek hats.

However, the plastic trophy of many a sky kid's childhood was the fastest hunk of Corellian junk that is the Millennium Falcon. The physical embodiment of the matinee swagger of *Star Wars*, the Falcon was and still is a plump space nickel at odds with the jagged, industrialised angles of its enemies. It is a balletic station wagon, familiar to any kid of the 1970s and 1980s whose dad had an old banger of a car that needed a thump and a prayer to make the corners. The Palitoy version of it was also £22.95 at Argos. And after countless requests, pre-written Argos booking slips with the order number carefully written out and overly obvious displays of just how much playtime I get from my current *Star Wars* toys, the Christmas Jedi Knights looked down on me kindly. I wasn't going to tell them I hadn't yet seen *The Empire Strikes Back* and the one instalment in the saga where the Falcon is a support character on its own. *Episode V* was not going to air on British television for another four years. It had only just recently been released to the home video rental market in America.

But on 13 November 1984, the last *Star Wars* film I had yet to see was released on British home video for the first time. The original May 1980 UK theatrical release of *The Empire Strikes Back* had passed me by. I was only 2 years old when *A New Hope* finally made its way to British screens in late January 1978. I was somehow caught between a second new television broadcast wave of them and the initial June 1983 theatrical run of *Return of the Jedi*. The global scope and success of *A New Hope* was soon lent further momentum by various reissues and a staggered release pattern (familiar for the time) that did not see it fire those blasters at once – or even only once. To be fair, the sound design and visual effects of the original trilogy were always a work in progress for Lucas. The theatrical campaign of *A New Hope* was not over when 1980's *The Empire Strikes Back* emerged. It could well be one of those films where – initially at least – the sturdier sequel was dealt a blow because of the might and brilliance of its original. *The Empire Strikes Back* was once the quiet, brooding and almost Nordic cousin of the original *Star Wars* movies – a midwinter rarity that didn't seem to be everywhere in the way the hot desert and redwood forests of *A New Hope* and *Jedi* were. It was four years after its release that

I finally saw *The Empire Strikes Back*. The will of the Jedha ancestors had clearly been working against me when it came to watching the Cloud City-flanked skies of *The Empire Strikes Back*. My own attempts to experience Irvin Kershner's rich benchmark of late-1970s cinema had actually become somewhat of an original trilogy of misfires and nearly-rans itself.

First off, I had only half seen a curious and very abridged version of *The Empire Strikes Back* sometime during December 1981. Mum was teaching at a Catholic junior school and I had been invited to the annual St Edmund's kids Christmas party. The pinnacle of the wet, dark and freezing cold afternoon that had no doubt been kicked off with a lengthy Mass or blessing was a showing of the official Ken Films Super-8 version of *The Empire Strikes Back*. In two reels with an accompanying audio tape for sound, the somewhat condensed version was a hasty thirty-minute but officially-sold precis projected on a wall in-between the PE climbing apparatus and the dinner lady hatch. The local priests had clearly bought the reels accidentally as *Star Wars* films – abridged or otherwise – were not normal fare in our Catholic curriculum. Though we did later have a Geordie high school headmaster who once randomly used Yoda's inspirational lines to try to lend some intergalactic clout to his weekly address to the kids. It was the same week he was quite rowdy and angered that aerosol sniffing had been discovered behind the church, so suddenly the 'do or do not, there is no try' Jedi master rhetoric was somewhat of a mixed message when it came to a can of Lynx deodorant. Back in 1981, I was completely lost by the film as the grainy AT-ATs aimed their fire at the school hall's dining hatch with blasters that were never quite in sync with that cassette tape. When I needed to venture out to the freezing cold outside toilets in the playground, wondering who these angry Empire men in black caps actually were, I took a pee in the dark outhouse as flashes from the asteroid battle and the Bespin approach flickered into the rain through the school hall windows. In hindsight, it was about as salubrious as a night in Dagobah – except we had Angel Gabriels, Marys and Josephs hanging from the ceiling rather than Mynocks or Snowspeeders. I can still see Carrie Fisher's concerned face and those Bespin locks as the rain pelted down her face through the glass and I dodged the icy puddles in the dark, only to come back to a hall that was dripping in condensation and slight confusion at the abbreviated, out of sync heresy before us. Suffice to say I had not really seen *The Empire Strikes Back* at this screening.

I would have to make do with the second truncated version I had access to – my *The Empire Strikes Back* Read-Along cassette and book. Those kids' Read-Along twenty-four-page glossy square books and cassettes were as near to ownership of the movies we had in a burgeoning VHS terrain that we were not yet part of. 'You can read along with me in your book,' urged the stately American voiceover man instructing me to turn the page when I heard the faux R2-D2. 'See the pictures. Hear the record. Read the book.' With official sound effects and John Williams cues mixed rather gratingly with terrible replacement voices with B-movie enthusiasm and rather basic narratives, I still lapped up these threadbare attempts to get kids to read the films, as they often had 'Story, Music and Photos from the Original Motion Picture'. Apart from the Palitoy boxes, storybooks, figurine cardbacks or the odd *Look-In* magazine cutting we had zero access to any supporting imagery from these films. When these cassette books were the lucky dip gift surprise at our church Christmas parties, I was one of the few who was not left disappointed.

The third in my trinity of *The Empire Strikes Back* setbacks was perhaps the toughest. During the late summer of 1983, and on the tailwind of *Return of the Jedi*, an official *Star Wars* trilogy triple-bill was doing the cinema rounds and the local paper announced it was coming to our Odeon in Guildford. At last – this *Star Wars* kid was within a Tauntaun's breath of a rousing send Hoth like no other! I didn't need *The Force Awakens* to tell me that the saga didn't end when the Ewoks held their open mic night for all deceased Jedi. *The Empire Strikes Back* was the finale I had been waiting for. No more would I be the sky kid who had to lie in the playground about seeing the AT-ATs getting destroyed by the Rebel Alliance. No more would I dismiss the confident claims that Darth Vader was Luke Skywalker's father as some personal slights against my own familial traumas. No more would I be denied the sight of the real Princess Leia Organa in her Bespin finery.

I had it planned down to the wire. My stepdad was going to accompany me with plenty of sandwiches, Dr Pepper and my own weight in Opal Fruits. My post-Crete replacement Han Solo figure in his navy-blue Hoth parka was on standby and the Saturday was looming fast. Any excuse to see *Return of the Jedi* again on the big screen was a bonus, and the chance to properly and finally see *The Empire Strikes Back* despite the 'Han Solo in carbonite' spoiler from seeing *Jedi* first was just too much. So to get grounded by the galactic parental senate that was my mum's last word was somewhat of a crushing defeat. I cannot recall the incident or sequence of events for sure, but it may well have involved a C-3PO hissy fit about not going to Mass, not getting any pocket money that week or using a swear word because of a combination of the first two examples. The maternal empire had really struck back and there was no new hope in hell this mop-haired Jedi was returning to the Guildford Odeon any time soon. There were tears, tantrums and at least one slamming of my bedroom door per hour until hostilities had faded. This was even worse than losing all my *Star Wars* figures and a Snoopy backpack to an unlicensed Luton cabbie who would never appreciate Princess Leia in her Bespin best. Having already seen *Jedi* twice at the pictures didn't help my cause either. Yet again, *The Empire Strikes Back* evaded my cinematic skies. Help me, Christmas 1984 – you're my only hope …

My Santa list for that year was a curious one. A Lego Robot Command Centre, a copy of John Masefield's *The Box of Delights*, a PVC caravan play tent with tubular frame, the requisite *Blue Peter Annual*, a *Look-In TV Annual*, Roland Rat's *The Cassette of the Album*, a selection box, some blank BASF VHS tapes and a glistening red Sony Walkman WM-22. And a plastic Corellian YT-1300 light freighter with batteries.

When I entered the lounge in the early hours of the morning of Christmas Day 1984 like a disguised Princess Leia creeping into Jabba's Palace (minus the stupidly placed wind chimes) and the smells of new PVC and our real pine tree mixed with the warm ashes in our fireplace filled the air, I beheld that most glorious of sights. Yes – it was a PVC cartoon caravan containing a Millennium Falcon placed just a bit too near the heat of an unattended open fire. Carefully sliding the PVC door of the beige cartoon caravan aside, I crawled into my secret plastic den, opened my selection box, started on a Marathon bar and reached for a sizeable box with Palitoy and *Return of the Jedi* visible through the thin snowman wrapping paper.

Having peeled off the wrapping paper, I laid the box safely on the floor before carefully taking a pair of scissors to the Sellotaped packaging to prise it open, without tearing a sizeable Millennium Falcon ® Vehicle box that had a future life of its own as a diorama on my bedroom shelves. Despite the Cloud City recreation from *The Empire Strikes Back*, the box was a gift in itself with its *Jedi* logo, glossy photographs of Kenner kids and that matinee movie merchandise promise of a 'Swivelling Radar Dish', a front cockpit that would hold two action figures, a Space Chess table, a Lightsaber practice room, landing gears that would fold and lock into place, secret compartments, a rotating laser gun *and* a real 'Battle Alarm

Sound'! This packaging was almost as special as the vessels inside and would be kept for as long as it would endure, even if the boxes often intriguingly featured the EU-savvy French translations of *Le Retour du Jedi*. Of course, the action figures were 'not included'. But suddenly my Han Solo and Chewbacca figures had a home of their own and were no longer required to illegally squat in a X-Wing neither of them clearly had any experience piloting. There was a sticker sheet too – full of sticky circular flourishes one must add to the Falcon's interiors, panels, that ion engine rear burning strip and a Lightsaber practice stick, tiny plastic ball and string that was all lost way before Mum put the turkey in the oven.

That fastest plastic hunk of junk in the galaxy was not even the main prize that Christmas morning. Aside from that PVC caravan-shaped kids' tent that was going to revolutionise my sleepover ambitions, 25 December 1984 had a greater glory. It was 124 minutes long, had all its original dialogue, there was no ninety minutes left on the school hall floor, no cancelled screenings due to unruly behaviour, and Princess Leia was at long last in that Bespin robe for real. I was *finally* going to watch *The Empire Strikes Back* in its entirety. It was not on television nor had we hired a 35mm copy exclusively from Lucasfilm HQ for the season. It had been released on home video rental the month before in both the UK and the US. And after some fortuitous desperation and planning on my part, Mum had reserved the only copy from the Gaston Gate Garage for the season. Breaking free from *One of Our Dinosaurs is Missing* on TV, Mum drove me to the garage in the early evening of Christmas Eve to pick up a new *Star Wars* film that was our property for three days. Part of my design realised that the garage was closed for Christmas Day and Boxing Day. For the price of one day's rental I could bask in an *Episode V* glory all of my own for three whole nights! Once the fear that the previous renter may not have returned the bulky black VHS box in time for the holiday closure had thankfully vanished, I stepped into the Gaston Gate movie reserve and nervously scanned the plastic shelves and carousels for that *The Empire Strikes Back* logo and icy *Gone with the Wind*-style poster design that always promised so much to this *Empire* virgin. It wasn't there. But thank Ben Kenobi. It had been kept for safety in the booth always manned by the owners' cigarette-ash dropping mother. And emerging from the smoke of that video booth like Darth Vader emerging through the carbonite mist, and with a quick scan and touch of that deliciously slanted *Empire* logo on the VHS cassette itself, I took hold of that black-boxed splendour. I could have so easily have taken it home and watched it there and then. But time and Midnight Mass did not allow it. I had waited four and a half years for this moment. Another day wouldn't hurt. With no one yet up on Christmas morning and my freshly minted Falcon taking pride of place on the hearth rug, I shut the curtains, turned off the lamps, switched on the tree lights and carefully fed *The Empire Strikes Back* into our front-loading Hitachi VT-33A.

As soon as those Viper probes drop from a Star Destroyer like Imperial pollen, *The Empire Strikes Back* and its Rebel heroes are on the run. With the collective might of the Empire's fleet dancing above them like a ballet of armageddon, director Irvin Kershner's defining space adventure plays out like a nervous road movie without any roads. Like any road movie, every rest stop has its dramas and every wrong turn its predicaments. The Rebels are only just catching breath on their icy Hoth outpost when *Episode V* starts and barely catch up until halfway through *Return of the Jedi*'s next episode. Nothing is quite ready. Nothing quite works. 'We're having some trouble adapting them to the cold,' remarks a deck officer about the Snowspeeders before Han Solo is soon haphazardly swinging about a lightsaber he has never used before to gut a Tauntaun snow creature for warmth. Because of this improvisation, the swashbuckling drive of *The Empire Strikes Back* becomes ever princely in its heroism and wholly noble in its emotions. These are beats of resistance and makeshift invention that gloriously find their way into *Rogue One: A Star Wars Story* thirty-six years later. Scaling back the sci-fi pomp and fantasy trappings of *A New Hope* is a brave move on the part of George Lucas, director Irvin Kershner and writers Lawrence Kasdan (*Raiders of the Lost Ark*, *The Force Awakens*) and Leigh Brackett (*The Big Sleep*). Instead of tripling the spectacle and widening the palette of characters as expected after the biggest box office hit of all time, *Empire* scales itself back. It becomes the opposite of what the hurried *Star Wars* imitators are labouring naively to cash in on. Its early genius is how it wrong-foots *A New Hope*'s critics, copycats, and indeed fans. Whilst the famed attack on Hoth is expansive, ambitious and heroically achieved, all that is dramatically at stake is the Rebels getting to the emergency exits to escape. No tactics of war. No destruction of a mega weapon. It becomes just as narratively dicey as any planet-killer of a Death Star being readied in *The Force Awakens* or *Rogue One*. The temptation on the part of Lucas to go wider, bigger and more expensive is avoided like the Millennium Falcon shuns asteroids. The Norway-as-Hoth overture aside, the film has a great sense of containment, of being inside and letting the character dynamics and emotions widen the story rather than a constant flow of jaw-dropping visuals. There are no Greek-God-style Jedi temples of awe here. The HQ of a Jedi legend is a muddy swamp with a basic pan on the stove. We don't need another homage to Mos Eisley's hive of scum and villainy when the sight of a ragtag band of unsavoury alien bounty hunters aboard a pristine Star Destroyer is menacing enough. Unlike that *Star Wars* trope of gear-changing drama taking place on perilous Imperial gantries and metallic chasms aboard the Death

Star – admittedly *Empire* both writes and reinforces the book on that one – that all-important beat of Darth Vader finally being in the same room as Han Solo, Princess Leia, Boba Fett, Lando Calrissian and Chewbacca is here realised in a narrow, unimportant dining room. And just as Han's rather awkward *Meet the Parents* supper gets interesting, with Vader's cold buffet matching his guests' reluctance, the doors close. It is not just the Brodys, Nearys, Freelings and Kramers who settle things over the dinner table.

When American new wave cinema evolved and some of its Californian-based indie flagbearers fired the starting pistol on the modern blockbuster, some suggested that evolution saw the pared-down intimacy of titles like *American Graffiti*, *Klute*, *The Last Detail*, *The Last Picture Show* and *The Sugarland Express* sidetracked for the 16:9 might of *Star Wars* and *Close Encounters of the Third Kind*. With its small band of likeable rogues penned into one vehicle, bickering on the bench seat about the right course of action, rubbing the enemy's noses in it, cruising the back roads to avoid the authorities and a small, confined timescale of story – *The Empire Strikes Back* is actually more *Sugarland* and *Graffiti* than not. The whole of *The Empire Strikes Back* is told in the front seats of cockpits and stolen conversations in corridors. After the opening Hoth act, very little of the film even takes place on land. Unlike *A New Hope* and the prequels, there is no sense of home for any of the characters. Everyone is on the run. It almost plays out like a lost weekend for the Rebels. With their Death Star administrative hub destroyed in the previous film, Vader and his Imperial Officers are resigned to posturing aboard anchorless Star Destroyers. Being rudderless and homeless again becomes a later motif of *The Last Jedi* (2017) when the Resistance run out of both road, soldiers and fuel as the First Order's Dreadnought looms over the starry horizon like the truck in *Duel*. Instead of ranks of faceless Stormtroopers and officers intimating the magnitude of the Empire, in *The Empire Strikes Back*

The Port of Oakland container cranes and how (untrue) local myths suggest they inspired the AT-ATs of *The Empire Strikes Back*.

we see the personalities and weaknesses of individual commanders. There is the naivety of the short-lived Admiral Ozzel (Michael Sheard), the bullish and determined General Veers (Julian Glover) and the brilliantly patient resolve of Admiral Piett (Kenneth Holley) – the unspoken gentleman of the Empire's senior leadership team.

There is little excess in *The Empire Strikes Back*. For all its sci-fi scope and dramatic grandeur, it is ultimately a very intimate movie. The end result is a sharp, open-ended quest with airtight dialogue and a conquering sense of purpose. Just like *Indiana Jones and the Temple of Doom* (1984), Harrison Ford is easily at his most handsome, buoyant and narratively crucial in this second outing.

Han is forever crashing about like a nautical seadog with his crazed wrangling of the stubborn Falcon and a constant loss of face at its temperamental tricks. The glorious 'make do and mend' philosophy of *The Empire Strikes Back* is one of its glories. It is an eleventh-hour sense of character resourcefulness that the prequels missed, but which newcomers to the saga *The Force Awakens*, *Rogue One* and *The Last Jedi* realise is key to letting new audiences in. When Cassian Andor (Diego Luna), Jyn Erso (Felicity Jones) and K-2SO (Alan Tudyk) infiltrate Scarif's Citadel Tower disguised as an Imperial Commander and Stormtrooper pilot, it is not just a knowing nod to Han and Luke doing similar with Chewbacca on the Death Star in *A New Hope*. It is remembering how the inventiveness of characters in a *Star Wars* film is a vital trope which *Empire* set in carbonite. It is a heroism held together with duct tape, a wrench and a prayer – an endearing sense of pluck that is the spine of *The Empire Strikes Back* and why many non-*Star Wars* fans found *Rogue One* so revitalising and involving. It is the saga's Robin Hood sense of swagger and adventure. It is a team-effort grammar that director Rian Johnson uses to punctuate *The Last Jedi* and the Resistance's ever-shrinking resources and options. It is why that cosmic station wagon that is the Millennium Falcon becomes a character in itself in *Episode V*. It creaks and moans and buckles, but holds a valiant resilience until the final reel where the sight of it going after a lost Han Solo almost restores more hope than those piloting it. By the time of *The Last Jedi*, the Falcon is a cult foe to Kylo Ren as he relishes the last act gunfire pointed its way – 'Ah, they hate that ship!'. That nothing matches within the Rebellion of the 1980s – its disparate ships, bunkers and impromptu transporters – is always a spur of the moment contrast to the organised, methodical might of the Galactic Empire. And all the time this is mirroring the creative pluck of Lucasfilm and effects conjurers ILM – holed up in their San Francisco studios and

The real Rebel base – the counterpulse city and home of Lucasfilm, Star Wars, ILM and *Watching Skies* history.

warehouses and X-Winging it as they go along with an improvised Rebel zeal and a practical toil yielding great practical results.

For a *Star Wars* movie, *Episode V* is a deceptively grisly film. From a Hoth Wampa's vicious claws to Solo slicing open the intestines of a Tauntaun to the first peek at Vader's mutilated scalp, the suction scares of a Mynock bat and Luke Skywalker having his father slice off his hand – *Empire* is definitely a product of that turn of the decade sci-fi marked by *Alien*, *Altered States* and *The Thing*. The trippy cave skirmish between Luke and a version of Vader – and the first time in the saga we see young Skywalker in a saber duel – is intentionally vague and hallucinatory. It's a non-linear moment in a very linear set of films (cue *The Last Jedi*'s rather trippy 1970s rock video look into Rey's mind and motivations). And whilst the interplay on Cloud City between a caring Chewbacca nursing a dismembered C-3PO is a much-needed tender beat, the scene of the Wookiee trying to revive the damaged, confused tin butler always packs a sadness for this sky kid. *Empire* is a film that plays with its shadows – all shot by David Cronenberg's favoured cinematographer, Peter Suschitsky. In direct contrast to the rich, golden and arid hues of *A New Hope* and *Return of the Jedi*, the photography on *Empire* is bound to a stark, foggy and hopeless hue – a very European palette devoid of sun, space and even colour. The Dagobah scenes are wilfully grim and almost black and white as Star Destroyers gather like ominous storm clouds, the skies of *Episode V* are repeatedly flanked with snow, fog and rain. Norman Reynolds' production design of the Vader and Luke duel is almost impressionistic in its abstract shapes, bursts of vapour and false perspectives echoing the rooftops and angular shadows of *The Cabinet of Dr Caligari* (1920). The blue and the neon orange of Cloud City's industrial underbelly compliment the blue and red of the battling lightsabers and it is as if the whole swordfight is unfurling on the underside of the mothership from *Close Encounters of the Third Kind*.

Unlike every other *Star Wars* episode and spin-off yarn to date, nothing is destroyed at the end of *The Empire Strikes Back*. It is almost a *Star Wars* movie in reverse – with the Hoth opener as good as any climax. Instead, Lawrence Kasdan, Irvin Kershner and George Lucas opt for the devastation of everything Luke Skywalker has ever known. Movie history continues to circle it as one of the biggest twists of cinema, but those six words – 'No Luke, I am your father' – also indefinitely changed the saga itself. It was suddenly also about dynasties and families rather than just a 'crazy old wizard', goose-stepping troopers and some rusting robots. In an era of the big-dollar American soap operas, the Skywalkers are now playing the Ewings at their own game. But it is less 'who shot J. R. Ewing?', more 'who shot first?' In a movie era of absent fathers – *The Sugarland Express, Jaws, Close Encounters, Superman, Star Trek II: The Wrath of Khan, E. T. the Extra-Terrestrial* – *The Empire Strikes Back* very quickly becomes the overnight daddy of daddy-issue films. Although – is the narrative shockwave of that revelation still not as solemn a conclusion as the suspension in carbonite and abduction of Han Solo? There is many a sky kid and now adult that learnt a cruel lesson in loss and separation from that particular rug-pull from writers Kasdan and Lucas.

Whilst the spine of this film is a downbeat, intergalactic Grimm fairy tale about the dangers of wandering too far into the woods, it is countered by a rich, glorious and wholly noble score from John Williams. It is easily his most accomplished *Star Wars* work with a collection of motifs and cues that define the sound of the saga for evermore. 'The Asteroid Field', 'Yoda's Theme', 'Yoda and the Force', 'Han and Leia', 'The City in the Clouds', 'The Finale' and of course 'The Imperial March' are all now standards of movie composition beyond the *Star Wars* canon. The Oscar-nominated score for *The Empire Strikes Back* is a buccaneer opera of gallant strings and heroic horns. When the Falcon cascades through an asteroid field, when a humble flotilla of Snowspeeders searches the snow sheets for a missing Luke and Han, when a Jedi master lifts an X-Wing out of a swamp, when Leia, Chewbacca and the androids finally flee Cloud City in a hail of blasters, when the Falcon finally achieves the jump to lightspeed as everyone's energy is spent – these are all afforded majestic, career-defining cues by John Williams. Just as the composer later achieves with *E. T. the Extra-Terrestrial*, the trust and dignity of Yoda is especially realised through Williams' strings and that stirring leitmotif. With a diminutive playful puppet performed by *The Muppets'* Frank Oz, it is down to Williams to portray the transcendent might of Yoda and the Force. We do not

The famous Yoda statue welcomes staff and visitors to Lucasfilm Ltd's Presidio Park home.

fully know we can trust this 900-year-old pallid green Jedi goblin with the voice of Fozzie Bear until John Williams tells us via his comic horns and eventual wall of noble strings that – like Luke pondering the twin moons of Tatooine in *A New Hope* – is key to the sanctity and valour of these films.

For a film that is ostensibly about the splintering of a resistance without narrative closure, it is Williams that voices those senses of victory and defeat that play with the themes of garrisons and friendships, heroes and fortitude. Just as the Rebel forces are bedecked in ivories and whites, so too are their musical refrains full of gallant strings and impish brass as the stomping percussion of the AT-ATs crunches heavily through the visuals. It is not as blatantly signposted 'Second World War' as Williams' rousing work on *1941* (1979), but that sense of air force strings and twisting aviators is gloriously realised in *Empire*. In a single roll of the Millennium Falcon, Williams' musical urgency switches to a romanticism and wartime adventure that keeps *Episode V* soaring and undulating as one of the great scores of the *Watching Skies* era. The arrival of the Falcon at the almost heavenly, sun-flecked Cloud City is met with a choir, and the closing finale aboard the Rebel medical convoy is an emotional cacophony of harps and romantic strings sliced apart by the *Star Wars* theme and one of George Lucas's 'Directed by' iris outs which are as old as cinema itself.

The Empire Strikes Back created the idea of the movie trilogy as both a creative enterprise and a monetary behemoth. Countless series and movie serials were often the mainstay of the early decades of cinema. George Lucas famously cites Universal Pictures' 1940s serial *Flash Gordon* as one of his influences for *Star Wars*. By 1980 and *The Empire Strikes Back*, movie trilogies were nothing new to cinema. Satyajit Ray wrote and directed the *Apu* trilogy in the 1950s, Ingmar Bergman completed his *Faith* trilogy in the early 1960s (starring *The Force Awakens'* very own Max von Sydow), Hammer Films had *Quatermass* and Sergio Leone produced his *Dollars* trilogy. But at the point of 1977 and *Star Wars*, movie trilogies were new to big box office and the returning dollars of younger audiences. *The Bad News Bears*, *A Man Called Horse* and *The Adventures of a Plumber* trilogies were hardly inspiring kids' birthday parties and duvet sets across the world. Suddenly that middle note could become the defining chapter. Without *A New Hope*'s prologue and *Return of the Jedi*'s epilogue, *The Empire Strikes Back* can just get on with telling the story in-between without an introduction or closure. The narrative core and drives of the entire original *Star Wars* trilogy are all there in *The Empire Strikes Back*. The real tutelage and scope of the Force, the farm boy who becomes a man, the romance between Han and Leia, the Rebel Alliance on the back foot, the muddy dignity of Yoda, the caped swagger of Lando Calrissian, the vices and sub-industries of bounty hunters and space scoundrels, the cool intrigue of Boba Fett, John Williams' 'Imperial March' and 'The Force' leitmotifs, the real pull of the Emperor, a Millennium Falcon and an X-Wing as support characters, the 'make do and mend' philosophy and the vital father and son tragedy that defines the story pulse of *Star Wars* for evermore. They all come to a triumphant apex in *The Empire Strikes Back* like no other *Star Wars* film before or since.

Close Encounters of the Third Kind and *E.T. the Extra-Terrestrial* also both culminate on the mournful beat of a spaceship departing to one of John Williams' great finale cues. The brilliance of *Empire* lies too in its franchise trust that this is now the unavoidable second act of three. And very soon the blunt climax of *Empire* was a landmark motif soon echoed in other films – most notably *Rogue One* and *The Last Jedi*, whose directors are clearly well-versed in the melancholic curtain-down glories of *Star Wars '80*. Despite being a sequel to a heavily cerebral original film, *Star Trek II: The Wrath of Khan* (1982) was the first movie of one of the era's most glorious swashbuckling threesomes, later completed by *Star Trek III: The Search for Spock* (1983) and *Star Trek IV: The Voyage Home* (1986). It is a trilogy so clearly influenced by the tonal triumphs of *The Empire Strikes Back* it closes its first two instalments on a downer aboard a ship manned by a crew licking their wounds and mourning their fallen friend, and the third act ends with the protagonist getting demoted. Nothing was more successfully uplifting in the early 1980s than downbeat sci-fi. Step forward *Blade Runner*, *Tron* and *The Thing*. If the 1977 successes of *Star Wars* inadvertently forced the hand of Paramount Pictures to finally greenlight what became *Star Trek: The Motion Picture* (1979), it was the story impact of *The Empire Strikes Back* which arguably re-pointed it towards that triumvirate of *Khan*, *The Search for Spock*, *The Voyage Home* and the subsequent 1987 appearance of television show *Star Trek: The Next Generation*.

Yet, whereas the *Genesis* trilogy of the *Star Trek* movies each ended with a certain studio uncertainty about returning cast members and profits, *The Empire Strikes Back* is a marvel of movie confidence. Its quiet assurance that it can conclude on a melancholy beat is now a blockbuster trilogy mainstay. Regardless of their source material, just look at the middle movies – *Mad Max 2: The Road Warrior* (1981), *The Two Towers* (2002), *X2* (2003), *The Dark Knight* (2008) and *The Last Jedi* (2017). All are darker-hued tales which close on a downbeat note because *The Empire Strikes Back* proved you could. Whichever way you read it, *A New Hope*'s beauty lies in that it doesn't know if its seemingly random posturing as an *Episode IV* is going to be the first or last in George Lucas's proposed interplanetary saga. The tag was only added to the 1977 original by the time of a 1981 re-release because of the 1980 momentum of *Empire* as a next chapter. Lucas may have envisioned a string of Skywalker space operas from the early San Francisco days onwards, but until those audiences, critics, kids and the box office marched to his Imperial drum, that was far from assured.

Parting company with *The Empire Strikes Back* was bittersweet. After three days' grace, I was thrown back into a galaxy where we couldn't own our sky watching classics as hoped. Not yet, anyway. Such were the vagaries of a time where a private copy of *The Empire Strikes Back* would cost about £80 and the video store had its opening hour restrictions.

There was one saving grace, however. ITV must have known I would be in Jedi cold turkey as we ate our own cold turkey, because a day or so later a great hour-long documentary look at the trilogy satiated my pangs. *From Star Wars to Jedi: The Making of a Saga* was a behind-the-scenes, clips-heavy look at the production of *Episode VI* and its siblings. This was one Christmas 1984 programme I would not record over. This was a keeper. This got the special screwdriver out of the garage to remove the tab and preserve the tape's contents for the remainder of time itself. And very soon – and maybe once a day – I would put on that VHS tape with its carefully written label, 'The Making of STAR WARS.' A well-written label was unspoken VHS code for, 'This is important and must be kept safe and untouched.' And every morning for the remainder of the Christmas holidays I would pore over the production footage of *Jedi*'s sizeable skiff set in Arizona, the puppet work and links to Jim Henson, the Elstree Studios creature shop and the ornate model work of those California FX dudes with their messy beards, skinny jeans and sun-drenched enthusiasm. *The Making of a Saga* was gold to a wannabe Henson puppeteer like myself. I was fascinated that Jabba the Hutt's smoking pipe was realised by a real puppeteer off-camera blowing cigar smoke down a pipe and the diminutive Mike Edmonds was charged solely with being the sluggish gangster's tail. Years later, I had one of those on-set catering bus lunches with Edmonds, who was an extra in a comedy show I was working on at the time. I knew immediately what his *Star Wars* links were. 'You were Jabba the Hutt's tail?' I asked over a plate of catering-bus couscous and salad.

A couple of days later, and just before the new year, ITV showed *Star Wars* again on the last Sunday afternoon of 1984. Finally, I was able to meticulously tape it on one of my new VHS tapes and use those little sticky alphabet letters to spell out 'STAR WAR5' alongside the very broken tab. There were never enough 'S' letters, so an improvised '5' would often suffice. *Raiders of the Lost Ark, The Empire Strikes Back* and *A New Hope* … it was not a bad first couple of weeks for our first video recorder.

Four years later, the Christmas Day 1988 ITV broadcast of *The Empire Strikes Back* was the first time it was shown on British television. It was also the first time I was able to video record and own that film. But a combination of the worst flu I have ever encountered and the Lockerbie tragedy unfurling on the radio as I couldn't sleep meant Christmas 1988 was somewhat of a wipeout. Fortunately, I had replaced the PVC play caravan on my Christmas list for CBS/Fox's *Star Wars* trilogy and their glittering un-remastered versions of the saga with their glorious mono sound, a 4:3 picture ratio and none of those annoying, new-fangled extras and deleted scenes. But my revived *Star Wars* ownership fortunes came at a price and I was beginning to think *The Empire Strikes Back* was a curse. Four years into its life and our faithful Hitachi video player experienced its first full-on R2-esque technical meltdown. And it chose to do so on Christmas Eve as the festive bonanza of highly tape-able network movie premieres, behind the scenes documentaries, cinema specials and unseen classics commenced. I carried that video recorder into the TV repair shop like an injured puppy going to the vets. It is not impossible that I turned to the assistant working there – someone I used to bike around with in my *Red Hand Gang* days – and quietly implore *'you will look after him, won't you. We just can't lose him now. Not like this'*. And as he took Old Hitachi off me with perhaps less care than I handed it over with, I watched as that little rectangular grey machine of movie devotion had its wires wrapped around it with no grace and a scribbled house address and phone number plastered haphazardly onto its backside. I think I phoned up every morning to see if it had made it through the night and had been fixed. It wasn't yet. I had to wait until after Christmas and after all those broadcast movie treats had passed me by. To say I was in flu-ridden mourning was an understatement. I refused visitors, got out of Midnight Mass for the first time ever and the glossy movie images in the intermittently circled Christmas edition of the *TV Times* were like ice cold daggers. For four years I had been able to tape, keep and rent a wealth of movies. But now I was back to square one at the worst time of year. Kind neighbours rallied around with offers of using their video recorders at any time. But it was painfully apparent that their idea of *taping* a film meant not taking out the adverts, putting a tape in at any time and adding unfathomable bon mots as, 'Well, we can certainly try to record the best of it for you.' Cue the shield doors being closed on me as I am left freezing cold and alone in the movie-less badlands of Christmas 1988.

DANTE'S MOVIE INFERNO

GREMLINS

1984. As monstrous anarchy unwraps Christmas early for a small American town, a miserable local is catapulted somewhat triumphantly from her stairlift into the snow-heavy night skies.

○————————○

1985. *Cute. Clever. Mischievous. Intelligent. Dangerous.* That was not only the foreboding tagline on John Alvin's denim-clad teaser poster for *Gremlins*, but it was also partially what this 9-year-old thought of the British Board of Film Classification's decision to slap a '15' rating on Steven Spielberg's Christmas caper of 1984. Director Joe Dante's slapstick ode to cinema and small-town Americana was first released in Britain on 7 December 1984. It shared that weekend's theatres with its equally mock-scary partner, *Ghostbusters*. But unlike Ivan Reitman's comedy hit, *Gremlins* was denied to us British kids. We were certainly hungry for it. But the British Board of Film Classification had other plans – and wouldn't feed our appetites after or before midnight, kept the projector lights very much on and no doubt demanded we take constant baths to wash our video-nasty-addled souls. I am sure the BBFC had its reasons. There was certainly a government panic about video nasties, piracy, porn and kids getting their movie-crazed hands on material that was not deemed as wholly appropriate – around the same time in British history that smoking was still very much permitted in all cinemas, seat belts in the back of cars were not yet law, we were all actively encouraged to attend kids' TV show recordings at BBC Television Centre and the Cold War threat of nuclear war was somewhat raging on. The resulting headlines and scaremongering over summer 1984's *Indiana Jones and the Temple of Doom* hadn't helped either. Maybe the BBFC had to be seen to be making a stance. The ratings system in America certainly got addressed with the introduction of the PG-13 rating to try to keep those marauding gremlins at bay in any future youth cinema of the mid-1980s. Ultimately, alas, the only real horror the kids were haunted by was being denied access to a new Steven Spielberg-produced movie by a censor turning a bit Mrs Deagle as the holidays approached.

With *Return of the Jedi*, Ewoks and Rancor Monsters still on our minds via VHS, the fantasy storytelling and creatures of *The NeverEnding Story* (1984), the matinee scares of *Ghostbusters* and the very phrase 'Steven Spielberg presents' all filling our cinematic horizons of late, *Gremlins* was eagerly awaited to say the least. There was already great cultural and cinematic importance to anything Steven Spielberg put his name to. The collectable sticker producers Panini brought out the requisite *Gremlins* album, and I would try to ensure every drive to Wednesday night Cubs would involve a detour to the only newsagent in our village that was stocking the 10p sticker packs. But censorship has a price. And mine was that a lot of folk at school were not allowed the 20p-priced *Gremlins* sticker album because of its alleged slasher relentlessness and organ-eating horrors. Having few school pals to exchange those Panini swaps with was pretty much sticker album death – especially if you had hopes of completing the 'Birth of the Gremlins' double-page spread and only had half a Judge Reinhold so far in your character portraits. Any decent sticker cards of the mohawked scoundrel Stripe were like gold dust, and I never completed Gizmo sat in his Barbie car.

For a film that was theatrically not letting us very-under-15-year-olds feed after midnight, there was a curious volume of *Gremlins* merchandise trying to fill the gaps in the toy shelves slowly vacated by *Star Wars* movies. There was a bendable Stripe figure I so desperately wanted, likewise one of the wind-up cars and Mogwai. There were hand puppets, jigsaw puzzles, photobooks, transfers, lunch boxes and of course the mandatory and scarily abridged Read-Along book and cassette tape. But my real goal was one of the plush Gizmos. I attempted quite a few drafts of various Mogwai coloured pencil art and got quite fond of the comic book reading brown and white mini-Yoda. It was not until my 30s that I was finally given one and jokingly sat him near our bathroom sink. It was about eleven seconds before I genuinely corrected myself and removed Gizmo just in case. I did, however, snap up the censor-ignoring 'novelization for young readers' by George Gipe – who also wrote the novelizations for *Back to the Future* and Joe Dante's subsequent *Explorers*. Naturally, it came complete with the requisite '8 pages of full-color photos'. A few years later, I tried to impress my school grades and English language teacher by penning a whole coursework essay on film novelisations. As others argued for the merits of J.R.R. Tolkein, Margaret Atwood, Harper Lee and the representation of a British childhood in Barry Hines' *A Kestrel for a Knave*, I blathered on about the overlooked literary prowess of film tie-in classics such as Joan D. Vinge's *Santa*

A veritable squadron of childhood tie-in novels from an era when these were the only keepsakes we had of our movies.

Claus: The Movie, Ed Naha's *Ghostbusters II* and of course *Gremlins*. The tactic of amazing and educating my teacher mainly resulted in utterly confusing him. I think my 'B minus' was merely him being polite – despite the stuck-in addition of various magazine images of *Ghostbusters II* and *Gremlins*. It was around that time that the novelisation of *Gremlins* was firmly taken off the GCSE English curriculum forever.

With Christmas way behind us, *Gremlins* was finally released onto home video rental in 1985. The Gaston Gate Garage video club naturally responded by securing one copy for the whole area to fight over like hungry Mogwai. But like the three rules emblazoned onto movie posters and our playground attempts to impress each other by reciting them for a film we had not seen, there was a catch. The BBFC had not changed its stance on the '15' rating. Cue the beginning of a new era of cinema spectatorship for us nearly-teenagers or those – like me – that were nowhere nearly at all. A by-product of watching the cinematic skies of Steven Spielberg, Richard Donner, Joe Dante, Irvin Kershner and George Lucas was that not all their output was going to be aimed at the original *Star Wars* generation. Not every great film of theirs would have an accompanying lunch box. Though I would have loved to have proudly opened a plastic lunch box with crucifixes, priests, Billie Whitelaw and *The Omen* emblazoned all over it for all to see every lunchtime. I could have cut my daily sandwiches with one of Mattel's Seven Daggers of Megiddo for maximum effect. Maybe we could have had a Father Merrin and *The Exorcist* figurine range complete with a twistable Regan head and a Georgetown backstairs★ playset? (★Father Karras figurine not included.) I would pay good money now for a 3¾-inch Ellen Burstyn figurine complete with removeable scarves and high-waist pants that play the Tubular Bells theme when you pull them higher. And could you imagine *The Color Purple* sticker album?! Our movie appetites were being both slowly whetted and opened out. With a new *Star Wars* or *Superman* film every summer not forever possible, we remained faithful to these American filmmakers even if some of their subject material would not immediately be faithful to us. And without the Internet, older siblings or even a readily available supply of home videos, our resourcefulness would have to call in parental favours and test their willingness to rent out some movies whose rating did not always match our own birth certificates. Like Billy Peltzer, we broke the rules. And the first 15-rated film my mum rented out from the Gaston Gate Garage that I may or may not have been seen that early Saturday evening was Joe Dante's *Gremlins*.

The staff at the Gaston Gate Garage knew the score. They weren't going to let me rent out *Emmanuelle 4 in 3-D*, but that would be because they knew it was rubbish. Yes, I was technically too young when Mum suggested I really need to see *An American Werewolf in London* (1981) and *Blazing Saddles* (1974) on TV one summer's night or when she later let me rent out *Stir Crazy* (1980), *Police Academy* (1984), *The Fly* (1986), *Aliens* (1986), *The Deer Hunter* (1978), *Out of Africa* (1985) and more from the garage. The odds of me becoming a glue-sniffing werewolf or even a Dutch colonial heiress with a gramophone I would take on safari having watched *Out of Africa* aged 11 were slim. The *Police Academy* movies became a thing for Mum and me. I might have got all awkward when Steve Guttenberg first emerges in that dormitory towel, but the humour was great and the returning, repeat formula was perfect for a Saturday afternoon and eight-four silly minutes in the company of Commandant Lassard, Captain Harris and their 15-rated hijinks. The first time I saw a woman's bare chest in the company of my parents was when we all saw *Airplane* (1980) and I was barely 10. To this very day, I cannot pass through any airport's drop-off bay without thinking of the bickering tannoy announcers – 'Listen Betty, don't start off with your white zone sh★t again!' I didn't get all the gags. But I knew the bare chest was one of them. These *Watching Skies*-era movies gave us a love of American cinema in all its forms. It was not going to stop when Indiana Jones reeled in Willie Scott at the end of *Temple of Doom* (1984). I wanted to see more of Harrison Ford. And before I knew it, I was furnishing my movie soul with rental copies of *Blade Runner* (1982), *Witness* (1985), *The Mosquito Coast* (1986) and *Frantic* (1988). I am sure my pocket money almost singlehandedly kept the fortunes of Warner Bros video afloat in the 1980s. And if you respect your local video store and its films, they respect you. Like Keye Luke's grandfather character in *Gremlins*, the garage only had three rules when it came to their video library. Keep the videotape out of light. Especially sunlight. It will ruin it. Don't get it wet. Not even in the rain. And no matter how much the club member cries, no matter how much the club member begs – never, NEVER bring a film back after midday.

With that ragged font and crisp poster paintwork by John Alvin still very much a symbol of 1980s cinema, fantasy and denim usage, *Gremlins* is one of the landmarks in the Amblin Entertainment production project. Taking on that trademark Spielberg domestic baton with some fun Frank Capra-smashing Americana and wry caricatures maybe not yet seen in a Spielberg stable movie, *Gremlins* is both a gentle, loving satire on the bearded one's 1970s and early-1980s tropes and a great addition to that canon. And it is not every teen film whose poster features the spot-lit, denim-wearing crotch of a hot young dude in a tight T-shirt with sexy hands that would certainly not have been out of place on a club-night flyer pinned to a lamp post in San Francisco's Castro neighbourhood circa 1984.

The creepiest notes of *Gremlins* are nothing to do with the body scares on offer from a director not long off *Jaws* satire, *Piranha* (1978) and werewolf chiller, *The Howling* (1981). The real unnerving beats are overlooked by adults when they try the futile task of assuming they know what scares you. There is still nothing more terrifying – after naïve censorship – than a motionless department store, an abandoned swimming pool and the corridors of your school at night, being shoved into a microwave, an open kitchen-top liquidiser and random Johnny Mathis music you cannot work out the source of. Yes, the bubbling death of Stripe and the microwave-ready gremlin was unsettling if you were 9 years old. But no more so than a quarrelsome alien's arm being lightsabered off in a Tatooine dive bar, a trainee Jedi hero having the same done to him by his father, a kind extra-terrestrial being found freezing and face down in a suburban stream and the melting, exploding faces of Nazi villains. What stayed with me more as a 9-year-old watching *Gremlins* was none of the knives or the jumps or the slapstick violence. It was the then 19-year-old Zach Galligan as all-round backpack-wearing hero Billy Peltzer. I was most jealous of Corey Feldman getting to hang out in Billy's bedroom, swapping drawings and watching movies. Just as the thought of Phoebe Cates was responsible for turning a few adolescent boys into gremlins after midnight – her poolside stint in Cameron Crowe's *Fast Times at Ridgemont High* (1982) had not helped much either (or helped quite a lot) – only-child Billy Peltzer very nearly gave me a lifelong thing for naïve bank clerks in denim. In many respects, it was great being on the cusp of becoming a gay kid in the 1980s. As the censors and their prudish scissors were nervously circling Daryl Hannah's PG-rated flesh in *Splash* (1984), Kelly LeBrock's midriff sweatband in *Weird Science* (1985) and of course Carrie Fisher's U-rated golden Wonderbra in *Return of the Jedi* (1983), they totally ignored the boys and their films which were already filling the video shelves – Timothy Hutton and Tom Cruise showering down in *Taps* (1981), Kiefer Sutherland in Nova Scotia in *The Bay Boy* (1984), Rob Lowe's jock-wearing jock in *Youngblood* (1986), most of the cast of Francis Ford Coppola's *The Outsiders* (1983) and any guy that wasn't Freddie Kruger in the homo-fest that is *A Nightmare on Elm Street 2* (1985). Whilst Billy Peltzer's denim world is not maybe as aware of its female and queer audiences as some of the other Brat Pack skewed films of the

Stay Gold – a street-art tribute to Francis Ford Coppola's *The Outsiders* on Ventura Boulevard, Los Angeles.

same era, Zach Galligan's boy-next-door charm was certainly an endearing substitute.

Gremlins is rarely terrifying, because kids have a sense of humour. When the synth-gothic sounds of Jerry Goldsmith's barbed score are mocking a scene before the visuals really kick off, the kids get it. When a vicious busy-body of a Republican widow is finally served her just desserts by a group of carol-singing gargoyles door-stepping her in knitted scarves and earmuffs, the kids cheer. When the hero's kind, but moaning neighbour is finally proved right about all those tales of Second World War gremlins and his own snowplough interrupts his TV dinner, the kids laugh. Gremlins is a cartoon. Gremlins is a parody. It is a tribute to the Looney Tunes influences of

Joe Dante and writer Chris Columbus (*The Goonies, Young Sherlock Holmes*). Bugs Bunny crops up in a TV cameo warning of gremlins from a 1940s Warner Bros *Merrie Melodies* short, animating legend Chuck Jones cameos and – like myself – the first film the green-skinned punks see at a movie theatre is Disney's 1937 classic, *Snow White and the Seven Dwarfs*. In many ways, *Gremlins* feels and plays like a companion piece to Joe Dante's 'It's a Good Life' episode in *Twilight Zone: The Movie* (1983). A compendium tribute to Rod Serling's 1959 TV series of mystery and intrigue, the ill-fated movie is structured around four standalone stories directed by Dante, George Miller (*Mad Max*) and producers John Landis (*An American Werewolf in London*) and Spielberg. 'It's a Good Life' features a cartoon-obsessed boy keeping his family in a tight grip by way of cartoon demons and a domestic space that is increasingly unsafe. He is a kid in a recognisable world of arcade games and plaid shirts, late-night movies on TV (still no one has a video machine) and a bedroom floor strewn with comic books and movie posters.

Gremlins is of course a total cacophony of in-jokes, movie references and the trigger for about a quarter of a million 'Did You Know?' articles in film magazines and websites the world over. Aside from the precursor to this very book's title, *Watching Skies*, by way of a small-town movie theatre marquee proudly promoting *Watch the Skies* – a closing line from *The Thing from Another Planet* (1951) and a Spielberg working title for *Close Encounters of the Third Kind* (1977) – Kingston Falls' Colony Theater is also playing *A Boy's Life*, which was an early title for *E.T. the Extra-Terrestrial*. Billy and his dog Barney race to work through the pavement snow in a tracking shot lifted from *It's a Wonderful Life* (1946) which itself later plays on a TV in the Peltzer kitchen. B-movie posters from the 1950s fill Billy's attic bedroom, as does a rolled-up ad for *Twilight Zone: The Movie*, *Invasion of the Body Snatchers* (1956) spooks Gizmo on the TV, a barfly gremlin plays the Atari *Star Wars* video game, 'E.T. phone home' is mimicked as a phone wire is cut, the ringleader gremlin Stripe hides amidst E.T., Bugs Bunny and Sylvester the Cat plush toys in the Montgomery Ward department store, and Steven Spielberg himself wheels past at an inventors' convention also frequented by the film's composer Jerry Goldsmith (*Planet of the Apes, Alien*) and *Forbidden Planet*'s Robby the Robot. Gizmo gives birth on a bed of DC comics, he gets into car racing by watching Clark Gable in *To Please a Lady* (1951) and other robot toys run amok more than once as if Barry Guiler from *Close Encounters* still hasn't tidied up his bedroom floor yet.

Again, it is part Joe Dante in-joke, part wise remembrance of the consumer, merchandise-loaded world that Billy Peltzer, *E.T.*'s Elliott, Carol-Ann and Robbie from *Poltergeist*, *The Goonies* gang and a lot of us did once inhabit – even the less sunny, less fashionable British flipside. Under production designer James Spencer (*Poltergeist, Innerspace*) this is a familiar shopping mall world of Barbie, Smurfs, ghetto blasters, 1980s fitness gear, Garfields and television sets. Billy's mum Lynn (Frances Lee McCain) is actually saved from a marauding hoard of gremlin invaders by a kitchen of white goods and all that homeware apparatus we'd gladly skip past in the Argos catalogue on the hunt for *Star Wars* figures. And as someone dragged around garden centres and ornamental fountain displays for way too much of my childhood, I can only share Stripe's pain at finally being killed in one.

But just as *Gremlins* is a Panini sticker album itself of cultural references, there are wider references at play. Cinematographer John Hora (*The Howling, Moonwalker*) brings in a Dutch tilt for his cameras and a bit of a German Expressionist nod to Robert Weise's *The Cabinet of Dr Caligari* (1920). Just like *American Graffiti* (1973), the local radio disc jockey kicks the film off and pops ups throughout – in this case, Rockin' Ricky Rialto and his yuletide Motown hits. The school science lab gone wrong set piece is once again played with as *E.T.*'s escaping frogs are replaced with an escaping gremlin and no romantic embrace. And the motif of a mother defending the home invasion as forged in *Close Encounters*, *E.T.* and *Poltergeist* is enthusiastically updated here with Lynn Peltzer (Frances Lee McCain) not only defending her kitchen from gremlins, but also her husband Randall (Hoyt Axton) and his faulty inventions. Though had she not defended the homestead so ferociously and singlehandedly, Lynn very nearly deserves everything she gets for thinking she can get away with a home full of that many knotty pine walls, ornamental tassels, military swords, more ornamental tassels and unadulterated chintz. If only gremlins were allergic to pine furniture and unnecessary pine knick-knacks, Kingston Falls would be a lot more welcoming of Christmas today. It is all a crazy domestic pulse which Dante picks up again a year later in *Explorers* (1985), in *The 'Burbs* (1989) when he creates comedy hell for Princess Leia (Carrie Fisher), and the *Gremlins* leanings of *Small Soldiers* (1998).

Like *Jaws*, *Close Encounters* and *E.T.* before it, this is very much a movie written by someone in their 20s and early 30s. It has those Spielberg tics of discovery, curiosity and humour before the world is tied to having kids and maintaining marriages, homes, elderly parents and careers. Chris Columbus penned the screenplays for *Gremlins* (1984), *The Goonies* (1985) and *Young Sherlock Holmes* (1985), as well as directed his debut *Adventures in Babysitting* (1987), all before he was 30. They are all about impending adulthoods that do not want to leave childhood behind. *Gremlins* is a film which celebrates youth – as in *E.T.* – by making comments on the bad habits of adults. The Kingston Falls' Sheriff tries to blag a free Christmas tree to no avail. Local men waste their time and dollars in the town bars. The town Grinch Mrs Deagle scrooges down on young families' poverty at Christmas. The town's seniors and cops naturally ignore the gremlin warning signs and advice of the main kids. And no one really listens to Mr Futterman (Dante stalwart Dick Miller) and his anti-German paranoias and non-American technology fears as a bar-wrecking gremlin fires a pistol into a black and white photo of a framed B-17 bomber and another generation's Second World War fireside tales of green bugs in the system.

Even if it is technically Billy's drawing aspirations that accidentally cause the real birth of the gremlins when friend Pete (Corey Feldman) spills some pen and ink water on Gizmo, his artistic ambitions and comic book interests are supported. *Looney Tunes'* Chuck Jones pops up as Billy's kind artist pal, offering encouragement to a fellow illustrator. Invention too is celebrated – with Randall Peltzer forever not wowing the world and his family with his array of unnecessary contraptions, yet doing so with great passion and dedication. *Gremlins* is a celebration of what is fun about childhood – Christmas, having your first job but not feeling much of an adult, getting a gift of a pet, having a cool teacher at school, your mum filling your stocking with robot toys despite the fact you now work in a bank and nearly have your first serious girlfriend, and of course the beguiling influence of comic books, *Snow White and the Seven Dwarfs* and monster movies.

All of this is somewhat lost in the 1990 sequel, *Gremlins 2: The New Batch*. Instead of a bag of movie theatre candy, *The New Batch* is like being stuck in the sweet factory for too long. Or having Christmas strapped to your face for 100 minutes. It spotlights and overexploits the fun cult and following of *Gremlins* rather than creating a movie world in which they are the story threat. It parodies the parody, so Gizmo – who looks like fame went to his head as he went for a Beverly Hills facelift with his royalties – becomes the gatecrasher rather than his green offspring. And it ignores the new, fourth rule of *Gremlins* – whatever you do, however it seems a good idea at the time, do not set your sequel in a skyscraper. Clearly no one took notice of *Poltergeist III* (1988). The community-under-attack Spielbergian blueprint that serves *Gremlins, Poltergeist, Close Encounters* and *Jaws* does not work in a city. That sense of community is already lost before the lights go down. *Jaws 3D* and *Jaws: The Revenge* prove you cannot even leave the same town. Although, who doesn't want to see Golan-Globus's late-1980s corporate aquarium skyscraper gone wrong thriller, *Jaws: The Fifth Floor*?! However, *The New Batch*'s Clamp Center backdrop, inhabited by the narcissistic blonde billionaire Daniel Clamp (John Glover), his PR manager Marla and his constant reminders of how good his tower is and that he is the best at all he does, whilst worrying about ratings, is now rather prophetic stuff on the part of Joe Dante. As the world witnesses what happens when the commander-in-chief tweets after midnight, *The New Batch* could well be now rechristened *All the President's Gremlins*.

Shot predominantly on various Californian sound stages, the deliberate backlot artifice of the original *Gremlins* is part of its very charm and endurance. The banks of street snow and the white-flecked chocolate-box homes and front yard pine trees are deliberately cute. This is an America slap-bang in a December of parking lot Christmas tree sales, fluffy earmuffs, knitted scarves, candy canes, festive baking, blatant prop store snowmen, snow fights and home-for-the-holidays gatherings. But it is never cloying. Partly because of the unfolding mayhem of the piece, but also because Joe Dante won't let it. It is barely sentimental, nor is it a savage indictment of a Republican-era Christmas. The 1980s need for greed is soon avenged by Mrs Deagle's superb stairlift-to-hell death and resident wannabe yuppie and sycophant Gerald Hopkins (Judge Reinhold) fares no better. The creature effects and puppets by Chris Walas (*Enemy Mine, The Fly*) totally work as they have an analogue, Jim Henson quality and anarchy to them. The silhouettes of bouncy-eared gremlins pop up like Nosferatu Yodas and one green offender at Dorry's Tavern even brings in a puppet of his own for added irony. This is a Gonzo the Great world of sight gags, slapstick, catapulted sprites and merchandise-savvy gremlins in Mickey Mouse ears, mugger masks and 3D glasses. The gremlins laying siege to the town bar is just any office Christmas party gone comedically wrong. Though one does wonder why evening barmaid Kate (Phoebe Cates) never called Billy or the police when the first green gargoyle came in asking for a pitcher of Snowball and change for the jukebox?! The puppetry and artifice of it all is exactly why *Gremlins* should never have been denied to us British sky kids of 1984. The idea now of CGI mogwai or gremlins is enough to make you eat chicken drumsticks after midnight.

The 1980s was a time when more summer-minded movies came out at Christmas than Christmas movies. Yuletide-gone-wrong movies were nothing new. The likes of *Black Christmas* (1974), *Christmas Evil* (1980) and *Silent Night, Deadly Night* (1984) had all poured blood into the eggnog with varying results. But Joe Dante and his mogwai helped change that. *Gremlins* snowploughed a more cynical festive path to the December box office, which was soon enabling the more mainstream-minded, Yuletide-crushing likes of *Die Hard* (1988), Richard Donner's *Scrooged* (1988), *National Lampoon's Christmas Vacation* (1989) and *Home Alone* (1990) to all stand under the upturned tinsel-clad tree and tear Christmas and Christmas movies apart. And with them a whole sleigh's worth of warped Christmas movies continue to fall down the box office chimney. The cute, non-cynical and successful festive movie is now as much of a festive novelty as a British high street without tacky Christmas jumpers. Tacky Christmas jumpers which were, incidentally, all inspired by the imagery and hold of American yuletide movies that were kick-started by the likes of *Gremlins* in the 1980s. A December with an annual screening of *Gremlins* is indeed a wonderful life.

Flash-forward to a more recent Christmas, and a festive channel hop one Sunday afternoon. As we pop our Gizmo under our plastic fibre-optic tree, we look for a yuletide classic to be a movie wallpaper to our home decorating session. With the lacklustre animations and kitschy television movies about orphans in big mansions not really doing it for us – we find a Sunday afternoon treat whose scheduling is aimed specifically at children. It came out in 1984, was once rated '15' by the British Board of Film Classification, and tells the story of all those little creatures that multiply when you throw water on them.

ONCE MORE WITH FREELING

POLTERGEIST

1982. Labouring with the inexplicable disappearance of his daughter, a real-estate developer dad tours new land with his reckless boss as he looks to the skies above his house and realises the dangers of only removing the headstones in the suburban valley beneath.

○————○

With my use of our Hitachi VT–33A video player and its accompanying television set at fever pitch, my parents' patience was wearing thin. I was not only blatantly obsessed with watching every big movie and most of the smaller ones live on TV so I could punch out the tape-eating space on our ever-growing collection of disparate and no longer blank VHS cassettes. Our lone lounge television was also regularly resigned to those screenings. There was no multi-record or simultaneous channelling in those days. The novelty of having a video recorder was wearing thin for others as I was celebrating it more and more. My parents soon hit upon an

Argos-providing idea – get Mark a television for his bedroom. I was in my tenth year. I had still not had the birds and the bees talk yet, but apparently I was ready for such things as a television in my room, with instant access to the likes of Channel Four and its already quite eclectic, adult and confrontational programming policy in the mid 1980s. It would be one of the few instances where I was actually ahead of the technological zeitgeist. Timings may have precluded me from the VHS revolution, but for once in my life I was going to be at the cutting edge of something. Okay, my friend Inigo already had a television in his room. Another pal had a whole playroom with a television *and* video. And my aunt and uncle in Glasgow had more than one. Just like the houses in *Poltergeist's* Cuesta Verde, kids having a television in their room in 1985 was very much a controversial development with hell and damnation rising up like finger-wagging cadavers. Our parish priest was already wise to the demonic grip of modern media and would regularly try to exorcise our souls with cassette sermons from the local bishop backing him up about smutty TV, breast-filled tabloids and the dangers of selfish American soaps like *Dallas* and *Dynasty*. Maybe it was Sister Irony that helped our Irish Catholic bishop use duplicated audio cassettes to disseminate his tired cautions of modern media, always with the final caveat of praying for the sisters in Africa and the health of our good Papal leader in Rome. I bet Pope John Paul II had a television in his Vatican man cave. Besides, I'd spent at least one night in the former home of the inventor of television. Me having a TV in my room was not heresy. It was ordained destiny.

Either way, in the spring of 1985 a trip to the altar of St Argos saw me become the proud owner of a colour Goodmans television set. It did not curb my movie-watching habits in the slightest. The very opposite in fact. Nor did it stop me being a pain in the Hitachi to my parents every time they settled down to watch *All Creatures Great and Small* or *Mastermind*. Just as I was upstairs in my room and fireside peace would reign downstairs, I would crash into the lounge in a dog-scaring panic to change their channel, switch to the one I was taping, stop the recording in the commercial break, press play to go back to the moment the ITV screen posted its *Superman II – End of Part 1* caption, press *Record* and *Pause* and awkwardly wait the four minutes of ads for Bradford & Bingley, Una Stubbs talking about Nescafe and Hellman's Mayonnaise sketches starring Bob Carolgees before the last commercial would freeze just that bit longer as a sign the movie was about to continue, the *Superman II – Part 2* caption would appear, I would press off the *Pause* button and the recording would commence. I would then shoot upstairs to continue watching *Superman II* in utter pitch-black bliss only to repeat the procedure every twenty-two minutes over the next two and half hours. That was more or less the 1980s for any movie-mad kid raised on *Star Wars*, Superman and Bond.

Whilst our cinematic horizons and vistas were guided by the big screen, the actual big screen itself was not always where a lot of us watched those skies. We caught up with them on our television screens, via TV schedulers, video rental stores, borrowed tapes, self-copied tapes and our parents' goodwill and video membership signatures. The promotional clips, the behind the scenes interviews, the ad-break coming-soons, the publicity tour interviews, and all the movies scattered across all four of our TV channels all came through one source – the small screen. For me and many like me, that small, convex sky played a crucial role and often a more familiar, cheaper and easier vista than the monoplex and its one or two titles a week or three-screen Odeon ten miles down the road.

However, a petrol top-up at the Gaston Gate Garage and the caption 'A STEVEN SPIELBERG Production' on the shadowy cover of a MGM/UA video cassette managed to wreak somewhat of a revenge on my parents' behalf for all those surrendered hours of television and broadcast cinema. If a nineteenth-century library ghost in a New York City Library had the power to scare the ectoplasm out of me, you could only imagine what happened when I watched the suburban skies of writer/producer Steven Spielberg and director Tobe Hooper's 1982 horror masterpiece, *Poltergeist*. Not only did it reinforce all our fears of clowns, flickering lights and thunder and lightning at a time when storms in Britain could leave you without power all night, it featured a television set as the conduit and gateway to two hours of immaculately produced domestic shock. It was the supporting cast member of a TV whose inner phantoms came to life through the white noise known as 'closedown' – or 'sign-off' if you were watching from California. And if you were a kid with a TV set in your room watching movies late into the night and made the mistake of falling asleep before all programming ended and woke up to the fuzzy white noise of nothing illuminating the end of your bed, then – to use its own tagline – a film like *Poltergeist* definitely knows what scares you …

O say can you see, by the dawn's early light …

1982's *Poltergeist* and *E. T. the Extra-Terrestrial* are two sides of the same Spielberg coin. Whereas *E. T.* is firmly about children, the wonder of childhood and the separation of families, *Poltergeist* is a rare Spielberg movie from this era. It is about a family that stays together. Directed by Tobe Hooper (*The Texas Chain Saw Massacre, The Fun House*) from a story by Spielberg and a screenplay co-written with Michael Grais and Mark Victor, *Poltergeist* is almost a movie checklist of Spielberg tropes. Invaded suburbia? Check. A resourceful mum? Check. A wall of light? Check. A heroine thrown into a hellish pit of cadavers, slime and mud? Check. Long–limbed skeletal creatures? Check. Mop-haired kids with *Star Wars* toys and TV watching habits? Check. A Golden Retriever dog forever looking off camera at the boom mic? Check.

In the wake of the male-centric *Duel, Jaws, E.T., Close Encounters of the Third Kind* and *Raiders of the Lost Ark, Poltergeist* is instead a movie predicated on women, daughters and motherhood. Here in the suburban backdrop of California's Orange County – but filmed in Ventura's Simi Valley – the momentum of *Poltergeist* is driven throughout by JoBeth Williams (*Kramer Vs Kramer, The Big Chill*) and her wholly accurate, natural turn as ex-hippy mum Diane Freeling. With the sense that motherhood and kids fell into place for her without looking, Diane is wife to real-estate property developer Steven (Craig T. Nelson) in a marriage you suspect was heightened by the unexpected arrival of their much older daughter, Dana (Dominique Dunne) and sealed by the later advent of Robbie (Oliver Robins) and their youngest, Carol Anne (Heather O'Rourke). In a home bordering on chaos way before anything first goes bump in the night, the Freeling household is one whose improvised texture immediately sits proud at the table of 1970s American cinema. The feeling of the Freelings is a living, breathing photo album of family life. The kids flick food, talk and ignore each other all at the same time, Dana flirts and plays with construction guys building a backyard pool, toys are strewn everywhere, E-Buzz the Retriever clambers over the furniture and eats everyone's food, and husband Steven needs as much breakfast attention and dressing help as his kids. It is the Griswolds from *National Lampoon's Vacation* without the Wally World coupons and Christie Brinkley driving past in a Ferrari.

Kids in horror films were nothing new. One of the terror genomes of 1930s horror and the Universal Monsters cycle is when Boris Karloff in James Whale's *Frankenstein* (1931) meets a precocious, over-trusting Carol Anne of his own before scooping her up and hurling her into a pond to drown. *The Bad Seed* (1956), *Village of the Damned* (1960), *The Innocents* (1961), *The Nanny* (1963) and *The Birds* (1963) all later make differing creepshows of their juvenile characters – directly or otherwise. But then American cinema of the 1970s didn't so much push the envelope of kids in horror as strap it to a bed, pour holy water and buckets of blood all over it, make it tricycle down hotel corridors for its life and try stabbing it on an altar with seven sacred daggers. Spielberg's own *Something Evil* (1972) predates *The Exorcist* (1973), *The Omen* (1976), *The Amityville Horror* (1979) and *The Shining* (1980). In a telemovie tale written by Robert Clouse (director, *Enter the Dragon*), Sandy Dennis's Majorie is slowly convinced her son Stevie (Johnny Whitaker) is possessed by – yep – something evil. As a simpler but still key learning curve for Spielberg, it is no ILM-fest of visuals, nor even that evil. But with all its then recent influences – such as Robert Evans' *Rosemary's Baby* (1968) – that independent, studio-freeing cinema of the late 1960s and early 1970s was also allowing a young Steven Spielberg to flex his directorial wings, and can later claim another descendent in 1982's *Poltergeist*. And in the bloody wake of *The Exorcist*'s Regan, *The Omen*'s Damien, *Carrie*'s Carrie, *Halloween*'s young Michael Myers, *The Shining*'s Danny and the kids in both *Jaws* and *Jaws 2*, Hooper and Spielberg are totally freed up to throw the bucket of gore at the Freeling kids in a manner cinema would not have allowed them ten or fifteen years before.

One of the aptitudes of *Poltergeist* is how it is not – unlike *Something Evil* – about an isolated house, or even a mansion on the hill or grand Georgetown apartment. Spielberg's stories and movies of the time are often about stories happening in the plain sight of communities. That is how they got under our skins. *Poltergeist* is all happening in a built-up, busy Californian suburb the dad himself helped create, and yet the Freelings are cut off. They cannot or will

Paramount's Stage 12 and the production home of 1968's *Rosemary's Baby*.

not tell anyone about the disappearance of their daughter. Steven's boss notes how Carol Anne has not been at school, but not enough to really care and in the (first) final battle idle neighbours turn a blind eye and assume it is all a crazy family prank. Maybe the dangerous, inaccessible backdrop of Tobe Hooper's *The Texas Chain Saw Massacre* is not that different to *Poltergeist* after all.

Again, this may be a sun-parched California of new builds and arid road layouts, but this is our world too of neighbours, TV remote control jousts, dead canaries, ice cream vans, kids huddled on kerbs sharing remote-controlled cars, chintzy furniture, ruined homework assignments, panics to get the beer crate home before the game, and in-joke giggling about uncouth neighbours. As Spielberg's effortless story unfurls like one of those ILM phantoms and the women of the piece begin to take charge of the narrative, there is a notion that the men of the piece just cannot hack it. Son Robbie flips out in every scene, dad Steven just recedes into dark-eyed despair and the paranormal expert guys lose their bottle and appetites all too quickly. Cue the on-screen gravitas of Beatrice Straight (*Network*) and the beautifully whispered and written scenes between her Dr Lesh and the Freeling family. As the shaking expert Lesh is lost for ideas, it matters not as the women of the piece take charge, working out spectral loopholes, sorting out snacks and eventually calling in scene-stealing psychic Tangina Barrons (Zelda Rubenstein) to finally to claim 'this house is clean' with a comedy straightening of her hair to camera.

Like those cackling Milton Bradley toys orbiting Carol Anne's bedroom on a haunted loop, there are many urban legends spinning around *Poltergeist*. Aside from the later and cruelly premature deaths of the Freeling girls Heather O'Rourke and Dominique Dunne (whose writer-producer father Dominick Dunne produced pioneering queer film *The Boys in the Band* for director William Friedkin in 1970) there have always been discussions about who really directed the film – Steven Spielberg or Tobe Hooper? Various anecdotes of usurped creativity have jostled for attention over the years over who was on set first, who directed who, who was tied to contracts and who was in charge. Ultimately, it doesn't really matter. Over three decades on, *Poltergeist* is still one of the crispest, most sharply written, acutely acted and physically conceived horrors to come out of American cinema. And it is a product of both its captains.

The consumer-led world of the Californian Freelings and their Darth Vader figurine carry cases, American Football helmets, home stereo systems and television sets are of course pure Spielberg. As are cinematographer Matthew F. Leonetti's furnaces of light flecked with spindly, liquid-like ILM creatures, that steep-pitched-roofed suburbia and those concurrent conversations and almost improvised kitchen table chatter. Without ever being cloying, there is Spielberg's positivity about the goodness of people – which was possibly less of an attribute in *The Texas Chain Saw Massacre* (1974). Likewise, kids are not strictly a feature of Tobe Hooper's blood-and-flesh-thirsty cinematic horizons at that time. Yet, Hooper was not long off Warner Bros Television's 1979 adaptation of Stephen King's *Salem's Lot*. A two-part contemporary tale of haunted homesteads and vampires starring David Soul and James Mason, the emphasis was on spooks, a bit of Californian-shot Americana doubling up for Maine, sunny greenery and small-town locals straight out of Amity Island. It also features teen boys with lives, bedrooms and tight denim wear surrounded by horror movie posters from the 1930s. It was more of a haunted foundation course for *Poltergeist* than not.

And whilst the tale of why the Freelings will never have to worry about recording *Superman II* off the television without commercial breaks is not really the brutal bloody torture-fest that is *The Texas Chain Saw Massacre*, both films do share a prolonged incident in the one house, both films linger on the scantily-clad misery of a heroine left to fight on her own after the men have gone, and both make veiled comments on where American society is at the time – be it a post-Vietnam, post-Nixon disassociated America or a Reaganite consumerism usurping 1960s ideals and liberalisms. With *The Texas Chain Saw Massacre* kept off British TV screens for many a concerned year, *Poltergeist*, *Salem's Lot* and a whole graveyard shift of Stephen King movie adaptations later became a vital movie staple to British kids with TV in their rooms and those with parents who would go to bed early. Lewis Teague's *Cat's Eye* (1985) starring

Drew Barrymore was a particular favourite, as was *The Dead Zone* (1983) with director David Cronenberg and Christopher Walken on top-notch, post-1970s cinema form.

Poltergeist is one of the purest horror films ever committed to cinema, yet it is all about television. Part side-note on the dangers of kids watching too much of it – not a warning that reached my childhood – the film starts on the broadcast image of the (then) nightly 'Star Spangled Banner' TV sign-off, one of Spielberg's favourite films *A Guy Named Joe* (1943) and the later ghostly inspiration for *Always* (1989) plays on the bedroom set, neighbours bicker over reception issues, a television of course becomes the famed portal to a spirit world, Steven is worried the Freeling story hits investigative show *60 Minutes*, the TV becomes a communication channel to the missing Carol Anne and the paranormal investigators use television monitors to track the spirits in the house. The creepy clincher is the moment when the paranormal research cameras capture the TV monitor's ghostly activity before the characters do, and the resulting playback is a strolling spectral procession of nineteenth-century spirits. It may part-explain why the film continues to age so well – it never looks wrong on a domestic TV set or flat-screen, whatever the technology playing it, because it is about a household gripped in television. Again, this was an era of American cinema where our spectatorship across the pond in Britain was served particularly by television, and that box in the corner of the room with a vase bought from Crete sat on the top of it was not a portal to spirits, but a prolonged and welcome intrusion from American cinema, news and culture.

Carol Anne might climb out of bed in the first moments of *Poltergeist* and wander up to that television set with a blue-eyed wonder only her advertising agent can love (Heather O'Rourke was already a commercials veteran by 1982). But the film is not

In an altogether calmer lounge than the one belonging to the Freelings, ILM and Lucasfilm continue to be San Francisco neighbours.

told from her or the kids' viewpoint. They don't invite you into the drama in the same way *E. T.'s* Elliott, Michael and Gertie do. And why does Carol Anne have a poster for Ridley Scott's *Alien* (1979) on the wall near her closet?! It is hardly setting the right nocturnal tone for a 5-year-old girl. Maybe she knew that Swiss sci-fi bio-artist H. R. Giger, who helped design the creature and Space Jockey in *Alien*, would later join *Poltergeist II: The Other Side* (1986) and try to up the returning scares there with his somewhat unique biological vision of the world and what might lie beneath it.

Part of the movie fun of *Poltergeist* is how it sits very much in that Industrial Light & Magic visual effects world of *Star Wars*, *Close Encounters*, *Raiders of the Lost Ark* and *E. T.* Those practical effects, models of rotating and collapsing houses, opening portals, clawing phantoms and ethereal ILM haze is such a defining part of these cinematic skies. Their liquescent clouds and ghosts, peeling faces and suburban miniatures are heady stuff to kids. It is an era of cinema where the suddenly-dropped jaw of an eyeless skull thrown into the frame puts another $5 million on the box office. It is a basic form of scaremongering, no different to tacky seaside ghost trains. The richness, however, comes from how it is all dressed and conceived by these ILM men and women perched in cramped, light-free rooms in the side alley warehouses of Van Nuys and San Rafael. And it is all greatly abetted by composer Jerry Goldsmith (*Coma*, *Damien: Omen II*) whose fast, buoyant strings open out a California street childhood and suggest sanctuary, childhood and an American idyll not unlike John Williams' work on the same summer's *E. T. the Extra-Terrestrial*. But just before the channel is changed onto the fright setting, the encroaching woodwind of Goldsmith's oboes, piccolos and flutes seep and rise into the Freeling house before the ILM phantoms ever do. As different slivers of woodwind and trombones seep into the rooms and glide up the Freeling staircase with Leonneti's camera just that bit behind, it is all highly reminiscent of the aural freeway of spirits and sounds as conjured up by the bassoons and clarinets of Ivor Stravinsky's *The Rite of Spring* – whose influences, flourishes and pounding sounds can be heard all over John Williams' 1975 score for *Jaws*. And when hell tries to break loose and then achieves it, Goldsmith ramps it up into some Night on Simi Valley Mountain trauma as his score is promptly visited by the ghosts of Moddest Mussorgsky's *Night on Bald Mountain* and its rising, rushing ghouls and crashing orchestral demons. Both classical Russian pieces are key to Walt Disney's pet-project *Fantasia* (1940) and its compendium mix of nature and landscape, heaven and hell. As Disney's *Bald Mountain* sequence unfurls into a mist-ridden Dante's Inferno of spindly witches, wraithlike spirits and arched demons, the whole stream of ILM's undulating spectral effects writhes alongside Goldsmith's score to make total, eerie sense. Suddenly the horror skies of my childhood as benchmarked by *Poltergeist* echo those haunted influences of Spielberg and his generation of visual artists, effects folk and ILM painters. Add to that a childish choir, that almost microphone-feedback screeching, the prolonged brass notes and gaggle of laughing phantom-like children, and one of the best special effects in *Poltergeist* is Jerry Goldsmith.

One of the famed taglines for *Poltergeist* was, 'It knows what scares you'. And it did. Clowns. Blue ones with little bells on their hats and shoes and the propensity for things to get kicked under the bed and its vulnerable foot-high netherworld void. As an adult, *Poltergeist* also knows what scares us kids of 1970s and 1980s cinema. Remakes. Bad ones with too many bells and whistles hanging off them that were not there when we last looked. Hooper and Spielberg's ode to simple terror was the first of all the movies discussed in this book that was unnecessarily exhumed for a remake. It is not wholly awful, but lost this Freeling fan as soon as the trailer told us to believe a flat-screen television would have analogue reception issues, that the kids would still be playing with

1970s toys not amiss in Barry Guiler's Alabama home and that kids would be suddenly dragged upstairs echoing deleted beats from *The Exorcist* (1973). Its biggest trip is that it takes away the feminine drives of the original by putting Sam Rockwell centre-stage, pushes the missing sister dynamic to one of a guilty brother and ditches Zelda Rubenstein's Tangina Barrons for Jared Harris. Like VHS tapes of pan-and-scanned *Star Wars* movies or original versions of *Close Encounters*, time moves on nearly as quickly as ideas run out and bucks need to be made. It is possibly further testament to the creative strengths of these titles, as well as the legal fortitude and clout of the likes of Spielberg and Lucas to craft their own studios, labels and franchises and remove the legal tab for security's sake. Its fears and branding were all about other movies' similar jumps and bumps. The 2015 *Poltergeist* remake is merely holding hands around the séance table with all the other kids-centric mixed bag of movie terrors that were just trying to be 1982's *Poltergeist*.

Poltergeist was released in the UK on 7 September 1982 – three months before its American cousin *E. T. the Extra-Terrestrial* landed on UK shores. Both are grand, fantasy operas about suburbanites, both are valuable documents of a particular domestic and American social zeitgeist at the time, both are key embodiments of Spielberg's story tenets and tastes at the time, and both are big films about what happens to small people. *Poltergeist* is not just one of the best horror films to come from this era of American cinema. It is one of the most beautifully told, performed and realised. There is a kindness and a realistic soul to this movie despite the supernatural chaos and warnings of only removing the headstones. Story matter aside, it has the pragmatism and cinematic expediency of Mike Nichols' *Silkwood* – which also starred *Poltergeist*'s Craig T. Nelson – or even Peter Bogdanovich's *Mask* (1985), and both titles' fierce ability to capture an everyday America and point of time. Curiously playing up to the family-pushing mantras of President Reagan's first term circa 1982, *Poltergeist's* nevertheless liberal, open-minded protagonists nestled in Orange County as shot in Simi Valley do not feel that Republican – despite the historically Republican grip of both locations. Twenty-two years later, Ronald Reagan, the fortieth President of the United States, was buried in Simi Valley. For a film that warns of the dangers of only removing the headstones, I will just leave that one there.

Many miles from the California hills of 1980s America, in the Surrey Hills of Britain, a blonde child awakes in bed with a Golden Retriever lying on the floor. The child looks to the white noise of a new bedroom television set hissing in the corner and pulls back the sheets. The child climbs out of bed and notes how the Retriever is looking to the wall above the headboard. Instantly terrified, the eyes of the child squint and try not to look as a dressing gown is pulled up for a makeshift shield and slow, cautious steps are taken towards the billowing white screen. In a sudden but brave panic, the dressing gown is thrown over the child's head as a self-protecting gesture and a young hand reaches out to try to find the TV's off switch. As all recent memories of a newly seen American horror film float around the room like phantoms, the child finally switches off the set with relief. The room is plunged into instant darkness and the Golden Retriever panics. Half an hour later, the child and his dog are on the floor in his parents' room, with thoughts of getting the new TV set exorcised by the local parish priest who had already warned us kids of the dangers of too much television.

THE SITH ELEMENT

THE PHANTOM MENACE
ATTACK OF THE CLONES
REVENGE OF THE SITH

2002. The oranges of dusk and the blacks of night gather the skies together with great portent, as a silhouetted and vengeful young man stops a desert transporter for directions to a bandits' camp and a dark path with no horizon or dawn.

1985. With 1983's *Return of the Jedi* looking like very much like it was going to be the last *Star Wars* film ever, it was about time someone stepped up and tried to help Lucasfilm Ltd produce a sequel. Or even a prequel – if such definitions had even been coined in 1985. With no release date locked in, it was clearly down to me to singlehandedly plan and plot out *Episode VII*. When you are already marinated in American cinema and the merchandise that supports it, the 8-year-old you naturally believes he or she can make their own sky-watching classic. Just like Spielberg and Lucas, I wanted to make my own movies. I had watched *Raiders of the Lost Ark* enough times since last Christmas, had a *Return of the Jedi* photo storybook and didn't need to attend the USC School of Cinematic Arts as I had watched *Supergirl: The Making of the Movie* and had kept all my Palitoy *Star Wars* boxes. However, unlike that bearded duo, I was not in possession of any old 16mm camera lying around and brothers, sisters or even neighbour kids to enroll in my fantasy movie homage ambitions. Although I did have a 1960s 16mm projector my stepdad Rob had once bought, a pull-up canvas screen, some old Laurel & Hardy shorts and a boxed movie title letters set that was not dissimilar to the price board down our local fish and chip shop. Rob had also got an old American 1958 book called *How to Make Good Home Movies*. 'By the editors of the EASTMAN KODAK COMPANY,' it proudly promised, 'a harvest of ideas for better movies, profusely illustrated with 316 full-color photos and drawings.' It contained such sage-like Hoth-savvy advice as call your film *War in the Snow*, but be careful, 'anyone can make a movie of a gang of boys standing around and looking uncomfortable.' Quite right. Unfortunately, ours was a household that had not long saved up for a VHS video recorder. We were not going to be rushing forth into purchasing a video camera any time soon. Nor did we have an old 16mm camera. But why should no camera stop any kid wanting to reach for the stars or their movie wars?

Very soon the studios had been booked, at least one cast member had committed, John Williams was available and a return to Hoth was heavily rumoured. The finer production details, of course, leaked early as they always do and the studio truth of it was it was my bedroom, my acting skills, my *Jedi* soundtrack cassette and our back garden should we get snow during the next winter. Despite my limited resources, the first set on Stage B was Jabba's Palace –

there was no Stage A, but it sounded more Elstree Studios-like – in the spring of 1985, and spurred on by all things *Jedi* I endeavoured to recreate that Tatooine bolthole in my meager bedroom-cum-soundstage. It was going to be part homage, part prequel. I would keep the cardboard boxes from our weekly grocery shop to create the arches and walls of Jabba the Hutt's party chamber between my wardrobe and the airing cupboard. Instead of a smoke machine I used Johnson's talcum powder, I had a black gardening glove for my Luke Skywalker robot hand, my toys and ships would be playing themselves and any close-up work would be of my own TIE fighter recently made from a washing machine box I painted black and spent ages cutting out the pizza-slice-shaped cockpit windows with a Stanley knife. I hoped that the fact I had no Palitoy TIE fighter to match the larger, home-made cardboard one would be something we sorted in post-production. With my cassette player soundtracking this burgeoning Throne Room with John Williams and the full London Symphony Orchestra near to the only spare plug socket available in their full, mono glory, I would then pull the curtains tight and transform our garden torches into lightsabers cutting through the Dagobah mists of Johnson's Baby Powder.

Unfortunately, my first forays as an 8-year-old Lucasfilm executive were short-lived. Not only had I conveniently overlooked how the remake rights to *Return of the Jedi* had not yet been bought from George Lucas, some other overlooked technical concerns soon brought production to a crashing halt – not only was I was yet to find a video camera, my lead actor had overlooked his contractual obligations to the Cub Scouts, I was curtly informed our Golden Retrievers were not toys or even Rancor Monsters, there was no way that TIE fighter was coming indoors and Mum wised up to the amount of talcum powder being wasted on this movie. Production was swiftly shut down.

Without a title, a script or any crowdfunding culture to get this classic onto the big screen, it remained one of the unmade gems of the *Star Wars* canon. But twenty-six years, three prequels, two Ewok television movies, numerous animation series and one holiday special later, cinema finally got to see the *Star Wars* movie it was really waiting for. "You'll believe an X-Wing can fly," was our tagline, as a proper clear-out of my old bedroom of a lot of childhood boxes – including my *Star Wars* figures and ships and tiny blasters that hadn't ended up lost in the vacuum cleaner – coincided with a heavy snowfall in the south of England and what bungling transport officials, school principals and Hoth Rebel leaders call a 'snow day'. With everyone off work and without electricity, transport, social media and something to do, my man Elliot and I did what all grown men in sudden possession of an old ice cream tub of *Star Wars* figures and a bin bag of ships and vehicles do – we made our own *Star Wars* movie. Beginning as an amusing X-Wing photo shoot in our snowy street, the project is soon taking on a wintry life of its own with a loose story of two Rebel Admirals stranded on a frozen planet hoping a rescue comes before the Imperial fleet does. Called *Episode XI: Escape from Cold Moon*, the sixteen-minute short film becomes a no-budget labour of love that took in three snowy locations, all the toys and false perspective we could muster and descendent pups of those very Golden Retrievers denied their Lucasfilm legacy all those years before. Yes, our creature department budget stretched to some dogs – but you find me a sky kid with a dog that didn't use their pet in at least one lounge floor figurine stand-off?! Our sci-fi AT-AT detecting binoculars were an old View-Master, our green screen work was cotton thread and Sellotape and our costume design was some simple Hoth-like parkas and wellington boots. From the corners of their confused eyes, young kids pulling their sledges looked at us and our underarm AT-AT and Millennium Falcon –

utterly unsure as to why two grown men would be out walking their AT-ATs in these conditions and utterly unconvinced we were the generation who fought for the freedoms that enabled them to speed down hillsides on a plastic Darth Maul toboggan from Homebase. An elderly neighbour with sight problems wondered if my AT-AT was a new cat she hadn't yet met – a fun notion that despite my insistence otherwise went a bit weird when she insisted I come in for a cup of tea, a chat and to let my AT-AT get warm by her gas fire. And it turns out you do get a seat on a public bus en route to your Hoth location if you have an AT-AT poking out of your bag like a small dog off to the vets.

The end result of our gruelling one-and-a-half-day shooting schedule was a deliberately lo-fi, home-made nod to childhood and a tribute to how all us sky kids forever made our own mental films with the toys and figures we had. The story world, the film world and the toy world of *Star Wars* was an unbreakable trinity. We weren't just imagining ourselves piloting an X-Wing from Yavin IV to the Death Star. We were envisioning ourselves doing it in a film with a John Williams score, echoing the battle grandeur and cuts of *A New Hope* and the catchphrases of Harrison Ford and Mark Hamill. Before we knew it, we became juvenile experts on the pacing of a movie dogfight in space, our toys were our model department, our packaging cut-outs our matte backdrops, our figures our storyboards and our eyes were an instant Steadicam. Our toys were like a primitive pre-viz technology – where we would plot and block our own movies with such figure-placing dedication that was all about the perspectives, how things would swoop and swoosh in and when could we press the seat button that would splinter that Speeder Bike across all our bedrooms. The very fact we even knew terms like 'matte backdrops', 'storyboards', 'miniatures' and 'Steadicams' was because of *Star Wars*. We lapped up behind-the-scenes promo documentaries such as 1977's

The Making of Star Wars, 1980's *SPFX: The Making of The Empire Strikes Back* and 1983's *From Star Wars to Jedi: The Making of a Saga* and *Classic Creatures*. We were not just celebrating George Lucas and his layered worlds of myth and fantasy. We were celebrating cinema, its artifice, its reach into our childhoods and the studios of Hollywood and Britain's Home Counties.

One of the key legacies of *Star Wars* is how its movie future is now bolstered by the directors, writers, producers and designers who were once sky kids themselves: Gareth Edwards (director, *Rogue One: A Star Wars Story*), Rian Johnson (writer and director of *The Last Jedi* and a newly touted *Star Wars* trilogy), Ram Bergman (producer, *The Last Jedi*), Greig Fraser (cinematographer, *Rogue One: A Star Wars Story*), *Game of Thrones* show runners David Benioff and D.B. Weiss (currently earmarked to helm a new series of *Star Wars* titles), and of course J.J. Abrams (director, *The Force Awakens* and *Episode IX*) were all mostly born in the mid 1970s and hence are real *Star Wars* generation kids. Rian Johnson grew up in California and later studied at the University of Southern California's School of Cinematic Arts – as did George Lucas, Robert Zemeckis (director, *Back to the Future*), Bob Gale (writer, *Back to the Future*, *1941*), sound design guru Ben Burtt (*Star Wars*, *The Empire Strikes Back*), SFX guru Richard Edlund (*Star Wars*, *Poltergeist*, *Ghostbusters*), and those original American Zoetrope filmmakers who once hung out at San Francisco's Folsom Street – Caleb Deschanel, John Milius, Walter Murch, Howard Kazanjian and others. This new generation of filmmakers taking the lightsaber-shaped baton forward comes straight from the cinematic influence of *Star Wars*. Their work responds to the first wave of that original trilogy – as well as possibly their own recollections of running around the backyard with a Snowspeeder before being called in for supper. The replacement casting of director Ron Howard on 2018's *Solo: A Star Wars Story* is not just a solid call on the part of Kathleen Kennedy and Lucasfilm when the original pairing of Chris Miller and Phil Lord failed to work out. It is a potentially serendipitous move to put one of the original stars of the drive-thru youth pic *American Graffiti* at the helm of a speedster-minded Han Solo story about scoundrels and boy racers pushing their limits and the patience of the Empire. Less *Solo*, more *Corellian Graffiti*.

The filmakers and us are all part of an often-glorious mental ownership of these movies, their tics, details and triumphs. Some are very fortunate to make that ownership a very real one as they get to pursue their own moviemaking lives. It is crucial to remember that the first and biggest *Star Wars* fan in the world is one George Walton Lucas Jr. You do not put that much of your time, creativity, soul, money and life into one movie, let alone six, if you are not really a *Star Wars* fan. And that is not even counting the spin-off movies, TV shows, TV cartoons, online universes, literature, theme park rides, novels, computer games and merchandise both new and old. It is all a glorious universe of fandom. And just as for a great many people it is often a form of family, social groups, conversation shorthands, chat fraternities, vacation scheduling and romance makers – it was for him too. But sometimes – just sometimes – others' proprietorship comes with a territorial price. And that was never demonstrated more passionately than in May 1999 when George Lucas released the first of his *Star Wars* prequels, *The Phantom Menace*.

One of the crucial, essential legacies of the new wave of American cinema of the 1970s was the sequel. But what *Jaws 2*, *Rocky II*, *The Empire Strikes Back*, *Superman II*, *Star Trek II: The Wrath of Khan* and *Indiana Jones and the Temple of Doom* all did was to really monetise the sequel in big ways and with big bucks. Whilst Thomas Dixon Jr's *The Fall of a Nation* (1917) – the follow-up to D. W. Griffith's

The Birth of a Nation (1915) – is often circled as one of the first sequels, the truth is that the movie sequel and follow-ons are as old as cinema itself. So too are prequels. *The Good, the Bad and the Ugly* (1966), *The Godfather Part 2* (1974) and *Indiana Jones and the Temple of Doom* are all prequels. Although, until early 1997 it is fair to say the very phrase 'prequel' was barely part of movie parlance. It was barely used to discuss literature. Yet, in the early months of 1997 the rumours began pointing to a new *Star Wars* film that wasn't a reboot or a sequel to *Caravan of Courage*, but a fully-fledged new *Star Wars* episode that would begin to chart the rise and fall of Anakin Skywalker.

When we were young kids we would ponder the year 1999 and 2000 and work out just how old we would be. I was going to be 24. To the 8-year-old me, I may as well have been a 900-year-old Yoda. But time and movies you never thought you would ever see have a habit of creeping up on you. Britain was in the dying embers of Britpop. *Trainspotting, Lock, Stock and Two Smoking Barrels* and *Human Traffic* were where a lot of our movie minds now were, and my Bond fan head was happily full of a new era of Pierce Brosnan, *GoldenEye* and *Tomorrow Never Dies*. World-famous heroin addict and 1990s poster boy Mark Renton was playing Obi-Wan Kenobi, and that porcelain-faced young girl from *Leon* was going to be Luke Skywalker's mother. Celtic powerhouse Liam Neeson was mentioned too, as were the reassuringly familiar names of Kenny Baker, Ian McDiarmid, Frank Oz, Anthony Daniels and John Williams.

Us kids had waited sixteen years to watch the new skies of George Lucas's *Star Wars* world. The first teaser poster for *The Phantom Menace* heralded not only a new age of *Star Wars* and a tradition-shattering notion of a portrait-sized piece rather than the more British-skewed landscape-sized quad poster – yes, these things matter and get noticed – it suggested the age of the drawn movie poster had shifted. Rather than an initial painted image, here is a lone photographic image of a young Anakin Skywalker (Jake Lloyd) timidly leaving his Tatooine sand-igloo home and making those first few steps into a new future. With a cobalt blue sky, rich golden sand and a willfully undersized *Star Wars: Episode I* logo, this image would have been plenty on its own simple merits. But the added design stroke of a shadow looming away from Anakin forming the identifiable silhouette of his darker-sided future self Darth Vader was graphical genius. With perhaps more precision and expectancy than the series had seen before, it is a strikingly contemporary beat in the timeline of *Star Wars* lobby art. It is as landmark as a midnight highway for *Close Encounters of the Third Kind*, the moment of contact between a boy and an alien's finger for *E. T. The Extra-Terrestrial* and a lone girl swimming directly above a great white shark for *Jaws*. Those beautiful *Star Wars* posters surrounding the original trilogy the world over are naturally paid duties to the matinee adventure of a different era of movie promotion. Harrison Ford leaning over Carrie Fisher in the *Gone with the Wind*-style imagery for *The Empire Strikes Back* is a beautiful nod to old Hollywood. A photographic image would not have worked in the theatre lobbies of 1977 and its busy billboard world of very designed album covers, magazine covers exhibiting painterly effort unheard of nowadays and movie studios puffing up their chests with pulsating, lavish marquee art. Likewise, a painted design would have struck a retro note for some in 1999, but not the same vital and simpler visual declarations surrounding *The Matrix*, *The Sixth Sense*, *Magnolia* and *Notting Hill*. The poster for the Spielberg-produced *American Beauty* (1999) is a simple rose held against a young women's navel. That and the Anakin image are now defining beats of American turn-of-the-century cinema art. With an Annie Liebovitz *Vanity Fair* cover shoot officially whetting the appetites, the promise of new figurines and toys, and a lack of drip-fed news, images and updates in an Internet age that had not yet taken a widespread grip, us whipped-up sky kids were ready to Rebel party like it really was 1999.

The first trailer was going to be something special. Even more so when it became one of the most widely seen movie teasers not necessarily seen at the movies. And when the teaser trailer first emerged in Britain in December 1998, it took a further sixteen years for a great many of our home PCs to actually download it from the *Star Wars* website which was barely a youngling itself. As a few of us huddled round my mate Greg's faithful Pentium Pro processor on New Year's Eve 1998 to witness movie history via dial-up, we proved that you could indeed get excited by a downloaded video the size of a postage stamp whose sound was painfully out of sync and whose visuals froze at constant will. But to paraphrase Lucasfilm's end-of-the-century publicity push, every journey does indeed have a first step. Even on dial-up. And this wizardry was only available to us thanks to Greg's housemate who gave this new interweb a go solely because he wanted to keep in touch with his new international girlfriend via futuristically-minded Internet chat rooms. This was way before YouTube became a movie fan's refuge. This was way before we could watch a trailer for a much-anticipated movie on a phone whilst sat on the toilet. This was way before polls on Twitter began asking fans 'Which *Star Wars* fragrance is your favourite?' When Lucas's saga struck back, us sky kids – well, sky young adults – were still in an original era of analogue movie fandom, bound to trips to the cinema to see a new *Star Wars* trailer and lengthy waits on the phone to pre-book *The Phantom Menace* tickets with written instructions for our mums on phone holding stand-by should the front of the customer queue reach us whilst we were having a toilet break. Yet, as those Gungan warriors astride their Kaadu creatures shuffle into view through the wetlands mist of a Dagobah-like swamp, a sandy Tatooine vista unfurls itself to John Williams' 'The Force Theme' and a caption touts 'every generation has a legend ...', the teaser trailer for *The Phantom Menace* very quickly suggested that perhaps the golden age of the *Watching Skies*-era blockbuster may not have ended with that jubilant Ewok barbecue after all.

It is arguable that nothing was as good in the prequel trilogy as that first teaser trailer for *The Phantom Menace*. And that the first teaser trailer was arguably not as good as that first poster of young Anakin Skywalker in the sand. But here is George Lucas being acutely mindful of a new generation of sky kids. *The Phantom Menace* had to be their *A New Hope* or it was merely an exercise in fan nostalgia rather than extending the reach of the *Star Wars* movie world, audiences and permanency. Whilst there are many haters ready to tear your arm off in a Mos Eisley Wetherspoons if you disagree with them, ask many a young adult in their 20s what their keenest *Star Wars* memory is and they will say the Podrace, Darth Maul, a half-finished C-3PO, the Battle Droids and Anakin Skywalker. The reason we have *Star Wars* movies today, the reason we have a new trilogy and the names Rey, Kylo Ren and Finn feel like we have always known them, is because the prequels maintained and created new interest and dollars at the box office. If nothing else, they were a key bridge of business and commerce from the original trilogy to the confident emergence of *Episode VII, VIII* and *IX* from 2015 onwards. To use prequel parlance, the young padewan Jake Lloyd is an unusual addition to the *Star Wars* world we were all used to in 1999. Or even in 1983. Those far, far away galaxies and their theatrical movie world had not really featured children before. The creepy Wookiee children in the infamous 1978 *Holiday Special* do not really count, and Mace and Cindel from the two Ewok television movies – *Caravan of Courage: An Ewok Adventure* (1983) and *Ewoks: The Battle*

for Endor (1985) – are aimed squarely at the kids lying on their lounge rugs at home. Nothing wrong in that of course. We were all sky kids lying face down on the lounge rug with outstretched hands changing the channel and rewinding the Speeder Bike chase time and time again. But in *The Phantom Menace* here was a main character we had once long pondered the adult, child-bearing and dark history of now being pitched as exactly the mop-haired kid we were when we all first stood before George Lucas's Jedi Council and were accepted into the world of *Star Wars*. Here is a kid that came straight from a Kenner toy commercial and packaging and onto the big *Star Wars* screen.

With the focus on Anakin Skywalker, *Star Wars* shifts from the adventures of three pals to the rites of passage of just one. It grants itself a longer timeline and brings in inevitable beats of childhood, adolescence, courtship, marriage and parenthood. Add the vagaries of the frat house years, a new job and a bad boss and it is all a very new structure to the *Star Wars* world and to the *Star Wars* fan. All Luke Skywalker originally had to do was rescue a princess, get his Jedi stripes, and find out his father was someone he had to kill. With *Episode I* being more of a gradual overture to the momentum of story in *Episode II* and *Episode III,* both those later chapters are tasked with not just documenting the fall of a single man, but the fall of a Galactic Republic and the devastation of peace of an entire galaxy. There is a lot going on in those two films. The audience is pinballed about more than a protocol robot's head in a Bespin scrap metal unit. And since the American new wave and rise of the blockbuster, the movies changed. Part of that was ironically down to the likes of Lucas and Spielberg. The set pieces and adventurous grandeur they bestowed on our cinema screens created instant tropes, templates and hungers that needed ever-satiating and ever-bettering. And it did not take decades, but merely a few key years of queueing round the block. *Return of the Jedi* is a busier film than *A New Hope*. Likewise, *Indiana*

Jones and the Last Crusade is a broader film than *Raiders of the Lost Ark*. And *E.T.* is an emotionally sharper film than *Close Encounters*.

Narratively, the prequels' key selling point was also their weakness. The whole enterprise balances on the downfall of a man you already know becomes a kick-ass villain who finally dies with some sense of redemption. But that is a pitfall of the prequel, not George Lucas. A prequel is about adding punctuation to sentences already written. It is a treacherous endeavour for any writer or filmmaker – an exercise in joining existing dots with narrative lines that can only be so long or nuanced. Ultimately, the prequels miss the breathing space of a training retreat on Dagobah, a pit stop on Cloud City, or even the meeting of an Ewok on Endor. There is a big leap from the bowl-cutted hijinks of Jake Lloyd's Anakin in *The Phantom Menace* to the darkening of his over-petulant soul as played out by Hayden Christensen. Once he starts slamming his Jedi bedroom door and throwing his lightsaber out the pram we are into the story territory of joining up those dots. There is something bleaker about a little boy having the adults around him help initiate his later fall from grace than a teenager you just want to slap. The drama of Vader's downfall plays out more effectively through those around him – Obi-Wan, Amidala, Palpatine and the androids – than it possibly does with Christensen and his furrowed-eyebrow rage.

For a saga that has one of the most recognisable villains of twentieth-century culture in Darth Vader, the baton of treachery is bandied about a lot of antagonists in the prequel trilogy. It is a wholly new dynamic for an audience familiar with one baddie and one baddie's boss. From Christopher Lee's prim Count Dooku to Darth Maul's hip-twirling antics, the bio-hazard that is General Grievous, Jango Fett, Nute Gunray and Lott Dod to the off-story presence of Darth Sidious and of course the Senator, Chancellor and Emperor that is Ian McDiarmid's palpable Palpatine – one of the worst-kept and most prolonged movie twists in cinema history.

The villainous grace of *A New Hope*, *The Empire Strikes Back* and *Return of the Jedi* is that it has one uniform band of black and grey admirals, commanders, and Sith Lords. Ever-mindful of how the timeline decrees the wars in the stars have not really kicked off yet so conflict must be conjured up from elsewhere, the prequels sometimes labour to be *Star Wars* films. The threat of baddies in the original trilogy was not hinged on how caped, dexterous Sith trainees could kill you at thirty paces with a double-pronged lightsaber and a triple salchow. It was that the Empire was using them and had no sort of Geneva convention humanitarian qualms of overstepping the lines of decency in war. Whatever leaps of faith we need when accepting the sequel trilogy's insistence that the iceberg can strike twice and that the Empire didn't die after all at the end of *Return of the Jedi*, these new episodes understand the saga needs established villainy, not the founding seeds of it. The *Star Wars* movies are not about exposition, but situation. *The Empire Strikes Back* works so well because the momentum of villainy is already pushing the pace of the story. In the prequels, the story is still trying to create the villains so that familiar *Star Wars* pace is affected. And different. The idea of threes – a trilogy of films, three main heroes, three central tones of colour and three main backdrops – this modus operandi of *Star Wars* is sidestepped in the prequels. Incidentally, why have there been no senior characters or planets called 'Modus Operandi' in *Star Wars*?! *Darth Modus. Rise.*

We didn't love *The Empire Strikes Back* because it introduced us to the fantasy worlds of Cloud City, Hoth or Dagobah. We didn't love *The Empire Strikes Back* because of the Tauntauns or Ugnaughts. We loved *The Empire Strikes Back* because of its swagger, personality and soul. The backdrops and creatures were secondary. From the get-go, *The Phantom Menace* and George Lucas's screenplay is heavy on context. It assumes and places great story majesty on backdrops and characters who haven't earnt it yet. A beaten-up 1977-era world and its Empire-wary inhabitants were once explained away by the rusting contents of a Jawa's Sandcrawler. The presence of a black-cloaked villain and his accompanying dozen or so Stormtroopers in the simple corridor of a Rebel blockade runner once projected everything we needed to know about the bad guys. Here, that visual clarification and folklore shorthand is switched for senates, politics, palace meetings, Jedi summits, substitute teen queens, backstabbing congress, trade federation bureaucracy, hologram memos, a glut of obsequious advisers, duplicitous viceroys and a Palpatine who is hiding in such plain sight it becomes almost confusing. And this is all in the first act. The exposition of the original trilogy – a Star Destroyer chasing a Rebel ship, Vader powering through the smoke of a blasted door, the smoking embers of two slaughtered guardians, a robot emitting a hologram and Luke and Leia swinging across a Death Star chasm – they are major and succinct beats of twentieth-century American cinema. The prequels miss a little bit of that movie-minded precision.

With no Luke Skywalker, no Princess Leia and no Han Solo, the prequels also miss the very characters that took us by the hand and led us through the world of *Star Wars*. The motif of younglings and their masters is apt and necessary, but gone is the sense of ensemble, the triumverate of heroes and the improvised teamwork pulling through by the skin of their Hoth. In *Jedi* and *Empire* the screen wipes flit us to concurrent action and story threads that up the dramatic ante, with the final act of *Jedi* becoming a masterclass of action movie editing. Here there is no urgency predicated on characters. Obi-Wan Kenobi (Ewan McGregor) inspecting clone soldier factories like Jedi Ofsted packs less impact than an unsuspecting C-3PO being blasted into pieces off-frame on Cloud City. Leia and Han sharing a tender moment at a shield generator bunker surrounded by Stormtroopers is more romantic than adoring montages of Anakin (Hayden Christensen) and Padme (Natalie Portman) gamboling about on a large CGI beetle creature thing on a grassy hill. The difference of linkage here is that now the beats of the story are political and monumental rather than personal. Whatever dramatic interventions and developments are at stake, senate declarations and political filibustering do not pack the same drama as a collapsed snow tunnel and accidental embrace in a compromised Hoth Rebel base.

The prequels do, however, hold great moments and it would be wrong to push otherwise. The Podrace, Darth Maul and Qui-Gon's part vicious, part meditative duel, a spiralling Naboo royal fighter in space, the fluttering wings of a dodgy gambler and scrapyard dealer, Anakin and Amidala having one of their most romantic moments as they enter a gladiatorial arena and a John Williams orchestral flourish, the eerily calm Kaminoans greeting Obi-Wan Kenobi, the screaming creation of a cowardly, slippery Emperor, the collective slaughter of the Jedi and the literal rise of Darth Vader. But they are all still surrounded by a hell of a lot of bells, whistles, fireworks and plot. Their leading, perhaps most era-defining moment is still that teaser poster of the young Anakin Skywalker flanked by a shadow of his future self.

Part of the dilemma is possibly George Lucas and his under-standable baby-boom generation fascination with technology – and technology in entertainment. When you've pushed the boundaries, bought them, rewritten them, sold them to the world, digitally cleaned them up and watched them become an expected norm it is only natural to be compelled to do so again with a new trilogy. As the same computer imagery that Lucas and ILM evolved in the likes of *Young Sherlock Holmes* (1985) and *The Abyss* (1989) had taken a velociraptor leap forward with *Jurassic Park* (1993), the temptation is understandably to push the digital envelope again with the prequels. The digital upshot is that virtual sets, virtual characters, virtual armies, virtual ships and virtual filmmaking dominate. The predilection is then to make everything busy, elaborate and aesthetically different.

If not kept in narrative check, the very fantasy one wants to pioneer can run away with itself. And it was not just the widespread usage of all that virtual-ness that was the gamble. The timings of *The Phantom Menace's* technology were possibly not in its favour. With the dawn of a new millennium merely months away and all the hi-tech, social and global uncertainty that entailed, an *Episode I* poised in a gleaming silver, visually virtual world of computer-generated hillsides, goofy companions and over-busy cities was brave. Lucas is also often criticised for his supposed attitude to actors – that he is more about product than process and that the casting notions in the prequel trilogy could have been stronger. This fan agrees. However, that is to miss that in the prequels alone George Lucas casts Samuel L. Jackson, Liam Neeson, Christopher Lee, Ewan McGregor, Ian McDiarmid, *Mad Max's* Bruce Spence, the vocally dexterous Peter Serafinowicz, Ralph Brown, veteran Australian actor Jack Thompson (*Breaker Morant*), Joel Edgerton and Terence Stamp. That is not a bad line-up in anyone's universe. Oh, and one Jimmy Smits. Smits deserves full praise for bringing a much-needed gravitas and Rebel poise to *Attack of The Clones* and *Revenge of the Sith*. Of course, he is a key bridge between the original and prequel trilogies with the fan-savvy name of Bail Organa and an off-story figure we have known and trusted since the 1970s. The moment in *Sith* when a Jedi youngling sacrifices himself to let Organa flee the devastated Coruscant is a vicious and heartfelt beat of the prequels, as Smits' Organa steps into the narrative breach and bangs story heads together to start to tighten the tale into something more reflecting the *Star Wars* world we know. Smits' inclusion eleven years later in *Rogue One: A Star Wars Story* (2016) is a great tribute not only to the story responsibilities of Bail Organa, but the cape-wearing civility that Jimmy Smits lends those two – and now three – prequels.

Some of John Williams' best work is found in the prequel trilogy. 'Duel of the Fates', the stirring swirls of the London Choir and the

London Symphony Orchestra take that choral motif of the moment Luke finally pushes forward with his lightsaber against Vader in *Return of the Jedi* and turn it into a heavy, symphonic clash of the Jedi titans. And the love theme from *Attack of the Clones* (2002) is as quietly dignified, momentarily expectant and nineteenth-century as Williams' elegant work for the TV movie *Jane Eyre* (1970) with its fated romance cues and climbing strings.

The prequel trilogy changes the original trilogy. It enhances it around the edges and sometimes at its core, and not for the worst. What were once throwaway lines ('and he was a good friend'), looks from Alec Guinness, pauses by Peter Cushing's Moff Tarkin, sighs from Uncle Lars and cautious asides from Yoda – they all have a different, stronger resonance now. After the battle of Kashyyyk we now understand why Chewbacca roars at Stormtroopers. When Jabba the Hutt double-takes as Luke Skywalker marches into his chamber in *Return of the Jedi*, does the vile gangster remember the Skywalker slaves he once kept and the podracing humiliations meted out by Anakin? We are told at the end of *Empire* that Kenobi lied to Luke. But now we know why. And properly why. Obi-Wan willfully tried to destroy Anakin and left him for dead as the new Emperor was ready to give his employee of the year a Sith makeover and new office chair. When R2-D2 first sees Ben Kenobi stagger into view to rescue Luke Skywalker from a Sand People mugging in *A New Hope*, those cuts, looks and puppy-dog chirps speak volumes. 'I think he's looking for his master, but I've never seen devotion in a droid before,' remarks Luke, as there is now a feasible beat where both Ben and R2 know exactly who each other and the young Skywalker are. I never bought for one moment R2's memory systems were wiped as that ongoing project of a space saga seen through the eyes of robots that began in those awestruck movie theatres of May 1977 is possibly exactly how it will all end. Of course, a lot of this is our projections in hindsight and Lucas did not fully know if he would ever get prequels, let alone how they narratively padded out. But some of the greatest story strengths of the prequels are not in the films themselves but that which they have forever affected since. Now there is an altogether new Death Star trilogy of *Revenge of the Sith*, *Rogue One* and *A New Hope*. In closing 2005's *Sith* on the footnote of a newly-assembled Vader pondering the newly-commenced Death Star, Gareth Edwards' *Rogue One* becomes a fourth prequel and the first to just show the nine-to-five Darth going about his Sith

David Crossman and Glyn Dillon's *Rogue One* costumes on display at the wretched hive of scum and villainy that is Gatwick Spaceport.

business with menaces, a family-free workday and a humour. The prequels prepared us for the non-linear future of *Star Wars* films way before the flashbacks, flash-forwards and side-steps of twenty-first-century television and cinema made time-jumping experts of us all. As the likes of *Fantastic Beasts and Where to Find Them* (2016), *Star Trek* (2009) and *Casino Royale* (2006) prove, a franchise can endure and now expects prequels. *Star Wars* is responsible for that. When J.J. Abrams relaunches *Star Trek* as a prequel project, it is surely the *Star Wars* prequels whose legacy coat-tails they rest on? By the time of *Rogue One* (2016) we are all savvy to the time leaps at play. Gareth Thomas's first *Star Wars Story* even pauses for its own mini prequels in the form of flashbacks to Jyn Erso's childhood.

As a trilogy of movies, the prequels are perfectly acceptable bursts of entertainment. They are rich fantasy interludes that reveal the utmost dedication of the tireless hours, designs and artistry that went into them. They may in parts pale with any comparison to the original trilogy, but so do the altogether better received *The Force Awakens*, *Rogue One* and *The Last Jedi*. A Prius is never going to look and drive better than a Studebaker. Two decades later, *The Phantom Menace* fares well. The Tatooine interludes are where it really breathes and puts us back into that beaten-up world with the barest suggestion of that *Watching Skies* DNA. Anakin Skywalker lives with his single, but steadfast mum Shmi (Pernilla August) who has to learn to let go. Yes, there is that midi-chlorian sidebar to Jedi science and Anakin's possible ancestry. But the whole film is not about that. In a year that saw *The Matrix* and its labyrinthine plotting and bullet-time visuals wow audiences in a way some *Star Wars* fans expected *Episode I* to, here was a new science fiction movie that was an old science fiction movie of good and bad, a production statement of old Hollywood with an orchestral score by John Williams, two big British acting talents of the day and Celia

Imrie piloting a Naboo fighter ship. One could argue *The Matrix* is more dated today than *The Phantom Menace* ever is. Its plotting and dystopic twists certainly became too standard with two sequels that are now not nearly as rich or eminently watchable as *Attack of the Clones* and *Revenge of the Sith*.

Yes, the digital work in the prequels has aged faster than the original trilogy's puppetry, matte work, make-up and model work. But as curiously dated and awkward as a CGI Jabba the Hutt is, or a pratfalling Gungan clutching a spanner, or a computerised spinning Yoda, or indeed the furrowed 2002 millennial dramas of Hayden Christensen's eyebrow acting all are – they are ultimately as era-defining as a 1980 stop-motion Tauntaun, a 1983 decision to launch the puberty of all the heterosexual males on the planet by shooting Princess Leia in a tin brassiere in an Arizona desert, the Jar Jarring inclusion of an Ewok Tarzan gag or an occasionally boss-eyed 1980 Yoda puppet could be. I am not sure if George Lucas set out to make total perfection in every frame of either of his *Star Wars* trilogies. The joy of the movies is not just the artifice of it all, but seeing the artifice. It is scratches on vinyl.

This is not the young George Lucas whose crew would jump around town in the early Californian hours shooting *American Graffiti* on the hoof. This is not the 1979 George Lucas buffered by the success of *A New Hope* as he opens the hangar doors again at Elstree Studios. This is the George Lucas with the weight of technology and a global expectation on those check-shirted shoulders. The Podracing is of course George Lucas's *Tatooine Graffiti* moment – complete with trackside commentary from a Wolfman Jack pair of disc-jockey aliens, the boastful Sebulba filling in for Harrison Ford's racing rival and Natalie Portman's Padme bickering with Liam Neeson's Qui-Gon Jinn just like Mackenzie Phillips and Paul Le Mat in the back of that hot rod. And maybe Jar Jar Binks is just every half-bred Golden Retriever in every

Spielberg film of the 1970s – barking at the wrong time, looking off camera for laughs and just getting in the way. Okay, no – I am not going to advocate that at all in a chapter where I have already suggested *The Phantom Menace* is fine.

Along with Walt Disney, Alfred Hitchcock, Cecil B. DeMille, Orson Welles, John Ford, D. W. Griffiths and his friend Steven Spielberg, George Lucas is one of the leading American movie showmen of twentieth-century cinema. The fact he only directed six feature films in his entire career, but half of them were *Star Wars* prequels, surely necessitates a fairer rethink. The first six *Star Wars* films – even now that doesn't sound right to an older sky kid – are Anakin Skywalker's story and George Lucas's science fiction legacy. And time could well be good to them. The prequels didn't ruin our childhood as some of the annoyed fan mantras claimed. How can our childhoods be ruined when we had *Star Wars* so predominantly in them?! And the prequels let in new fans – new sky kids who later became money-earning adults who would be keen to see *Episode VII*, work on *Episode VIII*, bring their kids along on a Saturday afternoon to see *Episode IX* and create new movie theatre memories for new generations. This book is about legacies and what that initial run of films gave us all. The prequels are part of that legacy. But they also left one in their own wake – one that gets knocked and forgotten as three whole films and over nine hours of high-end moviemaking are reduced to hatred for a Gungan called Jar Jar Binks. Very much like the Bond movies – it does not matter where your entry point is. The importance lies in that you had one. And just like Bond, the wider moviegoing populace are what make box office hits, not just fans.

DARTH BECOMES HIM

THE FORCE AWAKENS

2015. A fearful astromech ball robot watches enemy shuttles drop into the night skies of a remote desert planet. With the mystery whereabouts of a legend at stake, the robot and his hotshot pilot master must move fast.

Dear 1984 me,

Please don't panic. And please don't rush to find Mum or Rob or a Golden Retriever or even a policeman. I didn't make a habit of writing to 8-year-old boys when I was one, so writing to myself as an adult in this way is a rather precarious endeavour for both us.

You probably won't get this letter until you return home from school. I hope it doesn't reach you on a Monday as I know that is *He-Man and the Masters of the Universe* day. And if it is a Tuesday I know you will probably not open it either as that is new *Look-In* issue day and nothing gets in the way of you poring over a new copy of *Look-In*. I do hope you win the magazine's video competition and become the proud owner of one of those three VHS copies of *Return of the Jedi* that you so desperately want and entered multiple times for. But there is maybe no need to check the letterbox every day for three and a half months – especially as you won't get a video player to play it on until the December of this year. Yep. That's right. You get a video player!! Don't worry. I imagine you will get a VHS copy of *Return of the Jedi* one day. If it is a Wednesday today, then maybe opening this letter will be a good thing as I know you hate Wednesdays because that means Cubs and you never felt like you fitted in there unless the weather was so bad that they did that thing of showing a video indoors and getting chips for everyone. And that magical night will only happen once. Oh, and don't worry – that cocky, but annoyingly athletic Cub with the good hair and cool trainers who said you would make a rubbish Scout and who loved himself more than everyone else loved his hair will not age well. The hair will be the first thing he loses before his waistline and taste in trainers. Obviously if it is a Friday then you will be at karate surrounded by all those much older boys with even more great hair, broken voices, stubble and slightly hairy chests that make you think of Harrison Ford in *Raiders of the Lost Ark*, but you will not be sure why for a little while longer. If it is a Saturday, then there is no chance you will be opening this letter. You will be up early, watching *The Go-Bots* on *Wide Awake Club* and drawing another *Star Wars* picture whilst leaning on your *Dangermouse* annual covered in pen stains. Oh, and please stop telling folk that *The Go-Bots* are the best ever and that no one will remember the *Transformers* in years to come. But when you tell folk you will one day see a CHiPs motorbike for real, you will. You will definitely not get this mail on a Sunday – which is fine as you will be eagerly awaiting *Terrahawks* in the afternoon, but quietly hoping Mum doesn't sit and catch it with you as I know you have a secret fear and total dread of the villain Zelda and cannot even look at her in the opening titles. Just so you know – like the library ghost in *Ghostbusters*, Mr Noseybonk from *Jigsaw* and Zelda from *Terrahawks* will never stop being terrifying so buckle up and get used to it. All things considered, I hope this letter finds you on a Thursday. I don't remember Thursdays being a thing.

A lot will happen between when you read this and when I write it. Most of it good. Some of it brilliant. Because of your love of cinema and America you will eventually get a degree in Film, become a writer and author, work with people you have long admired and be fortunate enough to be asked to write down and share all our stories of a childhood and adulthood through cinema. You will fall in love with someone who takes nearly every step into the real America with you and who shares those American friends, cities, streets and experiences that become as key to your life as *Star Wars* and *Superman* did when you were 8. You will also meet and befriend Octopussy, Roger Moore will send you a wedding telegram, you will bump into another Superman and you will one day truly regret not being quick enough to take up the kind offer of an afternoon with the elderly man that designed Chewbacca, Jabba the Hutt and Yoda. Yes, the make-up genius that is Stuart Freeborn will move into your home village when you move out. And whilst he will gift you some special mementos of his amazing working life, please don't ignore the invite for a cup of tea should it ever arise again in your timeline.

The real reason I have contacted you in this way is because written paper letters like this are the only way of contacting you in 1984. I cannot send an email as I don't want the Feds to think you are playing *WarGames*. And I know you always liked receiving written letters, but never got many – especially from strange future men professing to be your friend. Do you remember last year when you saw *Return of the Jedi* twice at the cinema? And do you remember how everyone told you that it was the last *Star Wars* movie ever ever starring Luke Skywalker, Han Solo and Princess Leia? Well, that is not entirely true. Okay, it is a little true. But only just. As you get older, you will find that life throws some curveballs. And some of them you might even catch. One particularly good curveball will happen in 2015. No. You won't still be watching films on the Hitachi player, nor will the Regal Cinema still be operating. In December 2015, a new *Star Wars* film will debut in the cinemas. It will be called *The Force Awakens* and star Mark Hamill, Harrison Ford and Carrie Fisher. The music will be by John Williams, Peter Mayhew will be back as Chewbacca, and there will be figures and toys, posters and a cute new robot. Oh, and the Millennium Falcon comes back. And the main character is a girl. You will not watch the trailer at the cinema before a Disney holiday movie – although oddly, *The Force Awakens* will actually be a Disney holiday movie. You will watch the trailer on a phone on a train with your husband. Each part of that whole last sentence will make a hell of a lot more sense one day. As will the return of three heroes you never thought you would see again. Trust me – it will be both strange and great with a touch of tragedy. A year after *The Force Awakens* – yes, just a year – there will be another *Star Wars* film. It will be the fourth prequel to *A New Hope*, but easily the best so far. And you won't call the first *Star Wars* film *A New Hope* for another few years either. Nor will you know what a 'prequel' is. It's a sequel, but backwards. And sideways. And sometimes both. But the fourth *Star Wars* prequel – and there will be more – sort of features Carrie Fisher a fortnight before she sadly passes away and Peter Cushing about twenty-eight years after he actually did. See – prequels are weird.

You will see *The Force Awakens* with two of your oldest friends you haven't met or made yet, your husband who you also haven't met yet and two god-kids who haven't been made yet. It will be the beginning of a grand new boys' tradition of watching new *Star Wars* movies where the younglings General Jack and Captain Finn will get new figures each time and give the future adult you a perfect excuse to go into toy shops and buy *Star Wars* figures. To be honest, all the toy shops will be full of dads and men your age who haven't really grown up, nor have any serious desire to do so as they puff up their chests and ask weekend staff if they are 'likely to be getting any more Poe Damerons in before Christmas?' Kids at the time will just look in confused awe as grown men in their late 30s and early 40s speed through the cardbacks of *Star Wars* figures looking for the rare ones in record time. Your X-Wing ensemble will be nicknamed Blue Squadron, will remain in tight formation throughout, always go for a cool dinner afterwards and – despite your attempts to let Empirical bygones be bygones – at least one of the god-kids will have a slight fear of the Stormtroopers wandering about the cinema lobby and not play ball in all photograph opportunities. The kids' *Star Wars* world is one now partly crafted of Lego. You will be a grown man jealous of your god-kids' *Star Wars* Lego Millennium Falcon. And no – they will not swap it with your early-1980s Lego police station complete with its own helipad and parking space.

You will obviously want to tell people some or even all of this. I would if I was 8½ years old again. I've certainly given you thirty-two years notice to get your name down in the bookings book for that first night's rental of *The Force Awakens* at the Gaston Gate Garage. As you find out, though, and partly due to their insistence of stocking only one copy of each new title, that is still cutting it fine and risking disappointment – especially as the garage will stop renting movies in the early 1990s. To be honest, by 2015 you will be either using a digital copy – which is invisible and cannot be put in a fake leather box from Argos – or a format called 'DVD'. This last one is not a tape and it's not an album. It is sort of like those cool 1970s coffee table coasters other houses had. There is also something called Blu-rays – which are neither blue nor have rays coming out of them. You cannot, must not put a bet on this information like this. Just look at Biff in *Back to The Future Part*

II. Oh, that's right, *Back to the Future* gets a sequel. Two of them. And as I suddenly remember the original film is not out until next year in your time, maybe forget I said any of that last bit. Just don't put a bet on any of this. No one will believe you anyway, despite the odds being amazing. Actually – and just between us Marks – if you were to put a bet on all of this, please ensure I can find the betting slip. Leave it in the old ice cream tub of *Star Wars* figures. That will never be lost.

Yours sincerely,
You in thirty years' time x

P.S. You will never get the Bespin Princess Leia figure replaced so stop looking. And rest assured, you will not be lonely. That recent dream you had about becoming Elliott from *E.T.*'s best friend … yeah, don't forget that. Oh, and Luke Skywalker dies.

To its eternal credit, *The Force Awakens* feels like a missing *Star Wars* movie that came out in 1985. Blessed with a cracking first half that beguiles and reminds of those Kenner and Palitoy-addled childhoods with magic, dignity and a heraldic swagger, *Episode VII* is a willfully old-school swashbuckler whose ultimate success is how it may have not even needed the returning veterans to work. From that opening canary-yellow crawl and a careful wording that promptly suggests it has been part of our cinematic skies for decades already, the first act of *The Force Awakens* unfolds as if barely a parsec has passed since the end of *Episode VI*. Director J.J. Abrams (*Star Trek*, *Super 8*), producer Kathleen Kennedy, returning screenwriter Lawrence Kasdan (*The Empire Strikes Back*, *Return of the Jedi*), composer John Williams, designers Darren Gilford, Rick Carter and their fellow Lucasfilm / Bad Robot creatives achieved just what their two-year damage limitation publicity campaign promised – they made *Star Wars* analogue again.

A new hope and new traditions – school pals, husbands and god-kids gather at the local Odeon System, December 2016.

Guess what – a rubber space vulture puppet picking at some sandy roadkill packs more impact than a bustling marketplace of mugging mouse-mat creations hanging off every moment and each other. A nosey B-movie alien noting a passing BB-8 astromech unit packs more of a *Star Wars* punch than a somersaulting sight gag with a Gungan. And sometimes someone desperately trying to fix a spluttering Millennium Falcon just needs to drop into the floor with a wrench and some tech-talk to properly make a hunk of junk really work. This is a special-effects universe that almost starts out as if CGI was never going to be invented to awkwardly 'beguile' us for a whole decade's worth of villainous metallic liquids, cartoonish Spider-Men, Ten Commandments sandstorms and exploding White Houses. The *Star Wars* saga has always been linear. The pieces or episodes might now pitch around different timelines. But the individual films do not. Aside from its scene wipes and concurrent narratives, *The Force Awakens* does not play with its timelines. Yet, unlike the prequels and their preordained narrative dots that were already there to join up with a lightsaber, here we do not know what they are. Social media rumours aside, *The Force Awakens* is the first *Star Wars* movie in thirty-two years where the characters and their story are not a foregone conclusion. It is not just a reassuring return to the analogue glories of the original saga. It is a welcome reminder that in this age of teasers, convention panels, set reports, extras and featurettes, the tricks and beats of a film's story can still remain a handsome surprise. The simple skill of *The Force Awakens* is that it dismisses all that non-cinematic surmising about fan-fuelled spin-offs and extended universes for a story and production that is pure, basic cinema. *The Force Awakens* feels like a movie where more effort went into preserving its sense of integrity and tone rather than ambitious visual effects and alien worlds created on a mouse-mat in San Francisco's Presidio Park. Granted, there are computer-generated key characters, particularly with Lupita Nyong'o's Maz Kanata and Andy Serkis's Supreme Leader Snoke. It is not devoid of all digital light and magic. But their story purpose is not CGI. Unlike some of the prequel set pieces, *The Force Awakens* never feels like a demonstration for an industry tech show in San Francisco. The prequels are beats in the *Star Wars* saga. *A New Hope*, *The Empire Strikes Back* and *Return of the Jedi* are beats of popular twentieth-century culture and Hollywood history. *The Force Awakens* has to try to straddle both.

Aside from Roger Moore returning to Bond, Richard Dreyfuss donning his *Jaws* beanie hat again or maybe Michael Crawford being Condorman once more – maybe – seeing Harrison Ford, Mark Hamill and Carrie Fisher back in the roles that launched a million plastic toy ships is something akin to what Admiral Kirk remarks in the great *Star Trek IV: The Voyage Home* (1986). 'You're not exactly catching us at our best,' pleads Kirk, typifying the equally warm glory of seeing Luke, Han and Leia on our movie screens for the first time in over three decades with an altogether new 'best' that is barely flawed at all by the passing years. The fears and concerns over any of the returning crew donning their blasters and Endor ponchos again were all allayed the moment Harrison Ford ran into the Falcon and first trailer with a 'Chewie, we're home' relief. Harrison Ford is not still pretending to be an aloof heartthrob in his early 40s. Neither is Han Solo. Instead of turning him into an embittered veteran, Kasdan and Abrams' screenplay pitches Solo as instantly accepting and admiring of our new heroes Rey, Finn and ball of electronic sass BB-8 with a grizzled and fatherly twinkle in his eye. In a flip of *A New Hope*, it is now Solo's turn to convince the young upstarts aboard the Falcon that the Force very much exists. But unlike Solo's uncertainties in Episode IV, here there is no resistance to this Resistance. They believe him. And very quickly that group dynamic with Solo at its heart is back – augmented by John Boyega's cocksure Finn, Daisy Ridley's inventive Rey and an amazingly coiffured Chewbacca. And that old man run, lunge and punch of Han's is already the stuff of pub-chat legend.

In returning to those analogue *Star Wars* tenets of production and visual design – as Kylo Ren illustrates – *Episode VII* goes very non-analogue with its characters. In *The Force Awakens* it is Stormtrooper FN-2187 that has that all-important first-act change of heart. The old 1940s Second World War dogfights, cool-headed heroines and Third Reich dynamics of *Star Wars*' original trilogy have now evolved into a 1960s Cold War of blurring allegiances, exiled heroes and vicious newcomers refusing to learn from history as they build their walls and missiles. In this new era of *Star Wars*, old villains like the Stormtroopers can now be moral heroes. And new, moral-less villains can be Skywalkers. And Solos. That Cold War world of messages, maps and the bullying and purging of war dignitaries and heroes like Lor San Tekka (Max von Sydow) is ever so witch-hunt like.

Putting the corporate rebranding of the Galactic Empire aside, the villainy of *Star Wars* is always Darth Vader and ultimately his superior – Emperor Sheev Palpatine. *Rogue One* knows that. But *Rogue One* has a story timeline and *Star Wars* history in its favour. After BB-8, Domnhall Gleeson's vampy, camp and hissy General Hux is the film's second ginger stress ball as he snarls his path across numerous First Order gantries whilst doing that necessary 'looking down at very British deputy officers' thing the high-ranking villainy must always do in *Star Wars*. The most interesting malevolence, however, in *The Force Awakens* is a Vader fan-boy – the hipster-angry Kylo Ren, played with festering volatility by Adam Driver (*Midnight Special, Inside Llewyn Davis*). A more nuanced young actor than *Star Wars* is perhaps used to and – like Domnhall Gleeson – born the year *Return of the Jedi* first premiered, Driver creates an antagonist in Ren who generates as much audience sympathy as he does fear. A sort of wannabe Sith element with Instagram hair who breaks the *Star Wars* villain rule by peeling off the mask from the get-go, Kylo reminds of the dramatic opportunity and villainous baiting the prequels lost out on as he sneers and stomps his way around the brilliantly realised Finalizer Battlecruiser and its ever-so-1977 interiors. Perhaps that full-on juvenile meltdown will be better served in Vader's grandson than the past adolescence of his grandfather.

The familial dynamics surrounding Kylo Ren are almost as unnerving as his fatal last-act gesture towards a true icon of twentieth-century cinema. Adam Driver is *The Force Awakens'* biggest character gamble – and success. The celebrated dynamics of the Luke, Leia and Han trinity have now been rewritten –

The new *Star Wars* sequel trilogy awakens at London's famed Odeon Leicester Square in October 2015.

underlined with a new tragedy any future revenge will never rectify. The death of Han Solo is nearly as shocking as when he shouts out 'Ben!' to his wayward son moments before walking across a walkway mindful of Ben Kenobi's last act of courage from *A New Hope*. The tropes were never good for Ford's return. And they certainly set up a downbeat dread concerning Luke Skywalker's fate when *The Last Jedi* starts two years later and we all have a hunch a dropped brown robe could provide tears before bedtime. A lead mentor is always struck down by a lightsaber in the first episode of each trilogy, and in *The Force Awakens* Han made that destiny-gambling comment, 'we'll meet back here'. He may as well have showed us a creased photograph of his princess back home and explain how he cannot wait to see her again once this war is over. For this sky kid, the biggest regret of Han Solo's demise is that we will never see any new shared scenes between him, Mark Hamill and Carrie Fisher ever again. It was a particularly sad moment to be aboard a plane in December 2016 that had just touched down when the news of Fisher's very real passing broke, amongst the disembarking passengers as they turned on their phones. A little kid across the aisle tried explaining to his younger sister how 'Princess Leia has died' and everything on that bitter December night just got that bit colder. Despite the possible nods to Lucas's stark costumes of *THX 1138* (1971), those later scenes in *The Last Jedi* of a wounded and struggling General Leia adorned in white are now forever tinged with an off-camera poignancy. The hanging motif of John Williams' 'Princess Leia's Theme' hardly helps the nostalgic emotions either.

In the timeline of this new trilogy, General Leia now has to face a future where her young protégé Rey is to be trained by her brother to avenge her lover's death by killing the son obsessed by her dead father. See – *Star Wars* is a familial soap opera swathed in sci-fi clothing. Suddenly *The Empire Strikes Back*'s infamous 'No, I am your father' is less of the twist it used to be. It is going to be fun *Keeping Up with the Skywalkers* again – and especially under the acting auspices of Driver's fuming, lost and unpredictable Kylo. This is where *The Force Awakens*, Abrams and Kasdan fire the starting space pistol on this sequel trilogy with a flare of brilliance the prequels never experienced. Our heroes now have choices. Our villain now has choices. The story will now happen because of them, not around them. In the subsequent *The Last Jedi*, director Rian Johnson is then permitted to rug-pull the audience with a heroic switch of allegiances for Kylo - as a slo-mo twist on a red Pinewood soundstage sees 'the boy in the mask' fight alongside Rey as Johnson heroically lets the past of *Star Wars* assumptions die and a *Game of Thrones* sudden-death shock leaves the sequel trilogy's Snoke in a dead heap of gold bling. For the eighth *Star Wars* episode to end with zero indication as to both Kylo and *Episode IX*'s narrative path is one of Rian Johnson's unspoken triumphs.

We all thought we had *The Force Awakens* mapped out. In the eager, but refreshingly restrained publicity campaign for the film's December 2015 release we all assigned and imagined family links and mystery story arcs to Rey, super trooper Finn, stroppy villain Kylo and hotshot Resistance pilot Poe Dameron (Oscar Issac). We all assumed the narrative dynamics at play must be loaded with secrets and revelations. Box-set television, catch-up bingeing and multi-film comic book franchises had made us all structurally cynical – looking for plot turns and second-guessing twists over character. One of the screenplay tricks and tics of *The Force Awakens* and *The Last Jedi* is that when those credits roll we still know very little about any of them. After the plot-heavy politicking of the prequels, where lead characters were often chess pieces to be lifted and dropped by the events happening around them, here the characters are the plot. And one can almost touch the amount of toil, thinking and energy that went into those script meetings and drafts to make *Episode VII* not only play with organic grace, but the organic grace of a moviemaking style from another century. It takes a lot of effort to look effortless – especially in *Star Wars*.

The original world of *Star Wars* was always about fathers and sons. Now it fixes too on mothers, sons and surrogate daughters. The scavenging Rey is the eyes of the audience in a female *Star Wars* role that no doubt panicked some of those traditionalists who forget the first on-screen girl they ever cared about was Princess Leia Organa. Through *The Force Awakens*, *Rogue One* and *The Last Jedi*, this is now a freshly pointed saga that sees Jedi sisters finally doing it for themselves. And none more so than chief sister and producer Kathleen Kennedy.

Beginning as a working associate to Steven Spielberg, the California-born Kathleen Kennedy's first feature as producer was 1982's *E. T. the Extra-Terrestrial*. Having set up Amblin Productions in 1981 with Spielberg and producer, director and eventual husband Frank Marshall, Kennedy continued to produce *The Color Purple* (1985), *Empire of the Sun* (1987), *Always* (1989), *Hook* (1991), *Jurassic Park* (1993), *A.I. Artificial Intelligence* (2001), *War of the Worlds* (2005), *Munich* (2005), *War Horse* (2011) and *Lincoln* (2012). In 2012, Kathleen Kennedy became the president of Lucasfilm Ltd, with a new parent company in the form of Disney. George Lucas had clearly wanted to hand on his lightsaber legacy to a parent who could understand and safeguard his various movie bequests and story legacies. The initial padawan of a movie to emerge from that retirement deal is, of course, *The Force Awakens* – produced by Kennedy, who helped settle upon director J.J. Abrams who in turn brought in two women editors (Mary Jo Markey and Maryann Brandon), evolved Carrie Fisher's Leia from her 1970s feminine deity to robust Rebel matriarch, added a female Stormtrooper to the mix (Gwendoline Christie's Captain Phasma) and pinned a young female lead to its mast in the form of Daisy Ridley's Rey. Without fanfare, it is a marked female change of direction for the *Star Wars* saga and a welcome move which swiftly continues with *The Last Jedi*'s purple-rinsed Vice-Admiral Holdo (Laura Dern), a beefed up Lieutenant Connix (Billie Lourd), Commander D'Acy (Amanda Lawrence) and Rose (Kelly Marie Tran), spin-off tale *Rogue One* and Felicity Jones' Jyn Erso taking events full circle by handing on the literal baton and Death Star plans to a young Princess Leia. Such present-day movie progressions are less about pushing the possibility of a new, key feminine pulse to our childhood favourites and more about reminding how films like *The Sugarland Express, E. T. the Extra-Terrestrial, Poltergeist* and *Close Encounters of the Third Kind* already had just that.

When it takes its eyes off the BB-8 ball both figuratively and literally, *The Force Awakens* nearly does exactly what it shouldn't – it becomes a reheated soap opera based on the brilliant beats of other *Star Wars* films. A Death Star with a structural weakness for the third time in four successive episodes? And that is not counting *Rogue One*. Someone in First Order's management team really must review their contractors' safety records. Or at least dig out the old Galen Erso file from the Citadel Tower when it comes to corporate safety leaks. And whilst we all love a cantina band and a motley band of law-dodging alien émigrés, a hell of a lot of story-progressing homages take place in basically one happy hour in Maz Kanata's bar where everyone knows Han's name. A sliver of that breathing space Abrams lends Jakku may not have gone amiss here. In the span of what barely feels like five minutes, we have great Yoda-like wisdom from Kanata, avaricious gangsters, an empirical confession from Finn, the discovery of Luke's lightsaber, the awakening of the Force in Rey, a curious Jedi knightmare-cum-vision and aural cameos from Frank Oz's Yoda and Alec Guinness and Ewan McGregor's Obi-Wan Kenobi. The old saga was always successful because it had a cracking pace as well as those story beats. But Kasdan and Abrams still get that. There is a heraldic swagger to the whole piece that cinema just doesn't do any more. An ailing Finn is laid out like a Disney prince with a hopeful kiss from Rey, an elder like legendary actor Max von Sydow (*The Seventh Seal, The Exorcist*) is treated with great story reverence, flags and banners hang off castles and First Order rallies, and the idea of rebelling and resisting as a team is all restored after the fragmented exploits of the prequels.

Visually and artistically, *The Force Awakens* is top-notch cinema. It is a joyous about-turn to that 1970s sense of independent production flecked with a good old classical Hollywood sense of production, characterisation and physicality from all our youths and video rental altars. Harrison Ford and Han Solo's return to the saga aboard a smuggler's freighter is brilliantly draped with *Return of the Jedi* mid-shots, reds, golds and black metal. The Starkiller Base is a grey and disco-white nod to its 1977 DNA, and the alien dialect subtitles return to their late-1970s font. Rey climbing throughout an upturned and cavernous Star Destroyer flecked with dust and the shadows of empire became part of *Star Wars* lore before the first teaser ended. And the all-inclusive Resistance Rebels crowd round their command centre in a heroic Last Supper vignette – complete with a returning Admiral Ackbar brilliantly barking combat ideas like grandad in the corner.

And if the return of the monumental Mon Calamari admiral himself is not reason enough to slump back into your captain's chair with an Ackbar sense of 'they did it' relief about *The Force Awakens*, the costumes clearly take the last act of *Return of the Jedi* as their cue with lots of greens, khaki and dark royal blues mingling with the orange uniforms of Black Squadron versus the charcoal grey, cold silvers and blacks of Hux, Ren and Phasma with the generals of the First Order donning caps that curiously mirror Kylo Ren's Command Shuttle. The costume design by *Star Wars* first-timer Michael Kaplan circles each of the main characters with wardrobe motifs which became standard in the run-up to the film's release. Kylo has his phantom menace of the opera mask with its *Tron* decoration and tight-waisted frame making him almost look like a human lightsaber, Kaplan evolves his sense of torn, makeshift wraps and loose material for Jennifer Beals in *Flashdance* (1984) into Rey's Bedouin wrap top with leather wristbands and lighter colours for a lighter soul, he trades the green leather jacket he gave

Brad Pitt in *Fight Club* (1999) for a biker's jacket both Poe and Finn get some cool mod mileage out of, and Harrison Ford gets to swap the legendary trenchcoat Kaplan dressed him in for *Blade Runner* (1982) for a snazzy half-length, Hoth-ready parka and a great quip about being cold. Parkas are clearly this season's must-haves in this *Star Wars* revival galaxy as Cassian Andor (Diego Luna) is soon cutting a dashing figure in his own one in the following year's *Rogue One: A Star Wars Story*.

However, and this is *Star Wars* fan-boy sacrilege so do not come marauding like a boozed-up Tusken Raider, but maybe – maybe – the wider sweep of the film could have done with a tad … more … CGI. Seriously. The soaring work on Abu Dhabi's Jakku is beautifully sparse, tonally edifying and David Lean in widescreen ambition. Yet they are also scenes coyly punctuated with derelict spaceships, webuyanydroid.com shysters, alien gas stations, food bank stamps and prized drinking holes. After a while the vegetation of the British countryside locations in the last act come over as, well, the vegetation of the British countryside. The icy Hoth world of *The Empire Strikes Back* has a dramatic function – it was fatally cold and impossibly treacherous. Here the Starkiller Base scenes are not as earnt as the Jakku opener. They are maybe indicative of Abrams nodding a tad too much at the past like a Jedi motioning for his lightsaber over a Sarlacc Pit. And that is all totally understandable, as this film had to win over fans like no other film since *The Phantom Menace*. The Jakku overture gently bristles with a tactile and logical environment. The scavenging Rey values every drop of water, every inch of shade and improvised sand toboggan in this Star Destroyer boneyard. Yet, the last act's 'Third Reich On Ice' winter show of might may feel tonally right, but that is because it did before. The threat of the Empire in 1980 was because they turned up. Not because they were already there waving their own flags at their own supporters.

Rebel leaders General Jack and Captain Finn reporting for *Rogue One* duty, December 2016. The Force is strong with these god-kids.

Thank You

Dear Mark and Elliott,

Thank you very much for the Star Wars DVD. We watched it as soon as I opened it. May the force be with you.

From General Jack.

The Force is strong with these god-kids.

But before Yoda sits this sky kid down and warns him about where hate and fear lead to fan-boy suffering, when it breaks the tick-list shackles of all our expectations *The Force Awakens* is matinee adventure excellence. There is an understandable narrative choreography to the key beats. Nothing or no viewer is lost amidst the fictional technology and movie machinery of the siege of Jakku. The Rathtar attack aboard the Falcon has a logic and geography to its B-movie craziness. A moored TIE fighter in a flying panic aboard a Battlecruiser, a lone heroine lunching by her fallen AT-AT home, Lawrence Kasdan's cautious script-wrangling skills reducing the story to a look or gesture rather than the expositional minutes of trade union politics, Adam Driver's 'Darth Becomes Him' dilemma, a cinematographic decision to review and repeat the look, colour and visual depth of past glories, John Williams returning to his romantic glory – 'Rey's Theme' is as emotive as any cue from *The Empire Strikes Back* – and a Chewbacca that steals not only the Falcon at a powerful moment of tragic retreat, he almost steals the whole film – had that orange ball of astromech sass not got there first. These are all simple, yet analogue triumphs of storytelling – skills which some other examples of fantasy franchise cinema have dropped along the way. When the tsunami of superhero movies takes the open-ended nature of *The Empire Strikes Back* as licence to never end anything, they are forever teasing future films and dramas they haven't earned. *The Force Awakens* earns its Rebel Alliance stripes as both a reunion and revival. To quote Han Solo and 1977's *A New Hope*: 'Uh, we had a slight weapons malfunction, but uh … everything's perfectly all right now. We're fine. We're all fine here now, thank you.'

IN MARTHA'S VINEYARD,
NOT FAR FROM THE CAR

JAWS

1975. A new police chief sinks in terror as he watches the blood-spattered skies drop into a beach of Fourth of July swimmers, and a holidaying mother slowly realises her son is missing.

———○———○———

Today. Massachusetts. The grey of the Atlantic skies betrays just how warm it is in Cape Cod. As our ferry leaves the port village of Hyannis and the playground of the Kennedy family old and new, in the distance we pass the famous Kennedy Compound and its white clapboard structure. Indicative of much of the timber architecture dotted throughout Cape Cod and Massachusetts, it of course reminds us of JFK, Jackie Kennedy and many an early-1960s photo op. But already the Dutch colonial-style wooden homes and buildings, the steep drops of those sandy shores and those collapsing Cape Cod beach fences of this stretch of Massachusetts feel familiar for a very different reason. That reason causes me to forever scan the bobbing buoys, wooden jetties and the passing waters underneath with a familiar movie curiosity and an unspoken fear. We head towards the presidential and millionaires' bolthole that is the island of Martha's Vineyard and I count my blessings that we are already on a bigger boat. Eventually we pull into Amity Island and the unmistakable home of Steven Spielberg's *Jaws*. It was here in 1975 that new police chief Martin Brody (Roy Scheider) came to grips with the locals, summer business traditions, a stubborn mayor and the Boston dialect. It was here that a shark changed how the world looked at water, beaches, cinema and the summer blockbuster.

It is the beginning of our American honeymoon. Buoyed up by the friendships, movies and Californian vacations we had already been blessed with, I had long decided I wanted to propose in America. As it happened, it was only me that was in the States and Ernest Hemingway's house in Key West as I got on bended knee over the phone with about four and a half thousand miles between us. It now made apt sense that we honeymoon in America too. A month before Martha's Vineyard, my partner Elliot and I got married at the famed movie factory that is Pinewood Studios, London.

As a 007 fan, *Star Wars* kid and writer, Pinewood of course chimes with my filmic pursuits, our cinematic loves as a couple, as well as being a place where Elliot's dad had worked as a studio carpenter and where my grandfather Jimmy spent a lot of time catching bullets and working for the Bond family, EON Productions. More importantly for us and our endeavours to avoid a rainbow-strewn My Little Pony wedding full of covered chair nods to what others think the bride wants – it was a brilliant boys' playground for any kid raised on *Star Wars, Superman, Supergirl, Batman, Alien, Santa Claus: The Movie* and of course James Bond 007. Oh, and *Krull*. Definitely *Krull*. The dream palace I longed to visit as a kid was where I was now marrying a man my 9-year-old self would not

'I do.' Treading the same warm Pinewood paths as Bond, Superman and a galaxy of far, far away heroes.

have thought possible as I drew endless pictures of Luke Skywalker whilst not fully understanding why my heart would beat every time Clark Kent walked into the *Daily Planet* typing pool and Indiana Jones getting his shirt ripped off was always more interesting than him putting it on. Not only did we have an *Octopussy* top table – thankfully the mothers of the grooms barely flinched on that one – *A Force Awakens* table for the best men and that kind telegram surprise from Sir Roger Moore, but the 'Love Theme from Superman' played as our friends and family took their seats to dine in the same room Christopher Reeve and Margot Kidder would take lunch in when shooting *Superman, Episode VII* had not long shot on nearby soundstages and the Paddock Lot, *Episode VIII* was gearing up and *Spectre* was shooting its Westminster Bridge scenes that very night. One guest claimed a passing Daniel Craig had almost photobombed one of our official photographs at the front of the studios, and I quietly hoped Carrie Fisher and a dozen Stormtroopers would burst in like Dustin Hoffman in *The Graduate* to announce why the marriage ceremony could not happen. And all this sun-blessed aptness was lent further poetry by the fact we were the first gay couple to have a full marriage on the Pinewood lot. A place which wears its history at every turn now shares our personal history.

A week into our East and West Coast honeymoon and barely a fortnight shy of the Fourth of July, Elliot and I disembark at Oak Bluffs marina on Martha's Vineyard. I desperately wanted to arrive on Amity Island clutching a yellow lilo under my arm, a creased Kintner mom straw hat and a fake shark fin on my back whilst calling out for a missing black Labrador called Pippit. But there was plenty of time. At mid-morning, the town is already awash with arriving vacationers, biking couples and families, bustling historical cottages, tourist eateries and car rental units. As we are soon waiting for our own rental car in a hire shop manned by a curious amount of teen kids straight out of *Jaws 2* working their summer jobs, I am praying Robert Shaw's seadog Quint comes in and scratches his nails down a blackboard for a bit of peace and attention. Although mine is already on a beautiful silver convertible Chevrolet Camaro RS, complete with a shark fin radio antenna, parked up in a part of the garage that already looked out of my pre-booked price bracket. When it is our turn to sign and collect, the rental guy is immediately apologetic about giving our car away earlier in the day. He is so sorry. He asks if we are okay with driving the Chevrolet Camaro RS convertible complete with the shark fin radio antenna instead.

Laying on extra Imperial security at our Pinewood Studios wedding.

Cut to the husband and I cruising out of Oak Bluffs towards Chilmark and the fishing village of Menemsha in a Camaro RS with a shark fin antenna. For the first time in my entire life, I am at the wheel of a car straight men are looking at with head-turning envy. Okay, we didn't drive out to Menemsha immediately. Not far out of Oak Bluffs we have soon pulled over to have what was our first and only honeymoon argument, about how exactly we opened the Camaro's sunroof without damaging said shark fin radio antenna. And barely ten minutes after that, we have pulled over again near to where President Obama and Michelle are on vacation to ask for directions to Menemsha from a parked-up cop who is more keen to have a manly chat about a car I don't own than help with directions to Robert Shaw's shack in *Jaws*. 'Yes, and it has a shark fin radio antenna,' say I, with no clue as to its horsepower or engine specs, 'which is sort of apt for this island, don't you think?' The cop was clearly not a *Jaws* fan. Or maybe he was a relative of the Kintner boy and it was just all too close to home.

So here we are. Less watching skies, more chasing them as our honeymoon broke off from its East and West Coast trails to follow in the briny footsteps of a film that was about a shark and a boat whilst also being an independent-minded bottle of bubbly hurled against the bow of 1970s movie blockbusters. Ever since I confused *Jaws* and *Jaws 2* via a brief crush on the older Brody son in the latter, I had wanted to visit Amity. Like all real-life film locations, the reality is that Steven Spielberg's 1975 masterwork was not shot in one town, one street or even on one beach. The shoreline of *Jaws* was actually at least four separate beaches strewn throughout the eastern side of Martha's Vineyard. Likewise, the town of Amity was the previous whaling hub that is Edgartown. And Quint's shack was actually sited way across the island.

Finally, on our way down the South Road and past the Abel Hill Cemetery where John Belushi is buried, we reach the sleepy fishing village of Menemsha. It was here that Spielberg, production designer Joe Alves (*Close Encounters of the Third Kind*, *Jaws 2*) and cinematographer Bill Butler (*The Conversation*, *Rocky II*) pitched up amidst the fish markets, jetties and boats to shoot seadog Quint (Robert Shaw) and his shack replete with shark head skeletons and all manner of seadog machismo. It was one of the few set builds on the Vineyard and one which is tragically no longer there, having no doubt been dismantled soon after production. The majority of the film's white clapboard houses, municipal buildings and civic landmarks were shot at existing locations – give or take a sign change or two. And the village of Menemsha with its ongoing lobster traps, shacks and tanks, ropes, timber cottages with their squat windows, groynes, wooden stairwells and walkways, oxygen tanks, rusting outboard motors and abundant fishing rods raised skywards has not changed at all. It is here that Quint's trusty seafaring steed *Orca* is moored up and awaiting her final adventure as Hooper (Richard Dreyfuss) and Brody (Roy Scheider) strive to out-butch Robert Shaw and his dogged, but playfully half-cut shark hunting know-how. This is where the *Orca* sets out to sea amidst a jaunty John Williams music cue. This is where the modern blockbuster sets sail for cinematic mortality and the era of watching skies properly rises like a fast-moving shark fin.

Of course, *Jaws* actually begins by a beach campfire at night when a young woman called Chrissie Watkins (Susan Backlinie)

The timber-clad fishing hub of Menemsha and the site of Quint's *Jaws* home has not changed in over forty years.

and her cute stoner boyfriend Tom (Jonathan Fillie) skinny dip to their detriment on South Beach. If anything said America and the movies to me as a young kid and teenager obsessed with *The Wonder Years* and all manner of US TV and cinema, it was this beach. It is here that the cool kids are hanging out at night with their guitars, sleeping bags, kaftans, beer and harmonicas. It is here that Spielberg followed his friend George Lucas and *American Graffiti* (1973) into making a movie for kids and young adults with an astute opening gambit featuring the target audience getting attacked first. And it is here that the independence of those early Lucas and Coppola steps out of Hollywood have gone all the way from Folsom Street on the West Coast to Martha's Vineyard on the East.

In Britain, this overture to terror would probably have played out like a 1970s information film warning kids of the dangers of swimming naked in shark-infested waters near an electricity pylon, firework sparklers and broken glass. Instead, Spielberg and photographer Bill Butler render it a beautifully shot Massachusetts night with the opening title portent of suggesting something is in those waters already. These few cinematic moments represent the last few seconds that a beach and an ocean at night did not mean terror for evermore. And the fences. To me, the look of *Jaws* is those haphazard wooden Cape Cod fences, half buried in the dunes and flecked with dry grass and the odd severed hand. As soon as we pulled up in the Camaro and trudged down the familiar sandy steep incline towards the water, I was walking a mental tracking shot with Roy Scheider, hearing a police colleague's whistle, and looking for bug-covered severed limbs washed up on the shore. And how encouraging to see that of all the Vineyard's beaches, it is the South Beach that has the busiest activity with numerous lifeguards, beach volleyball pitches, pumped music and families all replacing the folk music and campfires of 1975. It is the total opposite of the quieter Joseph Sylvia State Beach and the scene of the Kintner boy death and the only time a deckchair looked cool on film – with that now-landmark dolly zoom into and away from Roy Scheider's Brody.

Here on the Amity town beach, I instantly regretted not wearing a Mrs Kintner straw hat as I looked to the waters and clutched my pearls with fake fear in real reverence to where we were. To be honest, the few vacationing families and couples there were on this sandy stretch did not look like they knew of the *Jaws* connections. The fact their roaming toddlers were allowed to wade into the shallows was testimony to that. And the lone child making a sandcastle unnerved even my movie remembrances. The last thing this pallid, Limey Brit wanted to do on the *Jaws* beach was jokingly start a real-life shark panic. Honeymooning or not, I doubt the

'Did you see that?!' This Kintner mom wannabe panics on the Vineyard's Joseph Sylvia State Beach amidst lilo-carnage and a Chief Brody dolly zoom panic.

island's real Chief Brody would be quite so cool as Roy Scheider. Although, I bet an older lady called Polly still mans the front desk and won't replace her typewriter with any new-fangled tablets and wireless printers.

The American Legion Memorial Bridge astride the estuary pool on the Oak Bluffs Road has not changed since Spielberg and the *Jaws* circus arrived in 1974. This is where the shark enters the kids' pool undetected, and Brody's water-bound son Michael is left in shivering shock, having no doubt read the script for *Jaws: The Revenge* (1987) and dicovering his mother ends up falling for Michael Caine's South London sea pilot with such glorious chat-up lines as, 'When I come back, remind me to tell you about the time I took a hundred nuns to Nairobi.' Like a great many landmarks on the Vineyard, the Memorial Bridge is synonymous with one film and is now of course christened 'The Jaws Bridge'. T-shirts are sold in Oak Bluffs proclaiming 'I survived the Jaws Bridge' and, despite the blatant signs urging 'No jumping or diving off the bridge', doing just that into the shallows beneath is now a rites of summer passage for many a Vineyard kid, adult and visitor alike. I was tempted, but eventually passed. Not only did I not have my skimpy 'I Heart Amity Island' 1970s budgie-smugglers with me, but we are clearly the only vacationing newlyweds on Amity to turn up in July and forget to bring swimming shorts. That was also why I didn't do a Chrissie Watkins tribute strip on South Beach in the hope a cute blonde graduate would yank off his Levi's and follow me into the moonlit surf. To be all Ellen Brody about it, I had already seen the very real shark warnings a day before as we traipsed ourselves home from a Provincetown beach, and the opening suite from *Jaws 2* was all I could hear in my head as the film director and local resident John Waters passed by and quietly grinned at my pallid, sweating Celtic state. And no book, closing chapter or author needs a fitting, but slightly humiliating finale detailing how I was the first person

The Cape Cod summer rites of passage that is jumping off *The Jaws Bridge*, aka Edgartown's American Legion Memorial Bridge.

to actually be killed by a real shark on Amity Island. Instead, I did the next best thing and got a photo op of me running like Chief Brody in a tribute panic along the American Legion Memorial Bridge screaming at the kids and swimmers to 'get out the water!!' Maybe these kids were *Jaws* savvy or Mayor Vaughn had got to them already, but everyone very rightfully ignored me.

The innate dread of the waters here has not faded over time. It is here you realise how the 1970s and early–1980s blockbusters that followed the bloody wake of *Jaws* do so on an emotion that they themselves sideline – namely terror. As noted already, *Close Encounters of the Third Kind* and *E. T. the Extra-Terrestrial* toy with the peripheries of movie horror to unnerve and dupe their audiences. But the film that launched a million kids' hands pretending to be shark fins in the bath, shot down the sale of inflatable beach lilos the world over and retuned younger generations' minds to get out of the water and into the movie theatres remains the bloodiest sky of them all. And nothing was more unnerving on any of these pit stops than seeing kids ignore the safety signs in the month of July on Amity Island.

It is in the picturesque Edgartown, and a few doors down from the hardware store Brody storms into to collect provisions to make his makeshift shark signs, where an endearing hand-drawn notice is stuck to the windows of a newsagents. Promising the 'Amity Walking Tour', it commences every Tuesday pledging 'photos, stories and a walk around the scenes and production of the classic film!' Edgartown is like a *Jaws* ride for real movie fans that don't go on movie studio tours featuring mechanical E.T.s, R2-D2s and sharks all programmed to fleece visitors for a ride snapshot. Part of the district is the island of Chappaquiddick. With access bound to the tides, the familiar way to reach it is to use the quick 'Chappy Ferry' – which is exactly what Chief Brody and Mayor Vaughn (Murray Hamilton) do when arguing about the safety of tourists on Amity Island. When they are not repeating their colleagues' need to chat to me about the specs of a Camaro convertible – 'doesn't anyone think the silver fin radio antenna is neat?!' – the traffic cops are out in force to stop the ferry-bound cars blocking the summer streets of Edgartown quicker than a bad Fourth of July marching band. And nothing blocks those patient cars driving onto what looks like the same ferry from forty-odd years back like a British movie fan stepping in for a thumbs-up photo opportunity and realising it is not just Mayor Vaughn who gets grumpy on Amity Island when the flow of tourism is jeopardised.

It was a hot afternoon, but it was also wholly stifling to be in a small pocket of a corner of America that in the 1970s was all a great many movie audiences and burgeoning sky kids knew of America. Lucas, Spielberg, Donner, Williams, Dante and others chose to present an America to us. A great many of the titles discussed in

The most famous car ferry in movie history today – Amity Island's Chappaquiddick Ferry.

this book are as much American stories as they are science fiction, comic book or fantasy tales. We never had sunny beaches in Britain. We had to go to Crete with our *Star Wars* figures to get any waves and sand.

Edgartown was the hub of *Jaws* on-screen and during its famously arduous shoot. The production offices, casting offices and no doubt some of the crew's bed and board were all spread throughout the narrow streets and white clapboard buildings of this captivating former whaling town. Here is where Amity's town hall, hardware stores and Brody's police station can be found without looking. Apart from the modern metals of the abundant parked and passing cars and that everyone is in shorts – which they

Off to the store for bits to make a shark warning sign before a marching band cuts me up.

curiously weren't on the streets of a film that is one of the most famous July-based movies of all time – none of it has changed. Imagine journeying to Elliott's Tujunga house in *E.T.* to find the front-yard grass is still parched and no one's moved that crushed bike from the driveway. Or finding that Simi Valley house of *Poltergeist* and to see how that backyard pool was still unfinished. Or maybe trekking to the Devils Tower in Wyoming to find a pile of *Close Encounters* gas masks and roadblocks still obstructing the canary-yellow marked highway. Or discovering that real-life Ewoks now host gay-cation breaks in the redwoods north of San Francisco. Okay, maybe not that last one. Actually, I want that to happen more than the others.

Waiting to ask Amity's Mrs Taft where she gets her hair done – Amity's Town Hall, Edgartown.

It is impossible to wander the main streets and side roads of Amity without beginning to stomp around like Roy Scheider. Ambling down from the police station, past where Keisel's bicycle rental shop is now an empty wedge of grass and towards that very corner where a bad marching band posed more danger to Roy Scheider than a great white shark, you cannot help but get that determined Brody strut thing going on. I suddenly had no time for dawdling pedestrians or unsure drivers and it was all I could do to resist buying a placard board and paints and warn everyone of allowing sharks to breed sequels in warm waters.

It is apt that Presidents, their wives and families vacation on Martha's Vineyard. Barack and Michelle Obama were nearby during our Amity trip and the Kennedys continue to have a presence throughout Cape Cod. If any film is the commander-in-chief of the 1970s blockbuster, it is Steven Spielberg's 1975 thriller, *Jaws*. Taking that template of suspense from *Duel* (1971), a bit of summer roaming from short movie *Amblin'* (1968) and mixing it with the blue-collar community chatter and local police politics of *The Sugarland Express* (1974), Spielberg and his writers Peter Benchley and Carl Gottlieb took the former's novel and – just like Francis Ford Coppola's *The Godfather* (1972) – turned an okay book into a landmark movie. Did it seriously create the 'blockbuster' as our queues for *Rogue One*, *The Last Jedi*, *The Empire Strikes Back* and *Raiders of the Lost Ark* now know it? It certainly recalibrated it. Word of mouth, teens and young adults are a heady mix if a movie strikes a summer nerve and plays for a demographic rather than to them. But that fin did not rise from nowhere. The new batch of 1970s independent-minded American cinema had already been preparing the waters for *Jaws*. Titles like John Boorman's *Deliverance* (1972), William Friedkin's *The Exorcist* (1973), Michael Crichton's *Westworld* (1973), Tobe Hooper's *The Texas Chain Saw Massacre* (1974) and Francis Ford Coppola's *The Conversation* (1974) all helped lay the watery foundations for *Jaws*.

When cinematographer Bill Butler shot both *The Conversation* and *Jaws* he was working equally in television and cinema. The immediacy and spontaneity of the television frame is prevalent in both. As Gene Hackman's San Franciscan surveillance expert slowly unearths a potential murder through his wire-tapping activity in *The Conversation*, Butler's prying camera moves arbitrarily and without immediate reason. The crosshair targets of Hackman's directional mics search the crowds and sidewalks haphazardly. As Butler's camera follows the people walking in front of and around Hackman, city women, labourers and suits negotiate busy streets and crosswalks in unrehearsed moments straight out of *Midnight Cowboy* (1969). The visual affluence and aspiration of the Hollywood fantasy and its cinema frame is slipping away – eroded and challenged in the many cultural, political and demographical shifts of the previous decade. The *nouvelle vague* of 1950s and 1960s cinema – especially that coming from France, Italy and Britain – has told new American filmmakers that cinema doesn't always have to be cinematic to be cinema. As a new batch of moviemakers, photographers and editors are removing some of those painterly, over-placed cameras of Hollywood, 1970s American independent cinema was removing the static complacency of cinematography. The camera no longer had to make beautiful visual statements to make good points. The camera could prowl, search, trip up, focus on the chatting chins of unconnected locals and make the ordinary beautiful. And that is no more evident than in *Jaws*.

Just as the San Francisco of *The Conversation* has a particularly impoverished, pallid hue that could not be further from Burbank or Hollywood, Butler's camera in *Jaws* captures the people of an American summer rather than the golden hues of Cape Cod in July. The camera of *Jaws* is no longer the overly rehearsed widescreen canvas of old Hollywood, but – like *The Conversation* – a probing, reportage eye roaming through the people and visitors of Amity Island. It is an almost voyeuristic, local television news snapshot of East Coast summer life. Families dig about for packed lunches, young teens gambol into the surf, new couples kiss, elderly locals continue their year-round swimming rituals, graceless swimming costumes stomp around the sand, larger ladies don't care as they float inelegantly in the water and oblivious toddlers make sandcastles in a world of their own. Amidst editor Verna Fields' ever-bustling cuts, ferry loads of unspecific tourists arrive, cars drive off the Chappy Ferry, kids skip their parents' gaze and the conversations around a nervous Chief Brody are ever inane and idle, bitchy and gossipy. It's partly because of the countless re-runs of the film on TV sets across the globe, but there is a sort of television immediacy to *Jaws*. Its cuts are quick, the frame is about the now and the nature of the shark attacks is visceral with an almost 1970s wildlife documentary dynamic, not overly shot as to be rendered beautiful. One of the many accomplishments of *Jaws* is how it decides to function as a movie. The rubber shark aside, Spielberg cuts away all the artifice and all director-led grandeur for the key beats of moving the story on. The pace of the movie is as victorious as its score, cinematography or casting. *Jaws* is a tour de force of movie structure. Every scene moves the film on.

The beach cameras are not steady. The frame sinks at angles beneath the surf and water splatters the lens and it doesn't matter. What would have been outtakes in times past are now raw, contemporary slivers – new ways and suggestions of storytelling sometimes using the quicker editing styles of television and news reporting and the shorthand they hold for mid 1970s audiences. It often feels like Spielberg, Butler and his lens are miles off the beach, zooming in to catch the human minutiae of beach life – the blurred legs passing through frame, the kids' front crawl races and the gossiping, nodding faces of the country club wives trying to keep their high salon hair dry in the water. We now see the vacationers in and out of the sea as the shark does – a confused mélange of limbs, chat and screams. The texture of Butler's camerawork renders everything – and, ultimately, the film – much more immediate. And contemporary. It is very much a *cinéma-vérité* documentary style where improvisation and spontaneity is key. It creates that all-important verisimilitude which is soon telling us everything we need to know about the mix of locals and opinion Brody has to work with and against. However, it is never *not* cinematic. There are great brushstrokes of light and colour in this film. By the time a moonlit sea is filling the frame, the movie has earned that visual eloquence. The blood reds, canary-yellow barrels and blues of the sea and skies of the final act forever break the real simplicity of one lone boat on the high seas.

Just like *The Conversation*, the visual expanse of *Jaws* is widened and intensified through its use of sound, sound effects, dialogue or neither. The sound work of American Zoetrope alumnus Walter Murch on *The Conversation* is now legendary and one of the key staples of any discussion of 1970s American cinema. Ironically, it was *Jaws* that won the Academy Award for Sound Mixing whilst Murch and the previous year's *The Conversation* missed out. Just like Butler's visuals in both *The Conversation* and *Jaws* prove, the sound doesn't have to be specific to get its point across. Chief Brody may dominate the frame, but those wanting his time and attentions are often off-frame – chipping in with their local comment and petty worrying. Everyone is wanting a piece of Brody's time but no one is prepared to lend theirs. It is a relief when the final act of simply Brody, Hooper and Quint on the high seas enables all three just to breathe without local interruption. But that is the point. Street music, street conversations, off-frame phone chats, the world-weary banter of sailors and seadogs, the bickering of kids and the breathless prattling of nosey men and women – it is all as widescreen and vital to the dressing of *Jaws* as a beautifully captured reflection of the moon on the midnight sea. How none of the sound and visuals often align is part of the raw appeal of *Jaws*. A great many of these films ditched the perfectly post-produced Hollywood soundtrack for wilfully cluttered audio and chat, that was as manufactured as anything over the decades before but now seemed personal. And relevant. 1970s American cinema remembered how sometimes the less you hear, the more you listen. And vice-versa. That cacophony of conversation and local bravado is a great inheritance from *The Sugarland Express* and *American Graffiti*. All the Amity boatmen jostle for front-page glory and a quick end to the shark problem, their constant chat and loud ignorance crashing about the conversations as Robert Shaw's Quint remains coyly silent. And then of course there is that curious moment of Richard Dreyfuss's shark expert Hooper suggesting their initial catch is nothing more than a tiger shark. 'A whaaaat …?' remarks one of the sailors in the campest Cape Cod moment this side of Provincetown. It is not just Brody who ultimately needs Quint to memorably scratch his nails down a town hall blackboard to get silence. Us viewers do too.

With the renewed use of sound in 1970s American cinema, the frame didn't always have to tell the story. The drive and presence of the shark itself is created through a sound effect, one of the most globally recognisable of all time – namely John Williams' two-note musical motif. Influenced significantly by Ivor Stravinsky's 1913 work *The Rite of Spring*, the Academy Award-winning score for *Jaws* is beyond iconic. Unashamedly going for disaster movie big when there is no other option, the grace of Williams' second collaboration with Spielberg is found in the side dramas it musters. Just as those two notes can be the underwater heartbeats of a shark, its victim or even a prudent reminder of the movie shocks of Bernard Herrmann's *Psycho* theme, elsewhere Williams' score dives, powers across the waters, doubles-back and catamarans over Verna Fields' editing calls. Just as the relentless scything of those brief notes has not lost any of its strength or even aged a day, the resulting silence left behind as those notes fade packs as much as trepidation as when they are hung over the film in big canary-yellow musical notes screaming 'Death!' Shrill woodwind and jabbing flutes pitch about like benign nautical alarms and deep, heavy notes just slowly sink under many a scene of dinner table pianos and the tableau of a family eating. And just like the early, brass-led Americana of *Superman: The Movie*, Williams uses his brass here to denote the sanctuary of an American homestead. Harps billow a false sense of underwater beauty, deceitfully reminiscent of a 1970s world of deep blue documentaries and grainy 16mm sea-life wonder. Just like *Close Encounters* and *E.T.*, *Jaws* opens with frictional sounds – synthesized slivers creating an underwater sonar scape where our senses are changed, curtailed and ultimately cut off. Bill Butler's camera is soon pushing over the bottom of the ocean with a non-human pace and a hungry point of focus. Williams' main shark cue is powered onto the soundtrack and the title card from the outset. For a film that infamously holds back on showing the shark in any lengthy detail, John Williams suggests it with great aggression from the opening frames. Despite being one of the most dark-edged cues of movie music in the twentieth century, Williams does not judge. The two-note motif is about the violent majesty of nature, not a chain saw killer or a closet murderer in a hockey mask. Even when the shark is seriously coming in for a kill, Williams throws some of his jaunty, seafaring motifs over the bouncing yellow barrels and rope pulling antics of Quint and his crew. Musically, *Jaws* is always very aware of its geographical and historical reference points in the history of Cape Cod, Massachusetts and British naval seafaring shanties.

One of the skills of *Jaws* is how its lead protagonist Martin Brody is very nearly the least necessary in the film's final act. He panics and slips and is out of his depth until a last-minute, resourceful hunch allows him to swim back to shore for it to all happen again three years later in *Jaws 2*. A deliberate fish out of water in the definitive *fish in the water* movie, Brody is no different from the city guys in *Deliverance* (1972). Or Edward Woodward in *The Wicker Man* (1973).

Just like *Deliverance* and *The Wicker Man*, *Jaws* pivots around what happens when the urban world clashes with the natural. Or rather, the urban world clashes with a natural world that has been misused by man. Here, the abuse is the ignorance of nature versus the greed of local commerce. The shark has just swapped a redneck banjo for an underwater cello. Admittedly, Roy Scheider's Brody is more likeable than the characters played by Burt Reynolds, Jon Voight, Ned Beatty and Ronnie Cox in *Deliverance*. But *Deliverance* was never meant for teens. It is no accident that Universal's *Jaws 2* takes note of its box office demographic and fills the film with kids and teens and the optimism of youth. The warning of succumbing totally to the arrogance and streamlining of city life is not for students, but the rat race men from *Duel* and *Deliverance*. It is not nature, but man that very much derails the weekend in *Deliverance*. *Jaws* is a classic example of how non-urban spaces are very much to be feared in 1970s cinema. *Duel* (1971), *Badlands* (1973), *Deliverance* (1972) and *The Texas Chain Saw Massacre* (1974) are hardly encouraging urbanites to drive off-grid at the next holiday weekend. To be fair, the 1970s cityscapes of *Dirty Harry* (1971), *The French Connection* (1971), *Mean Streets* (1973), *Taxi Driver* (1976) and *The Conversation* (1974) were not much better. Sprawling, contemporary cities do not feature much in Spielberg's world. If they do, they are often a sample of nostalgic hindsight such as the Los Angeles of *1941,* the Christmas box London of *Hook* (1991), the Berlin side-streets and walls of *Bridge of Spies* (2015) or the Shanghai of *Indiana Jones and the Temple of Doom*. Washington DC is kept at bay in *Raiders of the Lost Ark* – so much so that San Francisco doubles up for it instead. *Jaws* certainly plays with Brody's New York City background as he battles the Bostonian accent, dogged fishermen and local foibles – Brodie's 'they're in the yard, not too far from the car' went straight through my mind as a Hyannis ferryman announced our travel to Amity that July Tuesday. I always half-imagined Scheider's role opposite Gene Hackman in the New York narcotics thriller *The French Connection* was actually Martin Brody prior to moving the family to Amity Island to take the heat off that previous case.

Fresh to Amity, Brody is attacked from all sides before the shark even rears its ugly mechanical head. Veteran locals pick him up for not being local – 'You don't go in the water at all, do you?' The mayor picks him up for not being local – 'It's your first summer, you know.' Even his faithful wife Ellen (Lorraine Gary) calls him out not being local – 'Martin hates boats. Martin hates water. Martin sits in his car when we go on the ferry to the mainland.' Yeah, thanks Ellen. But in *not* being the local as he struggles to get to grips with the high seas like most of the film crew around him on the notoriously tough *Jaws* shoot, Martin Brody is us. And in doing so, he is the first everyman in that vital, career defining Spielberg trilogy that continues with *Close Encounters* and *E. T.* A continuing trait of Spielberg's directorial work is 'what would you do in this situation?' *Jaws* could very easily have been all about Richard Dreyfuss's Hooper – a learned marine academic man who travels light and works hard. But no. It is about someone with less water skills than that. It is every member of that audience in 1970s Britain who hasn't visited that many beaches apart from the Crete package holiday or the freezing grey English coastline in November where no one and their bag of chips were venturing that far into the Brighton surf.

Before the science fiction and fantasy genres had one of their defining movie renaissances in the 1970s, the horror genre was already rising from its own 1960s grave of lazy, gothic-skewed body terrors, biker films gone wrong and the withering coat-tails of Universal Studios' *Monster* series and its imitators. Just like sci-fi, a dubious raft of sub-par titles was never going to go away. But now horror stories with a domestic, contemporary reality were surviving sunrise. *Rosemary's Baby* (1968), *The Exorcist* (1973), *Don't Look Now* (1973) and *The Texas Chain Saw Massacre* (1974) all hand a bloody baton to Spielberg and *Jaws*. Horror could now be extreme and physical. Horror could now be indiscriminate. Horror no longer needed us to spend a whole film with one group of characters. Horror no longer saves itself for the final act.

Horror also has the unnerving ability to reflect where we and our societies are at any given time. *Jaws* is very much a post-Watergate, post-Nixon thriller. It is about small communities occasionally dogged by small minds, not the Feds and might of 'the Man'. Murray Hamilton's Mayor Vaughn is an anchor-patterned, blazer-wearing civic fool disregarding science, academia, safety and the law as he ploughs on with Amity's summer tourism plans and a gameshow host's sense of local celebrity. Very soon newspaper headlines and civic bureaucracy are not to be trusted. Graffitied humour is frowned upon and everyone loses their sense of humour – 'I don't think that's funny,' remarks the deliciously coiffured and pearl-clutching gossip, Mrs Taft (Fritzi Jane Courtney), 'I don't think that's funny at all.' And rising above it all, and indeed the whole movie, is Robert Shaw's craggy, worldly-wise and hard-drinking sea hunter, Quint. Pitched as both a deliberate rule-breaking contrast to cop Brody and academic Hooper, the British Robert Shaw (*From Russia with Love*, *A Man for All Seasons*) also brings a deliberate clash of acting styles. There is a sense Shaw is playing with Dreyfuss and Scheider as much as he is Hooper and Brody. The scenes between the trio have a brilliantly charged awkwardness and one-upmanship about them – as experience counts for everything, especially when crushing a beer can versus demolishing a polystyrene cup. Both Hooper and Dreyfuss seem to be in fascinated awe of the good ship Quint. His wild, booze-addled eyes roll over the screen and seas, and just as Shaw almost loses breath and maybe even his line, he snaps Quint back into a wise, thorough, and deceptively sympathetic 'working-class hero'. Robert Shaw's Quint is the first of Spielberg's crucial authority figures – actors, characters and often a mesmeric mix of both who pause a film, take us to one side and quietly illuminate the real point and arc of it all. Francois Truffaut (*Close Encounters of the Third Kind*), Beatrice Straight (*Poltergeist*), Margaret Avery (*The Color Purple*), Audrey Hepburn (*Always*), Anthony Hopkins (*Amistad*),

Ben Kingsley (*A.I. Artificial Intelligence*), Lynn Cohen (*Munich*), Niels Arestrup (*War Horse*) and Mark Rylance (*Bridge of Spies*) all take on Spielberg's baton of the quiet gravitas that Shaw held first in 1975.

The Texas Chain Saw Massacre is a particularly pertinent comparison to *Jaws*. Not only is it directed by Tobe Hooper, who of course goes on to collaborate with Spielberg for 1982's *Poltergeist*, but both feature a silent but deadly main adversary, both inhabit a world of trucks, denim and blue-collar machismo, both use isolation for their fears, both dress their sets and early chills with the bones of animals, both play with the expected horror beats and denouements, and both use a pretty blonde victim in a vest-top in their defining imagery. Whilst *The Texas Chain Saw Massacre* features young adults as its protagonists and *Jaws* features its beach kids throughout before more teens take the story reins in *Jaws 2* (1978), both films are very much aimed at that demographic. Discordant screams and unconnected screeches tear through the soundtracks and the grotesque-ness of toothless locals, sweaty and overweight men and the sexist gaze of some residents are unnerving way before either film unveils its killers. And like *Psycho*, *The Exorcist* or *The Texas Chain Saw Massacre*, one of the key motivators for kids and their interest in *Jaws* was how the notoriously grisly festival of 1970s movie horror was initially kept just that bit out of reach. That censorious distance was key to building the myth, the hunger and the need to see *Jaws*. In Britain, the film initially received an 'A' rating for its Boxing Day 1975 release, enabling it to be seen by 5-year-olds and up – if accompanied by an adult. That later evolved into a 'PG' in the 1980s. Having first splattered onto American TV screens in 1979, *Jaws* premiered on British TV on Thursday, 8 October 1981. It received a massive audience of over 23 million viewers. That was nearly half the population of Great Britain at the time. And you just know every one of them did a shark fin hand as soon as they were next underwater.

I was not one of those 23 million. Maybe Spielberg's salty flying limb opera was not quite right for a child that had only cut his Muppets 6th birthday cake the previous weekend. For a while, this kid got confused as ITV's frequent broadcasts – often on a Sunday night in the summer – would flip about with both *Jaws* and *Jaws 2*. We didn't always get to sit down from beginning to end with these titles that were not strictly suitable for our age group. Like a great white shark in the Cape Cod waters, I would steal and stealthily catch bits of *Jaws* where I could. My mum would often get up to let the dogs out during the commercial breaks, but never be back in time when the film started again. So, I would sneak in and catch what Amity action I could before she clicked that watching skinny-dipping hippies getting decapitated was not really what she wanted her son to answer when asked, 'and what did you get up to this weekend?' by a nun on Monday morning. I once lay on the upstairs landing listening to the whole of *Jaws* from the downstairs television. For years I swore Spielberg's 1975 archetype was about a group of teen kids being helped by Roy Scheider after Robert Shaw and Richard Dreyfuss both get killed first because they were not as resourceful as the kids. ITV then made great holiday weekend drama out of showing *Jaws 3-D* (1983). And for a while we thought the shark was now the centrepiece of a sequined waterski display team at SeaWorld you could only see through the 3D glasses that came free in cereal packets. With success comes a demarcated audience demographic. And with that comes tailored sequels and marketing that swim even further from what was first achieved in 1975. Again, the slightly out of reach, 'not in full grasp of a full screening' nature of a film like *Jaws* only added to its lustre and mythology. Because of *Jaws 2* I was more fearful of being stuck underwater under a boat or floating polystyrene mat down the local baths than I ever was being mauled by a great white shark.

To play with people's natural predisposition to be near and in water is a stamp on the human psyche that no motion picture ever achieved before. If you change how people perceive something, that is not just being a blockbuster, or even an indie-minded piece of effective new wave cinema. That is making a mark that goes beyond cinema. Just as George Lucas changed and updated our engagement with going to the movies and bringing them home to us, Steven Spielberg changed how we look at our world. It cannot just be this writer who clocks an approaching lorry in my wing mirror and thinks of *Duel*? It cannot be just me who looks at a desert canyon and thinks androids and Tatooine.

And if Steven Spielberg had the savvy instinct and moviemaking constitution to get under and into audiences' psyches with *Jaws*, just imagine their expectancies when Columbia Pictures announce *Close Encounters of the Third Kind*, Paramount declare *Raiders of the Lost Ark* and Universal first mentions *E.T. the Extra-Terrestrial*. That expectancy and attention Spielberg gets as a filmmaker is because of *Jaws*. The stamp of authority he gives a production – be it his or someone else's – is because of that imprint he put on our associations with water, summer holidays, beaches and eventually looking to the stars and how and why we communicate beyond our world – the most basic preoccupations any kid involves themselves with, whatever the decade. When the squeaky, cigarette-stained movie theatre curtains of the 1970s went up on *Jaws*, *Close Encounters* and *Star Wars*, our relationship with the movies evolved from being thrill-rides, tear-jerkers, toe-tapping diversions and romance-reliant comedies. They got into our soul and how we mentally bracket the world. It continues to this very day. You can sense the ears and eyes of an audience perk up when a slow-fading trailer caption declares 'A Steven Spielberg film'.

Jaws personifies the essence that binds these *Watching Skies* titles – the vibrancy of youth. Part of the success and following of these films must surely come not just from the younger age of the audiences, but from the youth of their creators. Steven Spielberg was 26 when he came to Martha's Vineyard in that Cape Cod summer of 1974 to shoot his shark movie. He was only 23 when he shot *Duel* (1971). Likewise, George Lucas was barely 30 when he finally got the production momentum going on what became *Star Wars*. These films all contain shot choices, editing decisions, casting choices, design choices and directional choices made by the young guard. When director Richard Thorpe made *Jailhouse Rock* (1957) to try to maximise the teen movie market for all things Elvis, he was 61. He was born in the previous century. As was Alfred Hitchcock, who had not long made *Frenzy* (1972), which, as grisly and tonally wretched as Hitch no doubt planned, was still a film from a filmmaker who was 71 playing to younger audiences whose sense of fear at the movies was about to be transformed forever with *The Exorcist* (1973), *The Texas Chain Saw Massacre* (1974) and *Jaws*. *Jaws* reinvigorated the American box office and got people and younger adults back into the habit of thinking about *and* going to the movies as the movies themselves got back into the habit of thinking about them. Seeing *Jaws* at the local picture house was as key to an American mid 1970s rite of passage and culture as getting a copy of Bowie's new *Young Americans* album or finding a neighbourhood kid who owned *Pong*. And if *Jaws* got kids and young adults re-engaging with those darkened cinemas, it was *Star Wars* that kept them there. But *Jaws* was not just a well-made rollercoaster romp. To this day it holds a contemporary zeal and an acute grip on character, time and place. *Jaws* is both popcorn and art.

Back at Martha's Vineyard and the ferry town of Oak Bluffs, and with a truly beautiful sunset draping a Technicolor dusk all around the skies and a well-earned gin raised in the honour of the sunken *Orca*, we look around the dockside's wooden shack bar as we wait for the ferry home. Above us hangs a small handmade sign proving that rubber sharks and dubious sequels may come and go, but that first blockbuster catch of the day is still the bloodiest and most victorious. It is a recreation of a sign hanging in the film asking for hunting help – 'REWARD: a $3000 bounty to the man or men

who catch and kill the shark that killed Alex M Kintner on Sunday June 29th on the Amity Town Beach.' If they just waited three more films, Ellen Brody and that fierce 1980s bob of hers would have done it for nothing. I knew I should have got that Kintner mom hat sorted in time.

As the ferry took us off Amity Island and its Martha's Vineyard counterpart, those dropping, cascading John Williams piano notes

The July sun sets over Amity Island and its Martha's Vineyard alias.

and harps which accompany the underwater sight of the plunging shark carcass and the water-dispersed sun floating above it like a mothership were all I could hear. Few films or franchises have that final act 'it's over' motif like *Jaws*. Few films so blatantly proved it was far from over as the shoal of *Jaws* of sequels soon proved.

TO THE SPACESHIP

1982. A globular mothership lifts itself, its compassionate cargo and its ring of spotlights through the tips of the redwood trees and into the starry night sky. Underneath, a band of kids watch the skies

○────────○

If you told me Harrison Ford would play Han Solo thirty-two years after *Return of the Jedi*, would I shoot you and your crazy under the table first? If you told me that Harrison Ford would play Deckard again in a new *Blade Runner* film, would I have believed your crazy replicant mind? If you told me Harrison Ford would be in a fourth Indiana Jones film, nineteen years after *The Last Crusade*, would that be as ridiculous as another fifth adventure subsequently pencilled into Paramount Studios' diary? If you told me that Ridley Scott would return to the world of *Alien* and make not just one prequel, but two at last count, I would throw you one of Scott's cold Northern stares and ask you to politely leave the room and take that ginger cat with you. If you told me that the deceased Marlon Brando would have another *Superman* film cameo in him, alongside another new actor flying to John Williams' 'Superman Theme', I would have sent you to the Phantom Zone. Or a blackened set being churned up by a Pinewood Studios wind machine before the afternoon tea-break. If you told me that Sylvester Stallone would set parts of *Rocky VII* in Liverpool as Mr Balboa returns to the glorious Philadelphia freedoms of his 1970s heritage, I would stop you at 'there's a *Rocky VII*?!' before throwing the towel in altogether. And if you told me that a full-size Millennium Falcon and key *The Last Jedi* set would be built on the backlot of a Surrey studio barely fifteen miles – let alone parsecs – away from me right now for a shoot whose clapperboard read '*Episode VIII*', I would have laughed before my 8-year-old self would tell you rather pointedly that *Star Wars* films are made in America and the Planet Elstree.

Vacated seats in a California movie house.

And above any of that, if anyone ever told me how one day I would watch the skies of a new Steven Spielberg film in the presence of Mr Steven Spielberg himself, that would really be the moment I would turn into Amity's Mayor Vaughn and refuse to believe you. However, in January 2018 an invite from an old school friend did indeed yield a close encounter of a legendary kind.

It was the night of the European premiere of Spielberg's *The Post* at London's Odeon Leicester Square. My friend Paul had not only landed two tickets through his company responsible for the UK distribution of the film - but a last-minute invite to the pre-film drinks too. As we tread the red and the short expanse of press-flanked carpet past a lone Meryl Streep beguiling the gathered lenses, I realised my costume gamble of vintage leather and tie to match an early 1970s Washington Post reporter was no bad thing. If Steven Spielberg was going to return to the decade that made him, then so was I! And almost forty years on from when *Close Encounters* first premiered at the Odeon Leicester Square in March 1978, here was I ascending the same stairs seen in every 1970s and 1980s premiere TV broadcast to a circle lounge that had witnessed every monarch, James Bond, Hollywood star, unruly flower girl and ballgown since the famed theatre opened in 1937. Apart from watching the Washington skies of the prophetic tale of the *Post's* 1971 stance on press freedoms, my only goal was to at least glimpse the bearded movie captain from afar – a sort of close encounter of the first kind. What I did not then expect was to walk into a makeshift and sparse private reception room housing only a trio of wine waiters and a sprinkling of early guests to jump straight to a close encounter of the second kind.

Having procured a glass of fizz and tidied my paisley tie, I glance across the enclosed, slightly darkened space and freeze in a heartbeat of both wonder and surreal panic. At that very moment I realise how I am about two very casual metres away from ...

Mr Steven Spielberg. What do I do?! What do I say?! With almost zero warning I had now gone to the spaceship in the forest. The biggest movie light of them all was already here – and like Roy Neary in 1977 I had been invited. If there was a sly crack in the PR duties of the night a polite hello was apparently fine and then maybe this sky kid could really take this to a close encounter of a third kind. But what would be my opening gambit? The welcome hand sign from *Close Encounters*? 'I'll be right here' and an *E.T.* finger to his forehead? Hastily scrawling 'love you' on my eyelids like a lovesick archaeological student or releasing buckets of school frogs and grabbing the bearded god in a romantic clench? These all feel somewhat like security gambles. But then – as Paul is asking for advice on driving the Pacific Coast Highway and I confess I am not remotely listening and in some state of shock right now – a lone Meryl Streep wanders towards us both. She is clearly keeping tabs on her PR obligations of the night – and maybe thinks she recognises my leather jacket from *Silkwood* – before she stops alongside the pair of us to join Spielberg in chatting *The Post* and current Hollywood and American politics.

In one quick cut, I am each and every awestruck kid from a Spielberg movie. I am Barry Guiler as his toys start moving, Gertie walking into her brother's closet after school, Jamie witnessing a P-51 fly across a Japanese internment camp and a dumbstruck Elliott meeting an interplanetary traveller in his moonlit backyard. Paul scans me wondering if he needs to face slap me like Amity's Mrs Kintner. I am thinking he might have to. If he doesn't, Streep might well do it for him. And as I try to move beyond this freeze-frame moment and Mr Spielberg is sounding and acting with the same buoyancy he did in every documentary and interview of my VHS childhood, I clock another childhood movie icon. There - sat chatting as if we are all in a 1930s Shanghai nightclub - is none other than Willie Scott herself in the guise of actress and Mrs Spielberg,

Stephen Spielberg introduces *The Post* at its European premiere in London, January 2018.

Kate Capshaw. I momentarily wonder if I should blame or thank her for inspiring this sky kid to prance around his childhood lounge with a dubious rendition of 'Anything Goes'?! 'This was the man who made *E.T.*', 'This was the man who made *Jaws*', 'This was the man who made *Raiders*', and 'This is the real Willie Scott – *the* Willie Scott!' – all these realisations kept circling my head as more guests filled the small space and then an impromptu and official voice bellowed out, 'Can the stage group please make themselves available?'. That was premiere-talk suggesting the A-listers get ready to introduce *The Post* to its gathered audience. And as everyone grabbed their coats – including Spielberg – I was suddenly like Jamie in *Empire of the Sun* all over again. With my hand mentally held out, I'd lost contact with the mothership in the crowds and the moment to shake Spielberg's hand and say a simple 'Thank you' had gone.

But it was replaced with an equally privileged one – when Steven Spielberg, Meryl Streep, and Tom Hanks (it is a strange night indeed when Spielberg's most ubiquitous leading man is the lesser mentioned name on the bill) soon emerge to introduce *The Post*. As the on-stage Spielberg recalls the Odeon Leicester Square premiere night of *Close Encounters of the Third Kind* in 1978, I am just wholly grateful to have had any kind of close encounter. The fact I am watching a Spielberg movie presided over by the man himself in a film which returns him and audiences to the decade that truly made him (and this book), I am more than content with the poetry of that - and being able to photograph the great storyteller himself. And as Paul and I appear to be the only ones who laugh at the fun Spielberg has in introducing Hanks – 'Please put your hands together for the star of *Joe Versus The Volcano*, *The Money Pit* and *Turner and Hooch* - Mr Tom Hanks!' - and Streep just serves up that luminous gravitas without trying, the lights in the 80-year-old cinema dim and 'A Steven Spielberg Film' once again promises to illuminate the dark once more.

A Mossad agent meets his Jewish adviser as the Twin Towers of New York punctuate the skies with blunt foreboding in *Munich*, a camera searches out a new *Man of Steel* flying for the first time across the canyons of America as his father's words and newfound skills pull him into the skies with exhilaration, a pinkie promise is made into a golden English sunset between a girl and a benevolent giant in *The BFG*, a now-reclusive future-bound Los Angeles cop looks through binoculars at the orange dustbowl skies beyond his apartment glass in *Blade Runner 2049*, and a battalion of fighters soar across a white plain pulling up a sky of red dust in their wake in *The Last Jedi*. American cinema still watches the skies for its matinee dramas, box office might and escapism. These moments still define American movies because these titles are still key players.

But what America were we looking for when we watched those cinematic skies and imagined the trails, story paths and worlds beneath? And what America did we ultimately find?

Before the effects and the thrills and the anthems and the artwork, the likes of Lucas, Spielberg, Donner, Williams, Mankiewicz, Hooper, Reitman and Dante chose to present America to us first and foremost. *Superman: The Movie* is about an American nostalgia being usurped by an American metropolitan future. *Ghostbusters* is about the entrepreneur spirit and politics of American city life and the meeting of various American comedy campuses in one big creative frat house of fun. *Close Encounters* is about that American insistence and ability to see a science project through and a tacit, global understanding that America and the American psyche would very much be part of that first contact. Before it is a comment on new American families, *E.T. the Extra-Terrestrial* is about an American childhood and suburban community. *Raiders of the Lost Ark* is about American cinema's ability to take the backdrop to the darkest chapter in European twentieth-century history and appropriate it into a glorious and modern American western. *Gremlins* is about the nostalgias for small-town America and its fireside memories of Christmas and the home. *Jaws* is about different, clashing interpretations of American masculinity and the concerns of small communities with bigger issues. And *Star Wars* is not just about some androids, a desert planet, an ice planet, a family revelation and some X-Wings. It is about the vision of a Californian, post-Second World War-generation filmmaker to pass on the oldest of tales in the newest of ways — whilst simultaneously advancing American technology, photography, animation, audio, software and communication systems.

George Lucas and Steven Spielberg did not just layer our movie screens with visual effects, classical composing and soul-searing

K-2SO offering duty-free perfume samples at the wretched hive of scum and villainy that is Gatwick Spaceport, December 2016.

moments. They evolved the grammar of adventure filmmaking. When we watch *Rogue One: A Star Wars Story* or *The Last Jedi* or *Solo* or *Ready Player One* the legacy is more than just a collection of original trilogy heroes and figurines thrown together with newly imagined characters, planets and battles. The balletic cinematography and sense of visual choreography of *Rogue One* is an evolution of those motion control camera advancements that those Lucas-employed men and women first pioneered in various Californian warehouses and Greater London film studios. The physicality of *Star Wars* and *Raiders of the Lost Ark* evolved the syntax of mainstream editing, the speed of cuts and the choreography of information. You only have to watch a behind-the-scenes featurette for any new *Star Wars* film to see the balletic effort, ever-elaborate camera rigs and gimbols and sense of movement that now goes into these films. Whichever way you look at it, *Rogue One* is a far more creatively directed movie than *Return of the Jedi*. But it has time and forty years of *Star Wars* adoration and study in its favour. It was not just the dwarfing size and radical sense of domestic science fiction of that 1977 sight of a Star Destroyer pursuing that blockade runner through the frame and many a kid's childhood. It was the renewed sense of spectacle through movement. Forty years later, the structural velocity of the first wave of *Star Wars* movies is there in nearly every Marvel Studios title. The palette of characters, worlds, rivalries, hierarchies and the humanity of Lucas's galaxy is echoed in every season of *Game of Thrones*. And when each open-ended *Avengers*, *Thor* and *Guardians of the Galaxy* motion picture cannot concisely end and forever pitches its conclusions in future chapters, it is because *The Empire Strikes Back* did it first.

The history and legacy of watching these movie skies is part of all our histories and the personal, cultural and social wallpaper to a great many lives. From the death of a grandfather in our home as I readied my *Superman: The Movie* flask for a new life in school, via

Thirty-five years later my Luke figurine looks to the Forest Moon of Pinewood Studios, my wedding venue and the new production home of *Star Wars*.

a divorce accompanied by *E. T.* and a house move accompanied by *Star Wars* figures, to the death of a grandmother seven years later when all a kind cousin could do to change the focus was walk down to her local video store to rent out *Indiana Jones and the Temple of Doom* – these films took on our personal baggage, our individual triumphs, personal journeys and saddest memories. An old ice cream box of *Star Wars* figurines pulled from the attic is as evocative today as a box of family photos, a graduation scroll or a first pair of shoes. Yet these films were never just personal. *Jaws, Close Encounters of the Third Kind* and *Star Wars* helped underpin the burgeoning home video market. Theatrical became rental. And rental became retail. When *E. T. the Extra-Terrestrial* grew into one of the most pirated movies of all time, it also meant it was one of the most watched at home of all time. Movie fans get excited about a new trailer or teaser debuting online because the likes of *Star Wars* and *The Phantom Menace* pioneered taking the impact and purpose of trailers away from the movie theatres and putting that engagement and anticipation online and elsewhere. Computer technology didn't just evolve from the Second World War and the Cold War. It emerged too from tech companies wanting to help the creative industries of California. When the sky kids of the 1970s and 1980s become parents and grandparents and sit down to watch *Toy Story 3*, *Wall-E* and *Monsters University* with their little ones, it is partly because George Lucas and Lucasfilm Ltd took a punt on Pixar with the momentum of *Star Wars* behind them.

When a new *Star Wars* film is released today, it is not just turning the men and women of the audience back into the sky kids of their youth. It is an ever-rarer moment when the popular culture is shared en masse and is – to quote Francois Truffaut in *Close Encounters* – an 'event sociologique'. As kids, a new *Star Wars* film – or even an old one at home on a creaky VHS tape – was all about the personal and the social currency it yielded. Now it is about the global. Sharing the joy of seeing a movie theatre *Superman* poster for the first time with others on the school bus has now become catching that teatime first trailer online and realising millions are engaging with it too with equal fever. And it is much more than nostalgia. Popular culture has now evolved. Imitation will always be the highest form of flattery. And homage. But a good film still must be a *good* film. *Rogue One* works not so much because it is a *Star Wars* story, but because it is a rich piece of movie craftsmanship. And whilst every *Tron: Legacy*, *Star Wars Rebels*, *Alien: Covenant*, *Mad Max: Fury Road* and *Blade Runner 2049* are of course part-trading on the cash-yielding reminiscences of all us sky kids, adults, god-kids and offspring – this prime era of American cinema doesn't fade because, above all, it is good. The likes of Spielberg, Lucas, Donner, their peers and colleagues made it good. They ensured that spirit of late-1970s cinema still has a striking, relevant moviemaking validity to this day. Those canary-yellow road lines have never stopped.

Like a bauble in the Californian skies, the mothership pauses for a brief moment in time before zipping with intent across the stars. Leaving a streaming rainbow in its wake, it narrowly misses half a dozen TIE fighters and a Man of Steel flying in the opposite direction.

Written and Directed by

MARK O'CONNELL

THE END

Artistic licence at San Francisco's Castro Theatre.

CLOSING TITLES

To Mum and Rob - you never turned up the lights, never changed the channel and always let me record first. You bestowed a childhood with kindness, care, the movies, TV, a plastic AT-AT and video club membership. Thank you.

To Dad, Ali and the O'Connell family on all sides of the planet – may the force be with you. And for providing a portal to a world of VCRs, Dr Pepper and 1980s home-movie technology – I am forever indebted to The Quinns from the Glasgow System.

To my Rebel guards - Vivienne Clore, David Lazenby, Nick Canham and the team – thank you for always having this X-Wing pilot's back.

These films and recollections only stay alive when they are shared. To my band of fellow sky kids holding the BMX bikes – Alex Swain, Ajay Chowdhury, Pat Molyneux, Inigo Matas, Phil Summerton and the Nelson boys of Blue Squadron – we'll meet in the forest after school. Bring sandwiches.

For a book about those films whose cinema lobby artwork was always the vital overture to taking our seats in the dark, I cannot thank Scott Woolston enough for his soulful cover art, astute movie eye and the creative ease in which it all happened. And a Rebel pilot is nothing without their command team – so many thanks to Mark Beynon, Lauren Newby and the whole garrison at The History Press.

To our dearest Michael Johnstone and David Faulk from the planet Verasphere - thank you for making your San Francisco ours too. With every beat a view and every view a story, it is now more than a second home with friends who have become family.

And to Mark Gatiss and Mark Millar – two Krypton leaders whose kind support is both fortune and glory and very much appreciated. Additional thanks to Pinewood Studios, Mark Witherspoon, the International Spy Museum, Paul Lofting, eOne, Mark Trevorrow, Sam Russell, Peaches Christ, the Castro Theatre, Maxime Brulein, Mark N. Thomas, Shoba Vazirani, Steve Clark, *OUT* magazine, Doug Baulf, Matthew Lenda, and the creative people and pulse of San Francisco.

And my heartfelt gratitude to all the directors, writers, actors, producers, composers, designers, FX wizards and bearded gods whose work helped inspire this book, a childhood, and an attic full of VHS tapes.

Finally, to my Millennium Falcon co-pilot in life, Elliot … '*I know*'.

MARK O'CONNELL WILL RETURN

BIBLIOGRAPHY

Alvin, Andrea, *The Art of John Alvin*, Titan Books, 2014

Biskind, Peter, *Easy Riders, Raging Bulls: How the Sex, Drugs and Rock 'n' Roll Generation Changed Hollywood*, Simon & Schuster, 1998

Bizony, Piers, *The Space Shuttle: Celebrating Thirty Year of NASA's First Space Plane*, Zenith Press, 2011

Champlin, Charles, *George Lucas – The Creative Impulse: Lucasfilm's First Twenty Years*, Virgin Books, 1992

Digby, Anne, *Ghostbusters: The Storybook of the Film*, Scholastic Inc., 1984

Gipe, George, *Gremlins*, Avon Books, 1984

Harris, Scott Jordan (edited by), *World Film Locations: San Francisco*, Intellect, 2013

Mankiewicz, Tom, and Robert Crane, *My Life as a Mankiewicz: An Insider's Journey through Hollywood*, University Press of Kentucky, 2012

Perry, George, *Movies from the Mansion: A History of Pinewood Studios*, Pavillion, 1986

Rinzler, J.W., *The Making of Return of the Jedi*, Aurum, 2013

Rinzler, J.W., *The Making of The Empire Strikes Back*, Aurum, 2010

Sansweet, Stephen J., *Star Wars: From Concept to Collectible*, Chronicle Books, 1992

...amakers: The Early Years of American Zoetrope, directed ...eva, Warner Bros. Entertainment Inc., 2004

...Dreams, directed by Edith Becker & Kevin Burns, ...ilm Ltd, 2004

...irl: The Making of the Movie, directed by Peter Hollywood, Cantharus Productions, 1984

The Making of Indiana Jones and the Temple of Doom, directed by Frank Marshall, Lucasfilm Ltd, 1984

The Making of Raiders of the Lost Ark, directed by Phillip Schuman, Lucasfilm Ltd., 1981

Richard Amsel / richardamsel.info
Billboard 100 history / billboard.com
British Board of Film Classification / bbfc.co.uk
Josh Kirby / joshkirbyart.com
The Second City / secondcity.com
UK Top 40 history / officialcharts.com

The History Press

The destination for history
www.thehistorypress.co.uk